Transit States

Transit States

Labour, Migration and Citizenship in the Gulf

Edited by
Abdulhadi Khalaf, Omar AlShehabi
and Adam Hanieh

PlutoPress
www.plutobooks.com

First published 2015 by Pluto Press
345 Archway Road, London N6 5AA

www.plutobooks.com

Copyright © Abdulhadi Khalaf, Omar AlShehabi and Adam Hanieh 2015

The right of the individual contributors to be identified as the authors of this
work has been asserted by them in accordance with the Copyright, Designs and
Patents Act 1988.

British Library Cataloguing in Publication Data
A catalogue record for this book is available from the British Library

ISBN   978 0 7453 3522 3   Hardback
ISBN   978 0 7453 3520 9   Paperback
ISBN   978 1 7837 1220 5   PDF eBook
ISBN   978 1 7837 1222 9   Kindle eBook
ISBN   978 1 7837 1221 2   EPUB eBook

Library of Congress Cataloging in Publication Data applied for

10   9   8   7   6   5   4   3   2   1

Typeset by Stanford DTP Services, Northampton, England
Text design by Melanie Patrick
Simultaneously printed digitally by CPI Antony Rowe, Chippenham, UK
and Edwards Bros in the United States of America

Contents

List of Illustrations

Figures

Tables

Boxes

Preface

The intersection of labour, migration and citizenship lies at the core of understanding social life in the six states of the Gulf Cooperation Council or GCC (Saudi Arabia, Kuwait, Bahrain, United Arab Emirates, Oman and Qatar). The region was the largest destination for labour migration in the global South at the start of the twenty-first century, with a majority of its working population composed of temporary migrant workers. These workers have underpinned the spectacular development boom across the region in recent decades – involved in construction, maintenance and infrastructure work – as well as service, clerical, retail and domestic activities.

South Asian countries such as Pakistan, India, Bangladesh and Sri Lanka have become almost fully dependent on the labour markets of the Gulf for their overseas workforce, with the money sent home from these workers helping to sustain millions of families across the globe. At the same time, international media, human rights organisations and labour unions have become increasingly attuned to the dire working conditions faced by many migrant workers in the Gulf – demonstrated, perhaps most strikingly, in the barrage of newspaper reports critical of Qatar's treatment of workers involved in World Cup-related construction projects. For all of these reasons, the Gulf region takes a central place in contemporary debates around migration and labour in the global economy.

Despite the extreme significance of migration to the Gulf, much scholarly analysis of the GCC's political economy has tended to sideline the importance of these labour flows, focusing instead on capital markets, the distribution of oil rents and the nature of ruling families. Explanations for the heavy reliance on migrant labour most often adopt a neoclassical lens of low population levels, mismatched skill profiles or 'push–pull' wage differentials between the Gulf and surrounding regions. When discussed in this literature, migrant workers are frequently framed as policy *objects* rather than social actors in themselves – a 'potential problem' that can be solved through institutional or policy initiatives.

Within the migration literature, analysis of the GCC has emphasised the deprivation and exploitation to which workers have been subject in the host economies, or the impact of remittance flows on community, village and other social structures in the source countries. This literature typically highlights sociological and anthropological themes, looking at the ways in which networks of migration form and decisions to migrate are taken, drawing upon the life histories of migrants themselves. Despite the fact that this literature contains a wide range of useful and perceptive analysis that provides an important counterweight to the traditional scholarly literature on the Gulf, it often suffers from being overly descriptive and narrow in focus – failing to adequately situate the question of labour migration within the broader political, economic and social developments in the Gulf.

This book attempts to bring together and explore the tensions between these different sets of literature, which too often tend to speak past one another. Our key argument is that the relationship between 'citizen' and 'non-citizen' holds immense significance for understanding the construction of class, gender, city and state in the Gulf. For this reason, questions of migration and the status of 'non-citizens' are essential to interpreting contemporary political and social trends in the Gulf.

The precarious working conditions of labour in the Gulf have often facilitated exploitation of both migrants and citizens. They have also engendered a variety of forms of social mobilisation and resistance, presenting new challenges for political actors. Migration has been a principal factor behind the dramatic changes in the Gulf's urban landscape – closely tied to real estate regulatory reform and financialisation. Constantly evolving forms of migration have emerged, linked to highly skilled labour and the rebranding of the Gulf itself. By bringing together scholars on the Gulf, including academics based in the region itself, our edited book critically explores these questions – recentring the question of migration at the core of the social structures and political economy of the GCC states.

The Structure of the Book

The chapters in this book are based on a dedicated workshop on Gulf migration that was held in Istanbul in May 2012 and was generously funded by the Center for Middle Eastern Studies at Lund University, Sweden.[1] This book covers a wide range of themes and case studies,

---

1   The authors would like to thank Lisa Barrington and Eda Farsakoglu for their invaluable efforts in organizing the workshop.

including theoretical and historical perspectives; migration and the Gulf political economy; migration and gender in the Gulf; and new forms of migration to the Gulf. Through each chapter the authors critically reflect upon the dominant understandings of migration in the region, exploring the ways in which migration has helped to underpin the construction of class, gender, city and state within the GCC.

The book opens with an introductory chapter presenting an overview of the main historical phases of migration to the Gulf. The two subsequent chapters lay out different theoretical accounts of Gulf migration and labour flows. Chapter 2 focuses on the politics of the state as a way to understanding migration, while Chapter 3 emphasises the Gulf's place within the wider regional and global economic structures. Chapters 4, 5 and 6 examine the relationship between migration and the socio-economic features of the Gulf – looking at its significance to the rapid urbanisation processes that have taken place over the last decade, the means through which the subordination of migrant workers is deepened through the work permit system known as *kafala*, and the ways in which these processes are gendered. Chapters 7, 8 and 9 challenge the standard caricatures of labour migrants as 'male construction workers', mapping new forms of migration to university and education zones, the role of 'migrant-mercenaries' in the security forces in the region, and the impact of exile communities on the politics of the Gulf. The final chapter presents an overview of recent mobilisation efforts surrounding migrant issues, and argues for more solidarity across the Arab world and globally for the rights of migrants.

Part I

Introduction

1

Histories of Migration to the Gulf

Omar AlShehabi

Understanding Gulf Migration

This introductory chapter discusses the historical roots and evolution of the extreme reliance on temporary migrant workers in the six states of the Gulf Cooperation Council (GCC). It focuses, in detail, on the most important changes that the region's population structure has experienced from the start of the oil era up to the first decade of the twenty-first century. Hence, this chapter aims to lay out the historical backdrop that underpins much of the analysis covered in subsequent chapters. Particular attention is given to areas of similarity within the individual experiences of each of the GCC states. The intention is to present a broad framework for understanding the rise of a demographic system between citizen and non-citizen populations that could be best summarised as 'restricted citizenship with unrestricted migration', and to shed light on the most important factors that contributed to its development.[1]

The main focus will be on detailing the mutually constitutive relationship that exists between the GCC's modern population structure and the oil revolution that took place in the Gulf. Indeed, the economic and political system that accompanied the oil revolution formed the very foundations of the demographic dynamics we find in the region today. The chapter's main thesis is that the demographic structure was the result of two often overlapping but sometimes conflicting projects: the construction of a 'petro-modernist state' in each of the GCC countries, combined with the establishment of capitalism as the dominant (but not the only) economic mode of production. Both of these projects were to be driven by rising oil revenues and migrant labour flowing into the region.

The GCC economies are firmly embedded within the global economy, based primarily on the region boasting the largest and cheapest proven global reservoir of crude oil. Ever since commercial exportation of Gulf oil took off in the latter half of the twentieth century, the region has received the highest windfall of petrodollars of any oil producers in the world. This centrality to the global economy is mirrored domestically by the dominant role the state plays within the national economies of the GCC. The state, and particularly influential members of the ruling families, has large control over how the oil revenue is to be spent domestically. This is complemented with an elite class of investors, often also members of the royal families, who control the main economic opportunities that arose from the windfall of petrodollars.

The GCC's demographic profile came to reflect the internal and external aspects of this resultant economic and political structure, which, by opening the doors to unrestricted migration while restricting citizenship, segmented the population into groups of 'citizens' and 'expatriates', and used the region's population to service this political-economic configuration. From the perspective of citizens of the GCC countries, this post-oil historical period has been characterised by a decline in their political influence and their participation in economic production. This has reached a point where, by the start of the twenty-first century, nationals represented less than half of the workforce in any of the GCC countries, and their productive roles were primarily confined to employment in the public sector or financial services. However, the upside of this situation was that citizens, and only citizens, were provided with the benefits of an increasingly generous welfare state, providing free or subsidised services, opportunities for mass consumerism, as well as the ability to establish small and medium enterprises. These benefits were obtained through a notion of citizenship founded on loyalty to the state, which came to be largely identified with the ruling families, by now firmly embedded as the apex of the local political system.

In tandem, regional capital's growing need for labour was fulfilled by facilitating the entry of foreign workers. The GCC's doors were opened wide to migrant workers who not only became the central pillar of the region's workforce, but also came to form the majority of the population within most Gulf States. Strict measures, however, were put in place to control expatriate integration and to reduce their power in the region's economic and political activities. These measures served to prevent them, as non-citizens, from settling permanently, from forming trade unions, and from capital ownership. Thus, the population structure was formed by, and in service to, the demands of an economic and political structure that evolved in tandem with the discovery of oil in the region. This demographic restructuring continued until the region began to resemble what some scholars have called a collection of scattered 'labour camps', rather than a set of cohesive and integrated societies (Al Kuwari, 2004a).

The First Oil Boom, 1931–1973

The population in what came to constitute the GCC was estimated at the start of the twentieth century to be approximately two million, of which about 900,000 were concentrated on the western shores of the Gulf and Oman (Seccombe and Lawless, 1987: 4). The cultural, historical and geographical scope of the region sits within an Arab and Islamic identity, but within this overarching framework it is considered one of the most culturally, ethnically and historically diverse parts of the globe, encompassing three continents that formed the ancient world. By virtue of this hyper-connectivity to the rest of the world, the Gulf's economies developed predominantly around commercial and entrepôt trade posts. The region is also distinguished as an important religious centre, being the birthplace and containing the two holy sites of Islam. As an historic point of convergence between different cultures and civilizations, most of the region's settled communities developed based on exchanges with the wider world, which naturally included population exchanges.[2]

This population exchange occurred predominantly in areas in close proximity to the Gulf and the Arabian Peninsula, with social composition based upon a complex network of commercial, cultural, geographical and familial ties. Environmental variables such as droughts and epidemics also affected the regional demographics and migration movements.[3] Borders did not exist prior to the Uqair Convention of 1922,[4] when borders were delineated for the first time between Saudi Arabia and Kuwait, and there were no official immigration controls, passports or citizenship documents until well into the 1900s.[5] As such, an organic society developed over the centuries containing a mixture of ethnic groups, sects and beliefs, within the region's overarching Arab and Islamic identity.

The Arrival of the Oil Companies, 1931–1950

The systematic import of foreign labour began in the nineteenth century under British colonial rule, forming the starting point for a new type of population flow into the Arabian Peninsula.[6] What particularly distinguished this new type of migration was the organised import of a workforce by a 'sponsor' (in this case, the British administration) that did not necessarily have any cultural or geographical connection with the region. Migrants were systematically brought in by the British to carry out the functions of colonial administration. Thus we see one of the most important features of this new phase of migration: members of the migrant community were not required or encouraged by their sponsors to integrate within the local communities. In fact, often the intention was to import migrants that would *not* integrate into local society, and indeed could be used as a source of discipline and control. Often the purpose of this first wave of migration was to strengthen the security forces through which the British maintained their control (i.e. mercenary forces). Migrants also formed the administrative class, and the majority of these groups came either from the Indian subcontinent or from the United Kingdom itself. This process occurred mainly in the areas known as the Trucial States (the western coast of the Gulf stretching from Kuwait to Oman), where the British presence was strongest.

This migration phenomenon was limited in scope, being mostly confined to the state's administrative and security apparatus. The situation was fundamentally altered with the discovery of oil. The first oil well was drilled in Bahrain in 1931, and the rest of the Gulf followed suit over the next two decades, with oil exportation from the region taking off in earnest after the Second World War.[7] It would not be an exaggeration to say that the region's political, economic and cultural roots were shaken and radically transformed over the course of a few decades. The Arabian Peninsula was transformed from a desperately poor area on the margins of the global economy, supporting its sparse population through pearling, entrepôt trade, and agricultural and herding activities, into an integral link in the global economic system. The discovery of the largest proven global reservoir of oil in the Gulf coincided with oil's transformation into the most important commodity of the economic and industrial revolution that swept the globe after the Second World War.

As the region's oil industry was laying its foundations between the 1930s and 1950s, expatriate labour poured mainly into the oil sector. The administrative and skilled labour classes came from Western countries, in accordance with the preferences of the American or British oil companies. In areas with British colonial presence, oil concessions were signed on the condition that preference would be shown towards workers already under British rule, and so most of the skilled workers came from the United Kingdom. The same principle also applied to the class of clerks and semi-skilled workers, who hailed mostly from the colonised Indian subcontinent.[8] The situation was different in Saudi Arabia, which never experienced direct British control. Instead, American companies had a monopoly over oil exploitation agreements, and so most of the administrative and skilled classes came from the US, while the demand for semi-skilled workers was met by importing relatively cheaper Italian settlers from Eritrea. In all the Gulf sheikhdoms, unskilled workers were sourced from the local population wherever possible, a condition imposed on the oil companies by the local rulers. The region was engulfed by an economic crisis in the late 1920s following the decimation of the natural pearl market by Japanese cultured pearls and the onset of the global great depression. Employment of locals in the oil companies provided a timely antidote (Seccombe and Lawless, 1987: 18).

The number of foreign workers in the oil sector grew rapidly after the end of the Second World War, when most Gulf States began exporting oil commercially. From no more than 2,000 in 1940, the number of migrants working in the region's oil sector as a whole had grown to about 16,000 by 1950. The majority of them came from the Indian subcontinent and the West. Although the majority of workers in the oil sector were still citizens, their proportions were shrinking fast. In 1945, citizens working in Bahrain's oil sector represented 63 per cent of the total workforce and 68 per cent in Saudi Arabia. In Qatar, the percentage of citizens among the workforce had shrunk to 54 per cent by 1948, while in Kuwait the number of migrants in the workforce rose from 5 per cent in 1945 to 68 per cent in 1949 (Seccombe and Lawless, 1987: 18). Hence, immigration in this period was driven mainly by the requirements of oil companies and the needs of the British colonial administration, both of whom were the principal parties involved in establishing the oil industry and controlling the resultant revenues.

Commercial Oil Production and the Emergence of Nationalism, 1950–1973

A new wave of migration took place between 1950 and the start of the 1970s. Increasing amounts of revenues were generated by the extraction and sale of oil on the global market, in what can be loosely termed as the

Gulf's first oil boom. Oil revenues flowed directly to the oil companies and the rulers' accounts based on the shares stipulated in the concession agreements between the two parties. Throughout this period, the percentage of oil revenue allocated to the rulers gradually increased as a series of renegotiations of concessions took place, particularly in Saudi Arabia and Kuwait.[9]

With increasing amounts of oil revenue being allocated to the state, economic opportunities in the region started to expand outside the oil sector. The public sector was the natural driver, concentrating heavily on building the basic infrastructure of roads, education, health services and administrative bodies. Attractive investment opportunities for capital accumulation began to emerge in the private sector too. Most of these activities were in secondary sectors that grew out of the oil boom, especially in construction and the importation of goods.[10]

Demographically, the first discernable development was a huge increase in the number of incoming migrants. Between 1950 and 1975, their numbers grew from no more than a few tens of thousands, to around one million (Chalcraft, 2010: 11–12). Some continued to work in the oil sector, but the vast majority were in the public sector, construction and the various service sectors that mushroomed in tandem with the growing oil revenues.

Migrants came mainly from other Arab countries. This was a logical development given that they shared a geographical, cultural and linguistic affinity to the Gulf. The consequences of the 1948 Palestinian *nakba* increased the number of Palestinian immigrants, and popular sentiment locally as well as the rulers' inclination was towards the import of Arab labour. King Abdulaziz of Saudi Arabia, for example, ordered in 1949 that citizens, then Palestinians, then Arabs and then the rest of the Muslim nationalities should be preferentially selected for work (Seccombe and Lawless, 1987: 26). The growing tide of Arab nationalism in Kuwait and the policies of the ruler Sheikh Abdullah Al-Salem, led to a preference for importing Arab labour there too. By 1975, 90 per cent and 80 per cent of expatriates in Saudi Arabia and Kuwait respectively were Arab. In the rest of the Gulf States, where the British mandate was still in effect, the proportion of Arab labour was smaller due to British sensitivities about the political implications of employing large numbers of Arab migrants. Instead, migration there tended to favour states already under British colonialism, particularly the Indian subcontinent. In Bahrain, Arabs accounted for 50 per cent of immigrants, two-thirds of which were from the Sultanate of Oman. By the same year, Arabs represented only a quarter of expatriates in the UAE and the proportion was similar in Qatar (Chalcraft, 2010: 7–8). Overall, by the end of 1973, expatriates stood at about one million, the overwhelming majority of whom were Arabs.

The third striking development on the demographic front was the emergence of a strong labour and political consciousness within citizens, based largely on the experiences of the local labour force employed in the oil sector. Two main factors fuelled this process. To begin with, the income and living conditions of expatriate workers during this period were perceived as better than those of locals. At the same time, a strong political consciousness was emerging regionally, taking its cue from political movements in the rest of the Arab world (nationalism and pan-Arabism) and globally (such as Marxism and socialism). This led to the development of various nationalist and labour-oriented movements, with oil company workers demanding increasing economic and political participation in the various Gulf States. Between 1938 and 1965 strikes were a frequent phenomenon in Bahrain, demanding that the same wages and benefits be applied to Bahraini workers as to expatriates at the BAPCO oil company, with the biggest symbol of discrimination being the allocation of separate drinking water fountains for the British, Indians and Bahrainis (AlShirawi, 2005). In Saudi Arabia, local workers at Aramco oil company carried out several strikes in the 1950s and 1960s to demand better living and wage conditions (Vitalis, 2006). Qatar was no exception, with the oil strikes of 1950–1956 being the most notable, while Kuwait was an incubator for many of the region's labour movements between the 1950s and 1970s (Crystal, 1995).

Thus, the period from the beginning of the 1930s to the end of the 1970s, which encompasses the first and second phases of systematic labour migration into the Gulf, was characterised by the establishment of the region's oil industries and the development of a strong nationalist and labour-oriented consciousness among citizens. By the end of the 1960s, expatriate numbers stood at no more than one million, and the vast majority of them (about 80 per cent) were from neighbouring Arab countries. The next period was to have drastic transformational consequences for the Gulf's economic-political structure and its population makeup.

The Second Oil Boom, 1973–1985

Although the changes experienced by the Gulf States differed based on their individual histories of commercial oil exploitation and internal political developments,[11] a pronounced demographic imbalance was to become a uniting feature within all states during the course of what we can term the 'second oil boom' of the 1970s and early 1980s. By 1971, all GCC states had achieved formal independence, with many hurriedly ushered in by their former colonisers to join the global community of nations as independent states.[12] The ruling families were by now receiving the lion's share of the oil revenues after several rounds of renegotiations with the multinational oil companies. A dramatic oil boom burst on the scene in 1973, usually referred to in the West as the 'first oil crisis', as a direct result of the 1973 October war between Israel and the Arabs. A steady rise in global oil prices followed, and unprecedented amounts of oil revenues flowed into state coffers. This continued throughout the 1970s and was followed by the 'second oil crisis' of 1979–1980 in the wake of the overthrow of the Shah of Iran and the beginning of the Iraq–Iran war. This boom period radically restructured the region's population for the rest of the twentieth century.

The Petro-modernist State, Capitalism and the 'Demographic Imbalance'

An in-depth treatment of the political-economic structures that came to define the Gulf during the oil boom lies beyond the scope of this chapter. However, it is necessary to sketch an outline of these developments, particularly from the viewpoint of a demographic lens, in order to understand the profound shift in the Gulf's population structures. The thesis put forward is that two processes, often overlapping and at other times competing, shaped the political-economic path of the Gulf States during the latter half of the twentieth century. One was the drive to establish a 'petro-modernist state',[13] with the royal families situated at the apex of this state. The second is the firm embedding of the Gulf States within the global capitalist system. Although these processes had their foundations laid and were already developing in the previous period, they were to come prominently to the fore during what we have termed the second oil boom period.[14]

Over the next few pages, we will focus on detailing the network of relations and institutions that developed with the emergence of the modern state in the GCC, in conjunction with capitalism becoming the dominant, albeit not only, economic mode of production in the region. The particular way in which the population structure manifested itself on the ground depended on multiple factors, including push factors in migrants' sending countries, the interaction between Western powers in the region, demands of the global economy, local political considerations, historical specificities prior to the advent of the oil age and the influences these factors had on structuring the distribution of oil revenues. Indeed, the greatest power to dominate within local society lay with those who controlled the oil revenues. It is therefore necessary to look at who controlled oil revenues and how it flowed in order to understand how the region's society became structured. In order to analyse this radical transformation, the key actors in this socio-economic network should be identified.

Before the emergence of the oil industry, the key parties that had a stake in the economic dynamics of Gulf societies could be loosely categorised as follows: the ruling families, the local merchant class, the rest of the region's urban and nomadic population,[15] and last but not least the Western powers whose sphere of influence extended to the region (particularly Great Britain and the US).

Pre-oil, the Gulf region lay on the periphery of the global economy, with its economic activity mainly dedicated to a pearling industry that catered for the global market, in addition to trade within the British colonial maritime network, facilitated largely through a clique of merchants with access to this network. Within this economic structure, the ruling families were strongly dependent on tax income and financing from these merchants, in addition to the political and economic support of the British.[16] The state's dependence on merchants gave the latter some say in political matters, and so the power of the ruling families was in no way absolute. The power of the merchant class varied between countries. For example, in Bahrain and Kuwait, where intra-regional trade played a major role, the merchant class's political influence was significant. In Kuwait, the 1910 migration of the pearl merchants restricted the power of the ruler, Sheikh Mubarak, while in Bahrain merchants played a central role in the 1923 political protests that ended with the British removing the local ruler in favour of his son. In Saudi Arabia, the financial support of the Hijazi merchant class played a crucial role in the extension of Ibn Saud's rule from Najd to the Hijaz area.[17]

The ability of local rulers to exert control on the Bedouin tribes in the Arabian Peninsula was traditionally weaker in comparison to the urban areas, where the rulers' economic and political base tended to be concentrated. However, the power of the Bedouin tribes was severely curtailed during King Abdul Aziz Ibn Saud's military campaigns in the early twentieth century, successfully establishing his authority over the vast majority of the peninsula. The hegemony of the Bedouin tribes over the peninsula's hinterland areas (*Deirahs*) was severely curtailed, dealing a mortal blow to their main economic mode of production based on trade access to these hinterland routes (Krimly, 1993: chapter 1).

The regional influence of British colonial power also varied. It was much stronger in Oman and along the Trucial coast (e.g. Bahrain), where the British were effectively the joint rulers with the local ruling families. In Saudi Arabia and Kuwait, however, the ruling families were much more independent in local affairs. Even in the latter countries, the British still played an influential role, particularly through their control of global maritime trade networks which were essential to the Gulf and Red Sea trade routes, and through their furnishing of funds to the local rulers.

The ascendance of oil radically reorganised this power structure. With the influx of oil revenue directly to state coffers, the ruling regimes' economic dependence on merchants and citizens decreased, effectively ending the government's reliance on its national population for fiscal revenues. On the other hand, international dependence between local leaders and Western countries strengthened, since they (particularly the US) were the main architects and guarantors of the global oil market.

This situation restructured social, political and economic relations to revolve around a petro-modernist state that is heavily integrated in the global economy and enjoys strong Western backing. If a 'high-modernist state' is one that is characterised by 'strong, one might even say muscle-bound ... self-confidence about scientific and technical progress, the expansion of production, the growing satisfaction of human needs, the mastery of nature ... and, above all, the rational design of social order commensurate with the scientific understanding of natural laws' (Scott, 1998: 4), then a petro-modernist state was characterised by a strong, one might even say muscle-bound, self-confidence in the power of oil revenues – coupled with the fuel of imported labour – to reorder the social and natural world.

Four essential elements characterised the vision of this petro-modernist state in the Gulf. First, it had to ensure that the ruling families were at the apex of the state's political structure. Second, its aim was to produce a disciplined population loyal to the state and the ruling elite. Consequently, the construction of a 'super-welfare' state for its citizens was the third essential element. Fourth, it displayed a curious combination of a modernist state, utilising the latest advances in science and technology to reform nature and society according to its vision whenever necessary, while also relying on pre-modern relationships whenever such relationships were more suitable to its goals.[18] Most crucially, achieving these aims could be short-circuited and fast tracked by the massive windfall of oil revenues and the labour power of migrant workers.

The one all-important characteristic of the massive inflowing oil rents was that it allowed the transfer of a huge amount of purchasing power from the outside world to the domestic rulers, purchasing power that was way beyond the current productive capacities of the local economy. The question was how to spend this massive purchasing power acquired from abroad. Building the modern state became paramount – a process that might have developed organically, spanning several decades or even centuries in other countries, with a multitude of social struggles and technological evolutions. The vision was to have this process ultra-fast tracked in the Gulf using the newly found oil wealth.

Thus, at the domestic level, oil revenues came to be spent mainly through the quickly expanding state institutions, most of whose activities concentrated on establishing the elements of a modern state infrastructure and welfare services, including roads, education facilities, health centres, desalination and electricity plants, factories and the central and administrative apparatuses of the state that were staffed by ever-growing bureaucracies. A small army of technocrats ran these newly emergent bureaucracies, and this group often included some of the most ambitious and newly educated within society, many of whom were highly motivated by the vision of becoming a modern, developed nation. The rise of this unique version of the high-modernist state cannot be explained by capital dictates alone, and indeed it is essential to place its emergence within the context of the dire economic situation prevailing before the flow of oil revenues, as well as the desire of the local ruling families to cement their ruling credentials. As previously mentioned, the onset of the great depression globally and the decimation of the pearling industry had left the economies of the region in tatters by the end of the 1920s.[19] The newly emergent state was a product of this process: it was a reaction to the dire economic situation of locals before oil money, it reflected the desire of its political and bureaucratic elite to become a 'modern state' under the guises of the ruling families, and it acted as a way to establish control and discipline over most of the population.[20]

In tandem, constructing this new modernist state opened up lucrative investment opportunities for capital accumulation. These investment opportunities were redirected towards the region's traditional merchant families and other individuals close to the ruling elite, due to their close proximity to those with political power, but also as a way of placating and establishing control over this group. It should not be forgotten, after all, that merchants offered the most direct political challenge to the power of the rulers during the desperate economic situations of the pre-oil era, most famously in the 1938 political movements demanding constitutional and institutional reforms that emerged simultaneously in Dubai, Kuwait and Bahrain. Tenders and licenses for state-funded projects (infrastructure, buildings and factories) were distributed along with land plots 'gifted' from the state. The import business, which relied on granting exclusive agency licenses over import brands, was another lucrative business to induce capital accumulation. Thus, new and vastly enriching opportunities emerged for the economically powerful class in the region (Hanieh, 2011: 60–70). Happily enough, or so it was thought, the new-found oil wealth allowed both the pursuit of economic profit by the private sector and the establishment of the new petro-modernist state. There was no conflict between the two, and indeed both were often two sides of the same coin. State-driven modernism and capitalism ran side by side.

The economic projects that accompanied these new visions naturally required a labour force. The Gulf's working class had traditionally been constituted by local residents. However, the local workforce presented three major problems for the emerging economic and political elite. First of all, the sheer quantity of capital resulting from the enormous oil revenues, and the number of associated investment activities, exceeded the capacity and quality of the available domestic workforce. The numbers required to build this new high-modernist state and to put such large amounts of capital in motion simply did not exist locally, and neither did the experience nor the qualifications needed for the magnitude and quality of these projects. These visions, after all, were based on the ambitions and calculations of the economically and politically powerful, rather than on the capacities and interests of the local labour force.

Second, subjugating the local population to the dictates of capital, which ideally wanted a 'flexible' labour force 'freed' from any 'rights' that might impede the workings of the 'free market', went against the logic of the modernist welfare state that was supposed to pull local people out of the dire economic situation they found themselves in prior to the windfall from the oil revenues. It would have been a hard political sell to place locals under the increasingly hungry and urgent demands of the new-found capital, but neither would it have been desirable (from the viewpoint of capital) to place restrictions that would favour strong labour rights.

Finally, the reliance on local and Arab workers created, as previously explained, a political consciousness among the workforce that demanded a greater say in the distribution of oil revenues and participation in the economic and political decision-making process. Concerns about the emergent local nationalist and leftist movements were at their peak. Thus, as the oil boom continued, the dependence on local and Arab expatriate labour became a less attractive option for the Gulf's economic and political elite (Chalcraft, 2010). Similarly, Western powers with influence in the region, whose primary interest now revolved around ensuring the steady supply of oil to the global markets and ensuring the continual positioning of the Gulf States within their spheres of influence, saw the evolution of such leftist and nationalist-leaning movements as a threat to their economic and political interests.[21]

A much more palatable way of securing what was seen as a more compliant and less risky labour force was to import increasing amounts of non-Arab labour. This presented multiple advantages for those in power and for capital. The first is the quantity and quality of the newly emergent labour supply. The expansion of the labour market from a local to a global scale led to an increase in the available labour supply from a few thousand workers at the local level, to hundreds of millions of workers theoretically available globally. The cost of obtaining this labour was relatively low and was easy to attract, because of the push factors in home countries lacking sufficient domestic employment opportunities. After all, the importation of foreign labour to the region was not without precedent. The path had been well-trodden previously by the British colonial administration and the oil companies. This importation of foreign labour had the added advantage of ending the state's dependence on local labour. Thus the local workforce was to lose its economic influence, as it neither provided taxes or labour power, and consequently was to lose one of its strongest weapons for demanding active participation in political matters.

However, the importation of foreign labour was not without its own risks. The first lay in the national reaction to an increasingly foreign labouring class, which initially was viewed as displacing the local workforce. The second threat was the possible increase in the economic and political influence of foreign workers as their numbers increased. The solution to these two problems, and the method of discipline, was to be found in the Gulf's current 'demographic imbalance'.

The first feature of disciplining this new demographic structure was that many (but not all[22]) of the benefits of the modern welfare state were to be limited to citizens to the exclusion of expatriates. A citizen most often came to be defined as someone who was (or whose ancestors were) present in the country before the oil boom, thus someone who had lived through the dire economic situation before the petro-windfall.[23] The allocation of exclusive benefits to citizens was made possible by the enormous oil revenues. These included free education, healthcare, subsidised housing and employment in the expanding bureaucracies of the state. To obtain these privileges, however, it was not enough to be a 'citizen'. One had to be a loyal and disciplined citizen too. Proximity and allegiance to the ruling elites, and not capitalist economic dictates, often became a crucial factor in determining how the largesse of state were to be distributed. Thus local society increasingly became vertically segmented into different yet overlapping corporatist groups of sects, regions, ethnicities, tribes and interest groups, whose positions vis-à-vis the state, rather than purely productive-economic considerations, determined the type of access they would gain to the state's oil largesse.[24] Indeed, different tribes, sects and ethnicities within the citizen population regularly engaged in competition against each other, often by state incitement, as well as disciplining and self-policing members of their own groupings.

The second control method over the new demographic structure was that although the Gulf States flung their doors wide to migrant workers, their political and economic rights had to be carefully restricted and managed. The possibility to obtain property, form unions and own capital were outlawed, and it goes without saying that many of the welfare state privileges afforded to citizens were out of the reach of expatriates. Their presence in the region was based on the principle of *kafala* ('sponsorship'), where each migrant worker must be sponsored and guaranteed by a citizen or a local company for a specified period that can be terminated when the employer sees fit.[25]

Failure to adhere to these new rules of the game would result in deportation for expatriates, and the restriction of state benefits for disobedient citizens. Thus the welfare state and the *kafala* system became powerful tools for self-discipline and punishment (Foucault, 1977) for both citizens and expatriates. Indeed, citizens and expatriates often became embedded in a network of control against each other as well as against members of their own groupings. The segmentation of expatriates along different nationalities with different languages and cultural backgrounds made any cross-solidarity between them extremely difficult. The spectre of the flood of strangers that could provide an existential threat to locals via the 'demographic disorder', with the state being the only possible agent with powers to deal with the matter, provided a powerful mechanism with which to discipline citizens.[26] Furthermore, the state was often seen as the only bulwark against the potential abuses that could be carried out by citizens against expatriates under the *kafala* system. Hence, the state was positioned as the ultimate arbitrator in the affairs of the population, whether expatriates or citizens.

The Oil Boom Leads to a Population Boom

Expatriate labour flows increased exponentially with the first oil boom, and continued into the second oil boom of the late 1970s and early 1980s. Between 1975 and 1985, the annual growth rate for the citizen population was 3.9 per cent, while the annual expatriate population growth rate was about three times higher at 11.1 per cent. Based on this growth, the number of immigrants went from less than one million before 1970 to over six million by 1985 (see Figure 1.1). By the end of 1985, expatriates made up a total of 37 per cent of the region's population, and in some countries, such as Kuwait, the UAE and Qatar, expatriates formed the majority, a trend that would continue into the twenty-first century (Figure 1.2).

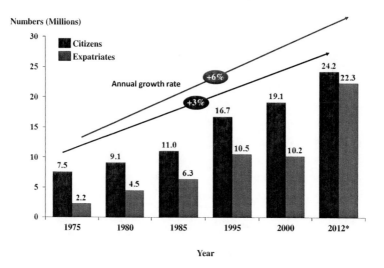

Figure 1.1   GCC population evolution, 1975–2012 (millions)

* 2011 figures for Bahrain, Oman and Kuwait. 2010 figures for UAE.

Sources: author calculations from 2010–2012 figures released by country statistical authorities. Previous years' figures are calculated from data in Shah (2004).

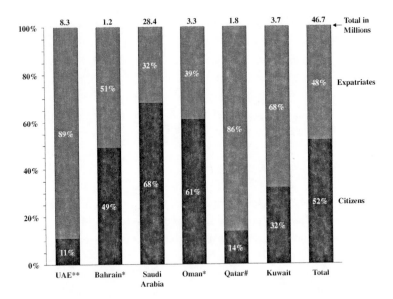

Figure 1.2   Citizens and expatriates' percentages within GCC populations in 2012

* 2011 figures
** 2010 figures
# Qatar does not release an official breakdown between citizens and expatriates. Hence, citizen numbers estimated at 250,000 for 2012.
Source: author calculations from national statistical authorities' figures.

Since migrants were overwhelmingly workers, with many not allowed to resettle their families with them locally, the expatriate percentage of the labour force was much higher than their percentage of the total population. Annual growth in the local workforce did not exceed 1.73 per cent between 1975 and 1985, while the annual average growth rate of expatriate labour had reached 14.8 per cent by the end of 1985. This raised the number of non-national workers from 1.1 million in 1975 to 4.4 million in 1985 (Figure 1.3). By the mid-1980s, expatriate labourers were equal to 70 per cent of the region's workforce. In some states, such as the UAE, non-national labour had reached 90 per cent of the total (Figure 1.4). Given that most of the migrant workers were males, GCC societies came to display one of the most unbalanced proportions of male to female ratios in the world. In the UAE, for example, male expatriates outnumbered female expatriates in 1985 by a ratio of 3 to 1, and the overall population was more than two-thirds male (UAE National Bureau of Statistics, 2005).

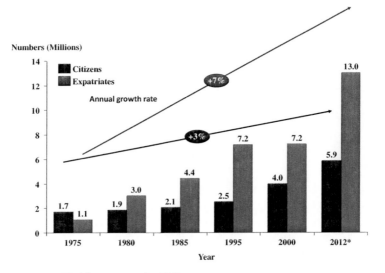

Figure 1.3   Workforce size in the GCC states, 1975–2012

* 2011 figures for Bahrain, Oman and Kuwait. 2005 figures for UAE.

Source: author calculations from 2010–2012 figures released by country statistical authorities. Previous years' figures are calculated from data in Shah (2004).

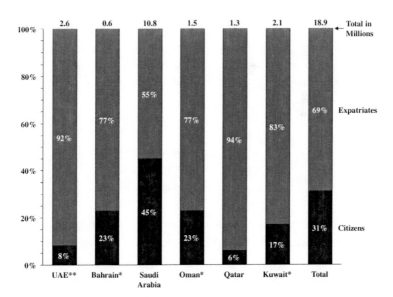

Figure 1.4   Citizens and expatriates' percentages in total GCC workforce in 2012

* 2011 figures
** 2005 figures

Source: author calculations from national statistical authorities' figures.

In addition to the unprecedented influx of migrant workers and the population's unbalanced gender ratio, two further features came to characterise demographic developments in this period. The first was the firm entrenchment of a network of vested interests that ensured the increasing demographic imbalance was now supported with a momentum of its own. No sooner had it begun as an official policy to restructure and utilise demographics for the purposes of economic growth and the building of the modern state that, with time, incentives had been established which embedded this population structure as an essential element of society, with a vast network of vested interests that had a stake in ensuring its continuity.

First, the economic incentives increased significantly for the private sector to rely on foreign labour when compared to the local workforce. The ever-rising economic and social benefits accruing to holding citizenship meant that the cost – both material and legal – of employing a local worker became increasingly unattractive, and importing foreign workers became a more cost-efficient option with less legal obligations. With the exception of some bureaucratic regulatory controls, there were no real restrictions on the ability of the private sector to import labour. Nor were citizens particularly eager to work in the increasingly harsh conditions of the private sector. Hence, citizens came to be concentrated primarily in the public sector, where the pay was much higher and the legal, material and social benefits of the emergent welfare state were to be found, and where citizens were protected from the vagaries of the private sector. Employment conditions in the latter were severely biased towards the interests of capital, with no minimum wages, no right to unionize and the threat of being fired an ever-present possibility. Jobs in the private sector came to be overwhelmingly filled by migrant workers.

Furthermore, citizens themselves also began to benefit from the importation of migrant labour. Some began to import labour for employment in their own small and medium-sized businesses, but the phenomenon in this period took off mainly in the domestic services sector (Al Kuwari, 2005). With the accumulating material and social advantages of being a citizen, the number of workers, particularly female, employed in domestic services began to increase steadily. Indeed, the dynamics of the migration process was in essence delegated from the state to the private sector and citizens, with each migrant requiring a sponsor, whether a citizen or a company, for entry to the country. Thus, a higher influx of foreign workers increasingly came to suit the interests of citizens, political decision makers and capitalists alike. Finally, a vast network of middlemen, agents and officials with vested interests in the migration process emerged in the sending countries too, who saw in exporting labour a useful source of hard currency and a solution to local unemployment pressures.

The second notable phenomenon was the marked decline in the percentage of Arab expatriates (see Figure 1.5). As mentioned previously, Arab labour was prevalent before the oil boom and constituted more than 70 per cent of the immigrant workforce (Kapiszewski, 2006: 9). As the two oil booms progressed, the attractiveness of Arab migrants decreased for several reasons. First, workers from the Indian subcontinent were relatively less expensive than their Arab counterparts due to the severity of the push factors in those countries. Second, investors and political leaders began to harbour suspicions regarding Arab labour, seeing them as a primary cause of Arab nationalism, Nasserism and leftism in the Gulf.

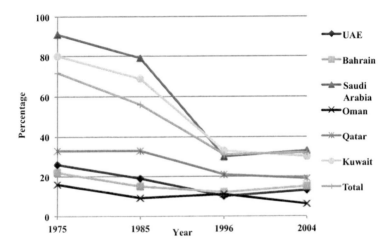

Figure 1.5   Percentage of Arabs in the GCC's immigrant workforce, 1975–2004
Source: (Kapiszewski, 2006).

As the oil boom progressed, nationalist and leftist movements declined in strength across the Arab world, with their centres of power in Egypt and Syria considerably weakened. This was met with the steady rise in the Gulf regimes' regional influence due to rising oil incomes. Concurrently, attention increasingly turned towards non-Arab labour that was seen as less expensive and less dangerous from a political and security standpoint.

There are no accurate statistics on the composition of expatriate communities in the GCC. This data are considered to be sensitive information with a security dimension in some countries. The following two tables provide unofficial estimates of the number of different nationalities in the GCC (Table 1.1), and the proportion of the various communities of origin within the labour market (Table 1.2). Both sources point to three main demographic characteristics concerning worker origin.

Table 1.1   Expatriate numbers by nationality, 2002–2004 (thousands)

Sending Country	Kuwait (2003)	Qatar (2002)	Oman (2004)	Saudi Arabia (2004)	Bahrain (2004)	UAE (2002)	Total
India	320	100	330	1300	120	1200	3370
Pakistan	100	100	70	900	50	450	1670
Egypt	260	35	30	900	30	140	1395
Yemen				800		60	860
Bangladesh	170		110	400		100	780
Philippines	70	50		500	25	120	765
Sri Lanka	170	35	30	350		160	745
Jordan/Palestine	50	50		260	20	110	490
Sudan				250		30	280
Indonesia	9			250			259
Iran	80	60			30	40	210
Syria	100			100			200
Turkey				80			80
Stateless	80						80
Nepal		70					70

Source: (Kapiszewski, 2006).

Table 1.2   Migrant worker percentages by regional origin in 2005

Sending Country	Kuwait	Qatar	Oman	Saudi Arabia	Bahrain	UAE
Arab	31	40	6	31	12	9
Asian	65	46	92	59	80	87
European	1	2	0	3	2	2
The Americas	1		0	2	2	1
Others	3	12	2	5	4	2

Source: International Labour Office and Arab Employment Forum (2009).

The first is that Arabs came to constitute less than half of the migrants in each of the GCC countries. The second is the multiplicity and diversity of nationalities and communities that came to makeup the migrant population. This policy was pursued as a method of discipline and control, in order to avoid particular groups developing a solidarity bloc based on national or linguistic ties. The third characteristic is the sourcing of the largest proportion of migrants to the region from countries with high levels of poverty and significant push factors, especially from the Indian subcontinent. Migrants from these countries constituted the bulk of unskilled and semi-skilled workers in the region. On the other hand, although Western expatriates formed a small proportion of total immigration, they exerted disproportionate influence by virtue of their concentration in the administrative and skilled classes. As was the case in the days of British colonialism, it was members from this group who frequently continued to manage, design and execute the plans and policies of the political and economic elite.[27] Arab migrants were mainly concentrated in middle-class technocratic and professional occupations, both within government and the private sector.

Thus, by the end of the first oil boom, what locally came to be referred to as the 'demographic disorder' became a striking and firmly embedded feature in all of the GCC states without exception. This, we argued, was the result of two often overlapping but sometimes competing projects of building a petro-modernist welfare state in conjunction with solidifying the place of the Gulf within the global capitalist system. The windfall revenues from the first oil boom meant that both projects could be pursued jointly with no apparent competition, and indeed circumstances meant that they complemented each other closely. Members of the royal family sat comfortably at the top of this pyramid of social relations, with their uncontested power grip largely based on Western backing and their control over the state's oil revenues, which they were able to distribute to further consolidate their rule. Their dominant position was complemented by an influential class of businessmen who used their close relations with political actors to benefit from the economic opportunities emerging from the oil boom. These groups formed a power bloc that was able to exercise hegemony within the resultant society. This domestic power bloc fitted rather well with the interests of the core Western powers, whose main concerns were the continued flow of oil on to world markets and maintaining the stability of the Gulf regimes under their political umbrella, avoiding the unsavoury consequences of any changes that may produce forces hostile to their interests, as had happened in other parts of the Arab world.

Demographics were reconstituted primarily to serve the requirements of this power bloc. Oil revenues led to a lopsided reversal in the historical relationship of dependence that had existed between the state and the local people who provided the main source of productive labour. Their role as labour providers was sidelined, as their involvement in most of the productive sectors of the economy diminished. 'Citizens' came to be concentrated in the expanding bureaucracies of the public sector, where they were becoming increasingly dependent on the state's largesse for their social and economic benefits, including salaries, access to housing and even birth and burial services, which were funded through the oil rent received by the state. These benefits were, however, reliant on discipline and loyalty to the state, and they were often distributed through a complex web of corporatist groups that helped to vertically segment and enshrine the policy of divide and rule over society.

Simultaneously, the growing demand for labour was to be met by the extensive importation of migrant workers, sourced from a variety of different countries to mitigate any potential solidarity issues. This migrant population was controlled by laws and regulations that restricted their ability to achieve political or economic integration. Thus most expatriates were in a state of permanent temporariness. As the region moved ever closer to resembling a scattering of transit labour camps, its energy as a society became primarily geared towards sustaining an omnipresent state that oversees the circulation of oil revenues and the execution of rapid economic growth, all the while carefully avoiding the formation of any significant political-economic power within the population, whether among nationals or expatriates.

Tensions Within the Petro-modernist State, 1985–2000

The extent to which the new population structure had become embedded in Gulf society became clear in the period that followed the first two oil booms, which we will call the fourth period of migration to the Gulf. This period was marked by economic stagnation and low oil prices, which tumbled from US$37 per barrel in 1980 to below US$15 in 1986 (U.S. Energy Information Administration, 2014). Despite the economic recession, the most important demographic feature of this period was the continuing increase in expatriate numbers, and the shrinking proportion of Arabs among them (see Figure 1.5). These developments leave traditional analyses of Gulf migration wanting – based as they are on push factors in sending countries and pull factors in the host countries – and instead point to deeper structural factors that the previous section explored. By the end of 1990, the vast majority of migrant workers were non-Arab, and their number exceeded 5.2 million

(Baldwin-Edwards, 2011), compared with the 2.5 million workers that same year who were citizens.

A 'structural break' occurred when Saddam Hussein's army invaded Kuwait in August 1990, with far-reaching repercussions for the demographic makeup of the Gulf. One of the more direct results of the invasion was that some 350,000 Palestinians were deported from Kuwait due to the Palestinian leadership officially declaring their support for the invasion. For the same reason, Saudi Arabia also deported hundreds of thousands of Yemenis from its territory, and the Iraqi communities in all the GCC experienced the same fate. It is estimated that up to two million Arabs were deported as a consequence of the invasion (Fergany, 2001: 4–12). Arabs were significantly reduced as a proportion of migrants, and the obsession with the security implications of the expatriate Arab presence became ever-more intense.

This period had consequences for the Gulf that extended beyond the immediate events of the invasion. From a political and security perspective, there was increased military dependency on Western powers, especially the US. During the operation to liberate Kuwait, foreign forces and military barracks were stationed across all the GCC countries for the first time, including countries that historically remained independent of direct foreign military presence, such as Saudi Arabia and Kuwait.

Locally, a series of increasingly glaring contradictions on the demographic front led to a process of internal reflection and reassessment within the Gulf. Although the number of migrants arriving in the Gulf was still increasing, the continued decline in oil prices restricted the ability of the state to absorb the growing number of citizens entering the labour force, with the official unemployment rates reaching double digits in several states (Al-Qudsi, 2006). How was the state to counter the paradox of a hungry economy continuing to demand imported labour, while witnessing an increasing level of unemployment within its local population?

Thus, tensions began to appear between the aspirations of the modernist welfare state and the goals of capital accumulation. On paper at least, the state seemed intent on attempting to force the private sector to share some of the 'burden' of providing jobs for its citizenry. The private sector, however, had little enthusiasm for the task. Initiatives, laws, incentives and restrictions were drafted by the state with the aim of 'nationalising the workforce' and raising the employment numbers among citizens. The official public viewpoint of the prevailing demographic structure was that it had become a 'problem' that needed to be dealt with (Kapiszewski, 2001: 7–8).

Having been accustomed to the pact established during the oil boom, the private sector did not want to employ citizens, and nor did citizens want to be turned into a labour class for the private sector. From the point of view of the private sector, citizens were costly, unproductive and demanding, while from the point of view of citizens, the private sector was greedy and exploitative, offering working conditions that were not fit for citizens. Thus, the state increasingly found itself attempting to force through an arranged marriage on unwilling partners.

Unsurprisingly, this largely proved unsuccessful. Despite a plethora of official initiatives and promises, the actual demographic profile did not change drastically, and indeed migrant numbers continued to rise (see Figure 1.3). By the end of 2000, there were over ten million expatriates in the Gulf, representing 35 per cent of the region's population.

It should be noted that the migrant figures mentioned above do not include the numbers of undocumented immigrants, which are thought to be large. For example, 700,000 undocumented workers were estimated to be in Saudi Arabia in 1997, 300,000 in the UAE and 100,000 in Qatar. These figures are equal to 18 per cent, 37 per cent and 41 per cent of the total number of expatriates in each country respectively (Shah, 2009). Thus, the phenomenon of undocumented labour became a widespread phenomenon throughout the GCC and occurred in various forms. Some workers remain illegally after their residence permit expires, while others enter the region through the illegal visa trade run by some GCC nationals, which illegally gives the worker *kafala* status.

The resultant unofficial pact throughout the recession was that the private sector continued in its practice of importing migrant workers (albeit at a slower pace), while the state did its utmost to ensure that the lower oil revenues were not reflected negatively in the wages and benefits its citizens enjoyed. Indeed, the largely Arab expatriates in the public sector were increasingly replaced by citizens as one way of alleviating unemployment pressures. What was drastically reduced instead was state spending on capital and infrastructural projects. Grandiose modernist developmental state projects were sacrificed for the sake of the welfare state and capitalism. Private sector employment patterns remained largely intact, and most attempts by the state to restructure it away from migrant labour towards the local workforce were resoundingly defeated (Chaudhry, 1997).

Alienation, Exploitation, Citizenship and Identity

The result was that with the exception of the oil sector, state-provided services and the financial sector, GCC citizens were largely unrelated to the rest of the productive sectors in the Gulf economies, with the private sector operating in its entirety with little active participation from citizens. Indeed, if all citizen-workers were to go on strike, the private sector would largely continue unabated.

This low involvement of citizens in society's productive processes is reflected in their very low participation rates in the labour force and correspondingly high rate of economic inactivity. For example, the labour force participation rate for the whole population of the UAE in 2009 stood at 73 per cent, not very different from the OECD's rate in 2009 of 71 per cent. This overall figure, however, masks a huge disparity between the rates for citizens and expatriates. The citizens' rate was 45 per cent (63 per cent among males and 28 per cent among females), nearly half the rate of 79 per cent among expatriates (94 per cent for males and 48 per cent for females) (UAE National Bureau of Statistics, 2009: table 2/42).

The consequences of marginalising citizens from much of productive labour go beyond the economic dimension, and have even extended into fraught issues around identity.[28] With citizens becoming a minority in most GCC countries (where in many cases Arabs as a whole are also a minority), a perceived sense of alienation has emerged among citizens of most GCC states, with many complaining that they are 'strangers in their own land'. The flipside of this perceived threat to identity was the emergence of intolerance and xenophobia, which manifests itself in the inferior perception and treatment that many citizens display towards migrants. The issue of the 'demographic imbalance' created a general feeling among many citizens that they were caught between a rock and a hard place, in a precarious choice between intolerance towards expatriates and the perceived threats towards their identity and culture. These phenomena are mostly two sides of the same coin, a product of the alienation and fear of identity loss that citizens feel, and the fact that being a citizen is in many ways constituted by the rights afforded to the citizenry to exercise domination over migrant workers.

Thus, most of the human rights literature on migrants in the Gulf has come to focus on the limited rights and privileges that are afforded to foreigners in comparison with citizens, especially the 'structural violence' generated by the current sponsorship system, which pits non-citizens in a position of social inferiority in relation to their local sponsors. This often leads to severe human rights violations and persecution against expatriates, leading some activists to describe it as modern institutional slavery (Union View, 2008).

We can summarise this situation within a society segmented into groups of citizens and expatriates as a severe type of 'hyper-alienation' that both groups experience, albeit in different yet mutually dependent ways. Hyper-alienation is taken here to refer to a person's lack of control and involvement in the production of their surrounding environment,[29] whether economically, politically, socially or culturally, to the point where they feel the surrounding environment and its production process does not represent them, and indeed is a source of oppression. If alienation on the economic front is usually defined as a lack of control by workers over the production process and the goods they produce, then what citizens experience is an extreme form of alienation: having minimal active participation in the production process and very little input into what is produced. Their primary economic role is confined instead to being consumers and beneficiaries of state-distributed or privately generated rent.

This often also means extreme alienation towards the built environment, where citizens have very little input into the construction and use of the urban landscape, an issue that will be explored in depth in Chapter 5 of this book. Indeed, involvement in the public decision-making process generally is virtually non-existent, with many citizens complaining that they had no choice or say regarding the 'demographic imbalance' in the country.[30] Socially and culturally, there is a perception by many citizens that their language, identity and culture is under threat as a result of becoming a minority in a population that largely does not share the same heritage or language. As for expatriates, their lack of political, economic and legal rights, the segmentation of society based on citizens versus expatriates with each group interacting largely in its own constructed spaces, and the treatment of many migrants as little more than a labour commodity in a temporary work camp, makes hyper-alienation a permanent condition for them. Thus the population as a whole – split into citizens and expatriates – suffers acutely from a severe state of hyper-alienation.

Concerns of the 'Population Imbalance' Reach the State

The ramifications of the population structure were not only confined to citizens and expatriates, but have also become a cause of growing concern at the state level. As outlined in the previous section, worries started to grow regarding the rising unemployment among citizens, the possibility of citizen unrest, and the weakening ability of the state to discipline citizens and maintain their loyalty through the distribution of oil rent. Added to this was the growing burden resulting from ever-increasing state subsidies. The vast increase in population size, business projects and the associated consumption activities meant an increasing burden on state budgets. Some of these subsidies supported citizens only (such as housing), but others supported both citizens and migrants (such as subsidised fuel, electricity and water prices). Indeed, citizens, migrants and local businesses have increasingly fuelled the burgeoning consumption of state-subsidised goods in the GCC. In Bahrain, for example, the price of petrol has not been raised since 1983, when a litre of '95 octane petrol' was priced at US$0.28, with the oil minister commenting in 2010 that subsidised petrol was costing the state treasury half a billion dollars annually (*Trade Arabia*, 2010). The UAE actually experienced a severe shortage of petrol at filling stations in Dubai and the Northern Emirates in 2011 (Pamuk, 2011), with the remarkable paradox of a petrol shortage in an oil-exporting state. There has also been growing official concern at the large exodus of currency from the local economy in the form of remittances abroad. One estimate put the total cost of expatriate labour born by GCC states – essentially as a subsidy to local businesses, citizens and expatriate consumption – at US$56 billion in 2002 (Ghaffar, 2004). Although citizens, local businesses, expatriates and local economic growth stood to gain considerably from these subsidies, the direct financial return from the point of view of the state is negligible, particularly considering that state returns from taxes are largely non-existent.

Furthermore, the presence of large numbers of migrants from certain countries that sometimes exceeded the total number of citizens created a perception of possible security and political ramifications within some official circles. In the UAE for example, Indian citizens represent 42.5 per cent of the population, while the percentage of all Arabs combined was 28 per cent (*Al Arabiya*, 2008). This led to active policing strategies to manage the different migrant communities, with many countries legislating laws that impose an upper limit on the percentage of workers local companies could employ from a particular nationality.

The role of international organisations and conventions that deal with migrant workers has also become an increasing concern of the GCC states. The International Labour Organization (ILO) and United Nations (UN) conventions, in particular, aim to give migrant workers all over the world (regardless of their legal or illegal status) similar political, economic and social rights to those enjoyed by citizens. We can mention here, for example, the 'International Convention on the Protection of the Rights of All Migrant Workers and Members of their Families', which was approved by the UN's General Assembly on 18 December 1990. This convention requires that migrant workers shall enjoy treatment no less favourable than that which applies to nationals of the state of employment in respect of remuneration and the termination of the working relationship (Article 25). In addition, there should be equality of social insurance (Article 27), migrant workers should have the right to form trade unions and worker committees of their own (Article 40), and they should have the right to enrol in those unions limited to citizens (Article 26). This is in addition to the right to take the necessary measures to unite the families of migrants (Article 44), the right to access education on an equal basis with citizens (Article 30), and it also stipulates that there should be respect for the cultural identity of migrant workers (Article 31) (Executive Office of the Council of Ministers for Labour and the Council of Ministers for Social Affairs in the GCC, 2008).

The Gulf States insist that these and similar agreements do not apply to them, because the expatriates in the Gulf are 'temporary labour' and are invited guest workers, rather than a 'migrant' workforce. International advocacy groups, however, insist that international conventions on migrant rights apply regardless of the length of the period that migrant workers stay in a country. Moreover, to what extent are migrants actually a temporary workforce, and how long do expatriates actually stay in the region? Although a comprehensive picture of expatriate settlement in the region does not exist, various statistics indicate that the percentage of expatriates who have spent a long time is relatively high, including many who have had children and raised their families for most of their lives in the Gulf. For example, migrants constituted 20 per cent of all children under 15 years of age in the GCC in 2007, and formed the majority of the children in some countries like the UAE. Expatriates also account for 27 per cent of over-65s, which indicates a high proportion of retired expatriates in the GCC (Fargues, 2011a). All these signs point to a degree of stable settlement. In the UAE for example, 28.5 per cent of arrivals spent ten years or more in the country, making it difficult to consider these migrants as 'temporary' (Baldwin-Edwards, 2011: 28–32). Regardless of the actual length of time spent in the host countries, a key factor in the continuing demographic structure of the GCC countries is that migrants *de jure* are not allowed a systematic and clear route towards obtaining citizenship.[31]

It does not seem, however, that any of these concerns at the official level were existential enough to induce a serious change in the Gulf States' policies towards the region's demographic profile by the end of the 1990s. Indeed, developments in the first decade of the twenty-first century exacerbated the population structure: the influx of expatriates steadily increased, confirming the deep embeddedness of the region's population structure in the socio-economic makeup of society.

The Third Oil Boom and 'Privatisation', 2000–2014

As the Gulf's third oil boom began at the dawn of the twenty-first century, the price of a barrel of oil rose from below US$20 in 1999, to US$60 in 2005, culminating in 2008 at over US$140 (U.S. Energy Information Administration, 2014). This led to the accumulation of huge oil revenues, estimated at more than US$2 trillion. The Gulf's foreign assets swelled, and by the end of 2009 they were valued at more than US$1.5 trillion, or the equivalent of 165 per cent of gross domestic product (GDP), the highest ratio in the world (Iradian, 2009: 1). This boom in oil revenues also coincided with a move by investors in the region to increase their local investment activities. The destruction of the two world trade towers in the United States on 11 September 2001 was followed by increased racism against Arabs and Muslims. Because of these developments, Gulf investors began to shift some of their money back into the region,[32] and copious amounts of capital were looking for a way to be utilised in the Gulf.

Demographically, this period witnessed an unprecedented increase in the number of migrants and the continued decline in the proportion of citizens and Arabs as a percentage of the total population (see Figures 1.1 and 1.5). The desire to mobilise such large amounts of capital caused the Gulf States to experience the highest population growth rate in the world. The contradictions enumerated previously continued to grow: rising hyper-alienation of citizens and migrants, vigilantism at the official level towards the policing of the ever-burgeoning population and concerns regarding the burden of state subsidies for citizens and expatriates. But this period was also characterised by a number of new changes that sharply distinguished it from the preceding eras.

The most notable was the wind of 'privatisation' that blew throughout the region and the ascent of the 'free market' mantra. If the recession period of the 1980s and 1990s saw the decline of developmentalist projects driven by the modernist state, the first decade of the new millennium saw their replacement with privatised mega-projects. Gulf markets were opened wide to private investment, with private and quasi-public companies and projects proliferating across the regional landscape. The intention was to steer the economy towards privatisation, reflecting the language of the newly adopted official economic visions and recommendations from the World Bank, International Monetary Fund (IMF) and like-minded private consulting firms.

Thus, development was no longer guided by grand projects driven by a centralised modernist state, but instead came to be identified with growth in the private sector. Indeed, development was simply to be equated with economic growth. As long as GDP was increasing then development was thriving, regardless of any other consideration. For GDP to grow, its main driver must be the private sector, and to stimulate the private sector, increasing amounts of migrant labour must be imported to meet its requirements.

The term 'private sector' is a misleading expression, because what developed in the Gulf does not correspond to the phrase's usual connotations. 'The private sector' often conjures up images of a plethora of private firms competing within well-defined and efficient markets, under the institutional framework of a neutral state that upholds the rules of the game. This most certainly was not the private sector in the Gulf. For starters, here the private sector was dominated by the activities of a small group of influential investors that are closely connected to, and often overlap, with those that exercise political power. This is therefore closer to what some economists term 'crony capitalism' (Baumol et al., 2007). Furthermore, the state continued to play a central role in this process, even if many of the projects and activities were labelled as 'private'. State-owned companies proliferated, with a considerable overlap between those in power and large investors, to the extent that in many cases the two parties were the same people (Hanieh, 2011). The line between 'public' versus 'private' was severely blurred, and increasingly the political and economic elite were fusing together.

Demographically, the most notable effect of this shift was to increase the size of the expatriate workforce, particularly in the 'private' sector. Feeding the prodigious building boom across the region, migrants were particularly concentrated within construction, with the sector accounting for up to a third of the expatriate labour force in some countries (e.g. Bahrain and Qatar). The rest of the migrant workforce was distributed between basic manufacturing, domestic labour, retail and wholesale trade, and the services and hospitality sectors (Baldwin-Edwards, 2011: 26). Although the financial crisis that struck the region in 2009 put a temporary check on economic growth, the number of migrants entering the region actually continued to grow, showing no signs of reversing the continuously upward trajectory that was established during previous booms and busts alike.

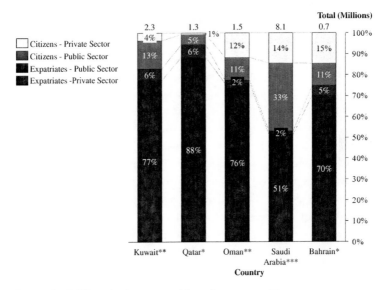

Figure 1.6   Public and private sector labour force composition, 2009–2012

* 2010 figures
** 2012 figures
*** 2009 figures

Source: author calculations from national statistic authorities, sourced from Gulf Labour Markets and Migration Project (2012).

It is worth spending a moment analysing the labour structure of this private sector. First, it is composed almost entirely of expatriates (see Figure 1.6). Even in countries where at first glance there might appear to be a sizeable amount of locals in the private sector (Bahrain, Oman and Saudi Arabia), this is actually misleading, as the overwhelming majority of citizens classified as working in the private sector are in reality employed in state-owned or mixed enterprises, such as the national oil or airline companies. This is in addition to the relatively high-paying financial services sector (which also has a high proportion of state ownership). As is to be expected, remuneration is very low in the private sector when compared to the public sector, with the average 2009 monthly wages in the Qatari private sector, for example, being less than half the average monthly wage in the civil service or publicly owned companies (Qatar Statistics Authority, 2009). Indeed, labour generally does not receive much of the value added in the Gulf economies, with the proportion of the GDP accruing to capital as a factor of production being approximately double that of labour. In Bahrain, for example, the 2010 ratio of the share of GDP going to capital versus that going to labour[33] was 1.4, while in Kuwait for the same year it was a whopping 2.6.[34] In Norway and the United States, two countries with relatively low proportions of GDP going to labour compensation by OECD standards, the figures were 0.6 and 0.7.[35] Thus, labour in the Gulf generally receives the shorter end of the stick when compared to capital.

The private sector expatriate labour force has relatively low skill levels. For example, 74 per cent of expatriates working in the Omani private sector in 2012 held qualifications that were less than a high school degree (Oman NCSI, 2012), and the situation is not considerably different in the rest of the GCC. Productivity is considered to be extremely low by international standards, and it seems it has actually been declining over the past few decades (IMF, 2010). Thus, the overall picture that emerges is that of a low-technology private sector with extremely high returns to capital, which relies on a relatively unlimited supply of comparatively low-paid, low-skilled, expatriate labour force with low productivity. At first glance this appears as quite the opposite of what economic theory would predict for countries that are supposed to be naturally endowed as capital rich and labour scarce. Given the story we narrated of the rise of the petro-modernist state and capital accumulation fuelled by oil revenues and unrestricted labour migration while restricting citizenship, this result is no longer perplexing.

One final characteristic of the labour force in the 'private sector' that is worth emphasising is the sizeable proportion of migrant labour working in small and medium-sized enterprises. This trend increased noticeably in the first decade of the twenty-first century, as dependency on migrant labour for income generation spread widely beyond 'big capital' and into the wider citizenry. As explained previously, demand by citizens for migrant labour used to be more concentrated on domestic services rather than income generation. At the turn of the twenty-first century, however, the allure of the public sector, where most citizens were employed, was fading. Government policy had given free rein to the private sector, and the public sector, or so citizens were told, could no longer be relied on to be the main engine of provision. Attention should be turned instead towards the private sector. Since becoming an employee in the private sector was still largely an unpleasant experience with relatively low pay that is best avoided by citizens (save for a few sectors in the financial services and state-owned enterprises), the solution was for citizens to become employers themselves. 'Small and medium-sized enterprises' became a buzz phrase, with the stereotypical image emerging of a citizen whose main goal is to either construct a building that can be rented out as apartments and shops, to rent out the commercial registration of a company under his name to an expatriate who then runs the business, or to use his *kafala* sponsorship rights to import migrants who would be given access to work in the country in exchange for a specified return.

These rent seeking practices had existed ever since the emergence of the post-oil economies of the GCC, but they took on a more intensive and prevalent form during the twenty-first century. Indeed, it would be a mistake to view migrants in the region as being solely employed under large, capitalist conglomerates. In fact, statistics show that a large proportion of migrants, often exceeding half, are distributed between domestic workers and small and medium-sized enterprises (which can be loosely seen as a citizen petite bourgeoisie). In Kuwait, for example, 2011 statistics show that nearly a third of the migrant population was employed in domestic services (Kuwait Central Statistical Bureau, 2011). In Bahrain, more than 80 per cent of workers registered under the social insurance organisation responsible for private sector employment in 2010 were in establishments with less than 50 employees (Bahrain CIO, 2010).

These developments were not unexpected, for if large investors and those in power stood to gain from the importation of foreign labour, then why should citizens not benefit too? If the rent directly received from the state no longer satisfies citizen aspirations in the way it used to, and if the state is actively encouraging the 'private sector', then why should citizens not also derive rent from the 'private sector' by recruiting migrants? After all, citizenship offers the right to extract rent via the *kafala* system and the importation of migrants that are directly sponsored by the citizen. In this way, the dependence on migrant labour was no longer in the sole interest of the state and big business, but also became ingrained within the wider citizenry for both domestic services and income-generating activities.

Thus, one is left contemplating the following paradox witnessed in Bahrain: labour-related protests by citizens in the late twentieth century were often opposed to the influx of migrant workers due to the perceived threat of employment competition, as occurred in the uprising of 1972

(AlShehabi, 2013). Less than four decades later, in 2010, the news was dominated by protests held by small-business owning citizens that opposed the levying of a US$28 monthly tax on importing migrant workers due to the extra costs this entailed for their businesses (*Al-Wasat*, 2010b).

One final development during this period that is worth emphasising is the newly emerging roles for migrants that extended beyond labour. Increasingly, GCC expatriates were no longer simply workers and sources of manpower, but they also became consumers, investors, owners of property and users of the urban space. The most prominent manifestation of these new roles was the emergence of a plethora of 'international mega-real estate projects' and 'free zones' in several of the smaller states of the GCC geared primarily to expatriates as their investors and final consumers. No longer were migrants simply seen as workers, but increasingly a different group of expatriates that could potentially act as a source of purchasing power which actively needed to be marketed to, attracted and recruited in order to buy, invest and live in the region. This phenomenon will be discussed in detail in Chapter 5 of this book.

Notes

1. The author would like to thank the Gulf Centre for Development Policies for funding support, Lisa Barrington for her translation assistance and Dalal Wad Eisa for support in data gathering.
2. For more on pre-oil society, see (Al-Naqeeb, 1987).
3. For example, 1904–1905 was known in Bahrain as 'the year of mercy', where the plague killed a large percentage of the population.
4. An agreement signed in Ibn Saud of Saudi Arabia and British officials that defined the boundaries between Iraq, Nejd and Kuwait.
5. For example, the first mention of 'foreign' versus 'citizen' in Bahrain, dates to a 1904 decree giving the British political representative the right to exercise judicial authority on 'foreign' subjects. The first law stipulating the conditions of citizenship was issued in 1937.
6. One could also cite the under-researched phenomenon of slavery trade as a pre-existing form of the systematic import of people for labour (mainly for domestic services). However, slaves formed an integrated and settled, albeit dominated class within Gulf society. This, in addition to the different mode of production that characterised slave labour in comparison to wage-earning labour, distinguish the slave trade from current forms of migration.
7. Bahrain was an exception, with commercial exports beginning in 1932.

8. There was also a significant flow of people between the southern coasts of modern-day Iran and the Gulf Arab States, continuing a process that predates the oil era.

9. For more in Saudi Arabia, see Al Seef (2007). For Kuwait, see Crystal (1995).

10. For Saudi Arabia, see Niblock (2007).

11. For example, earlier oil exports in Kuwait and Bahrain made them pioneers in regional modern state building.

12. Often this was against the wishes of the local rulers. For Bahrain, see AlShehabi (2013).

13. This term is a variation on the 'high-modernist state' (Scott, 1998).

14. Indeed, it is important to view the different periods as integrated rather than divided by hard cut-off points.

15. For our exposition, detailed stratifications within the local population are not addressed in-depth.

16. This applies even to Saudi Arabia, whose maritime trade, particularly through Jeddah, depended extensively on the British trading system (Krimly, 1993).

17. Krimly (1993: chapter 1).

18. Relationships within the 'private sector' labour market are a prime example of this, as shall be seen.

19. For example, it is estimated that Qatar's population decreased from 32,000 at the beginning of the twentieth century to 16,000 by 1945. (Crystal, 1995: 117).

20. For a Foucaltian examination of how the modernist state established discipline in Bahrain, see Kathem (2007).

21. A fascinating example appears in the dispatches of the British ambassador in Bahrain (British National Archives, 1972: FCO 8/1822). The British saw their main role post-withdrawal in supporting the fledgling state and countering the local threat that came from Leftist-leaning groups.

22. Migrant labour were to benefit too from subsidised water, electricity, food stuffs and in some cases healthcare and education.

23. In Kuwait, a Kuwaiti was defined in the 1959 citizenship decree as someone whose direct family was present in Kuwait before 1920.

24. Thus groupings based on sects, ethnicities, tribal affiliations, etc. came to play an important role in state politics. This has often been referred to as 'neo-patrimonialism' or 'corporatism' within the literature. For more see Al-Naqeeb (2012) and Khalaf (1998).

25. For more information on *kafala*, see Longva (1999: 20–2).

26. For an in-depth discussion of how this worked in Kuwait, see Longva (1997).

27. For Oman see Takriti (2013).

28. For example, the UAE pronounced 2008 to be the year of identity.

29. This is a more encompassing usage of the term when compared to that originally employed by Marx.

30. For an exploration of the attitudes of citizens in the UAE, see Herb (2009).

31. Bahrain is an exception, as its laws theoretically provide a systematic path for obtaining citizenship, but which often do not seem to be applied in practice.

32. Although the majority of Gulf investments continued to flow to Western markets.

33. As measured by the share of GDP accruing to operating surplus versus employee compensation.
34. Author calculations based from Bahraini (Bahrain CIO, 2011) and Kuwaiti data (Kuwait Central Statistics Bureau, 2011).
35. Author calculations based on (OECD, 2010).

2

The Politics of Migration

Abdulhadi Khalaf

This chapter focuses on migration as a resource for the rentier states of the Gulf region. It builds on various arguments I developed while attempting to understand what Gulf ruling families do when they rule (Khalaf, 2000; 2003; 2006). In studying how ruling families in the Gulf maintain the stability of their rule, one becomes aware of the diverse strategies employed by the ruling families to what Tibi calls 'the simultaneity of the unsimultaneous', in other words, 'the parallel existence of two social and political patterns with their social origins in crucially different historical periods: the old tribes and the modern nation-state' (1990: 128).

Theoretically, the chapter rests on arguments informed by contributions within the rentier state paradigm. Those arguments revolve around the proposition that abundant hydrocarbon rents received by ruling families have nurtured the growth of rentier regimes in the Gulf countries. Ideally, a rentier regime does not need to levy taxes from the population and is not required to grant representation. 'States organized around allocation would not have reason to create market incentives for development. They would also structure relationships with society vertically through chains of patronage dependence' (Springborg, 2013: 302).

The sudden oil boom of the 1970s generated a phenomenal expansion in the labour markets of the Gulf countries throughout the following decades. The availability of relatively abundant sources of labour force in the neighbouring countries provided Gulf countries with a straight-forward entry into the following four decades of infrastructural and economic development. Migrants from the Indian subcontinent and from Arab countries who migrated to the Gulf countries in increasingly greater numbers filled the hundreds of thousands of new jobs, most of which, at the time, were perceived as dangerous and undesirable by the locals. Migrant labourers were highly motivated, flexible, relatively cheap and replaceable. Those characteristics have warranted considering migrants as a reserve army of labour.

During the first two years of the oil boom, the influx of migrants seemed to spiral out of control of the government agencies that were in charge of issuing residency and labour permits, who were initially overwhelmed by the rising volume of applications. It did not take long, however, before governments gradually began to exercise full control over the flows of migration, its sources and composition.

Migration management has become a political necessity. In this chapter, I contend that migration policies have gradually been incorporated within the strategies employed by each of the ruling families of the GCC to maintain the stability of its rule and to reshape their societies. Migration has become a useful tool for social engineering, helping to reshape the GCC societies and redefine their social hierarchies.

Bringing the State Back In

Social science studies of migration have generally been concerned with how migration both affects and is affected by individuals, groups, communities and societies. Theories of international migration, laments Massey (1999: 303), did not focus on the nation-state as 'an agent influencing the volume and composition of international migration', and this neglect may have led to missing some important pieces in the international migration jigsaw. The case for bringing the state back in to the study of migration has been credibly put forward in several recent contributions to the field (Freeman, 1995; Hollifield, 2000; Castles and Miller, 2009).

Despite the many consequences of the globalisation of migration flows, the role of the state remains paramount. Cornelius and Tsuda (2004: 4–5) argue that the 'extent to which modern nation-state remains capable of regulating international migration and refugee flows – indeed, whether capacity to control such flows still represents an essential element of national sovereignty – is the subject of considerable scholarly debate'. The rationale for investigating the role of the state in migration is not limited to the needs of studying processes of border controls, visa requirements and issuance of residence permits. State authorities do more than that. They play active roles in encouraging or discouraging migration and in shaping its flows and directions of those flows. State institutions also shape a country's migration management regime, helping to moderate and even restrain the implementation of those regimes. Migration can affect the sovereignty and security of the receiving country, its ethnic makeup and the balance of power among its constituent communities (Wimmer and Glick Schiller, 2002).

Bringing the state back into the discussion is also necessary in order to understand how different politics of incorporation are formulated, and to explain their varied consequences (Castels and Miller, 2009). As Mabee notes, 'Since the development of the nation-states system, migration has taken on new significance. From the forced labour migration of slavery and colonialism to non-coercive labour migrations, the movement of populations as a result of war, and so on, migration has gone hand in hand with the development of contemporary nation states' (2009: 113).

Theoretical discussions and empirical evidence on the role of the state in shaping the migration flows, both in volumes and directions, have shown variations in states' intervention in migratory processes. Some sending states, such as the Philippines, Sri Lanka and India, have adopted a variety of strategies to promote emigration. These strategies include specially designed training programmes to increase the appeal of their emigrants in an increasingly competitive international labour market (Brush and Sochalski, 2007; Percot, 2006). From the perspective of receiving states, governments may decide upon appropriate regimes for border controls, visa requirements and issuance of residence and work permits. The institutions of modern states are also responsible for the design of those regimes and the measures that effectuate their implementation. Far from being a simple gatekeeper, the state actually controls migration through its monopoly over the right to proclaim and enforce its specific rules of entry and rules of exit in and out of the territories under its political authority (Weiner, 2006: 92–3). Control is not limited to the erection of restrictive barriers to free movements across state boundaries, but also a policy with respect to exit (Zollberg, 2006: 66–7).

The State

Weber (1978) characterises the modern state as a set of differentiated and hierarchical institutions and personnel engaged in political relations within a territorially demarcated area, over which it exercises a monopoly over authoritative binding rule, backed by a monopoly of means over physical force. This definition distinguishes the power possessed and exercised by the state institutions from the powers possessed and exercised by economic and ideological institutions. Its monopoly over the means of physical force gives it a superior authority over other institutions. It also gives the state the powers to control 'the total means of political organization' (Gerth and Wright Mills, 1945: 82).

The state, notes Mann, is a 'messy concept' since it can be defined in terms of both its institutions and functions, i.e. in terms of 'what it looks like, institutionally, or what it does, its functions' (Mann, 1986: 112). He discusses two meanings of state power. The first is the *despotic* power as represented by 'the range of actions which the [state] elite is empowered to undertake without routine, institutionalised negotiations with civil society, social groups and institutions' (1986: 113). It is primarily a repressive power and involves the autonomy of the state from social pressures, and it includes the capacity to control the distribution of resources without interference from society. The second is the *infrastructural* power represented in 'the capacity of the state to actually penetrate civil society and to implement logistically political decisions throughout the realm' (1986: 113). It refers, in other words, to the ability of a state to get things done, to administer and regulate, and effectively exercise its authority and achieve its goals within society. The infrastructural powers of the modern state have increased enormously. It has become capable of penetrating nearly every aspect of the everyday life in more ways than any of its historical predecessors. Through its capacity to penetrate, coordinate and moderate the activities of civil society, and economic and social collectives, the modern state can effectively and efficiently achieve objectives.

Weber and Mann refer to an ideal type of the modern state. Real-life state formations, on the other hand, are many and diverse. A central element that should be distinguished among these diversities is who actually dominates the state and controls its powers – whether through monopoly over the means of physical force as Weber suggests, or through control of the state's despotic and infrastructural powers as Mann suggests. While domination is not a simple term, Migdal argues that a closer study indicates the existence of 'various patterns of dominations generated by varying sorts of interactions among social forces' (1988: 9). These patterns, continues Migdal, are determined by key struggles that go on throughout the 'multiple arenas of domination and opposition' (1988: 9). In this regard, various sorts of states, writes Skocpol, give rise to various conceptions of the meaning and methods of 'politics' itself, conceptions that influence all relevant groups and classes in a national community (1985: 22).

The strength and autonomy of ruling families in the Gulf offer them the tools to both shape the institutional structures of their societies and pursue their own goals, either through transformative strategies or through coercive actions in pursuit of maintaining public order (Skocpol, 1985). Theirs is a strong state, par excellence. It is capable of penetrating society, defining internal relations among its constituent elements, regulating social relationships and determining how common resources are allocated. While there is a wide agreement, as Chaudhry notes, that the 'oil states have the capacity to create and destroy social classes', there is little work done on 'how and why' each country produces its own particular combination of despotic and infrastructural powers (1997: 187). This, suggests Chaudhry, leads to stretching the theory of the rentier state to fit almost any case at hand. This in turn results in analytical trajectories that neglect the impact of oil markets and of domestic reactions to budgetary policies.

The State in the Gulf Monarchies

Gulf monarchies have fared relatively better than most Arab regimes in terms of survival and resilience. This remains true even when one considers the eventful history of the recent four decades, with wars, invasions and border skirmishes; or its various palace coups, such as those in Abu Dhabi (1966), Oman (1973), Sharjah (1987) and Qatar (1995); or the chronic, and continuing, squabbles among siblings in Saudi Arabia, Kuwait, Bahrain and the various emirates of the UAE. The success of Gulf ruling families in holding out in the face of domestic and regional threats offers empirical and theoretical challenges to rentier state theory, and it has been explained differently (Heller and Safran, 1985; Lawson, 1989; Crystal, 1995; Long, 1997; Bryman and Green, 1999; Gause 2000; Tétreault, 2000; Gengler, 2011).

Mann's distinction between despotic and infrastructural powers is as interesting theoretically as it is empirically for examining how effective the ruling families in the Gulf have been in their endeavours to adjust to some demands of modern governance while maintaining their traditional forms of rule. Whether pursuing modern or traditional policies, the states of the Gulf monarchies maintained their capacity, 'to *penetrate* society, *regulate* social relationships, *extract* resources, and appropriate or use resources in determined ways' (Migdal, 1988: 5). Due to their ability to combine both powers, the Gulf monarchies gave their relations with their societies the distinct character they have.

It has become increasingly evident that the interests of the ruling families of the Gulf, and the stability of their regimes, is similar to that of many other authoritarian regimes, in that they do not depend solely on their modern and well-equipped security apparatuses (Brumberg, 2000). Rather than simply relying on coercion, the Gulf monarchies have employed various strategies of survival, including the manipulation of institutions and historical and ideological legacies in order to guarantee their hold over society and to undermine pressures from domestic challengers, including popular demands for a substantive transition to a transparent and competitive system of governance. In the Gulf, as elsewhere, the fortunes of authoritarian rulers vary. Autocrats of the world differ depending on how big is the political space open for them to manoeuvre; on how much time they have available for the manipulation of institutions, and historical and ideological legacies; on how responsive their public is, or at least a significant portion of it, to attempts to manufacture consensus; and on how far they can go in their attempts to diffuse emerging pressures from their local adversaries. Above all, they differ in terms of their willingness to unleash the full power of their security apparatuses on political adversaries.

Several students of the region have focused on the role of rent, while also accepting that several interrelated factors are at the core of the exceptional rise in the importance of the state's role and the power exercised by the ruling families over society. Rent – an already problematic term in economics – becomes more problematic when introduced to political sociology. Khan defines rent as 'an income which is higher than the minimum which an individual or firm would have accepted given alternative opportunities' (Khan and Sundaram, 2000: 21).[1] One of the problems with this definition is that it is too inclusive. Many real-world incomes, note Khan and Sundaram, have the character of rent. These include 'not just monopoly profits, but also subsidies and transfers organised through political mechanism, illegal transfers organised by private mafias, short-term super profits made by innovators before competitors imitate their innovations, and so on' (Khan and Sundaram, 2000: 5).

Rentier states, writes Mahdavy, are 'those countries that receive on a regular basis substantial amounts of external rents' (1970: 228). While revenues of each of the Gulf countries from exports of their main natural resource, oil, vary considerably, these revenues remain their main source of income. The ruling families in the Gulf control all sources of rent, enabling them to increase their autonomy from their social bases while expanding the system of political patronage. They have asserted their authority through expanding the state's active presence in almost every social, cultural and economic sphere, thus inhibiting the rise of competing social and economic power centres. Their financial resources and geopolitical importance helped the ruling families to increase their capacity to control serious internal dissent through expanding and modernising the military, police and internal security apparatuses at their disposal, and forge regional, inter-Arab alliances to enhance their stability. Rent, in other words, has facilitated, but not caused, the regimes' ability to combine the despotic powers of pre-modern states and the infrastructural powers of modern ones. Oil revenues, particularly following the oil boom since the mid-1970s, have enabled the Gulf monarchies to sustain their rule by combining coercion (maintained through the despotic powers of the state) with the loyalty of their subjects (maintained through the distributive powers of the state).

One of the immediate consequences of control of rent and its circulation is that loyalty to the royal family becomes a social as well as a political imperative. Unlike other society/state situations, what can be observed in the Gulf monarchies is shaped by two characteristic features of the state. The first is that the state is the ruling family; that is to say, more than simply stating that the state is an instrument of the ruling families. Rather, there is a distinct intertwining of state and the ruling families in a relation of indistinguishable organic unity. The second is that the state/ruling family unity is off limits to all other social actors. Nazih N. Ayubi (1995) discusses different political outcomes of the rentier state, where the state machine is the main engine for circulation and/or allocation of resources vis-à-vis various economic sectors and social groups. More specifically, he suggests the following outcomes of rent in the Gulf States.

As the rent is externally derived, the state becomes an intermediary between the world capitalist order and the local economy and society. In its turn, the state promotes levels of dependency by citizens on its agencies, its welfare services and other facilities. Within this relation of dependency a citizen becomes, according to Ayubi, 'disinclined to act economically or politically on his own behalf, let alone seriously criticise the state' (1995: 183). Citizens, including merchants, entrepreneurs and business people, become more preoccupied with attempts to access the rent circuit than aiming to build productive efficiency. Financial independence offers the state a high degree of 'relative autonomy' from the specific interests of the diverse collectives in society. Consequently, the ruling elites are able to change public policies, to reverse them, to select their allies and to change political allegiances with relative flexibility. Furthermore, its relative high degree of autonomy could enable the state to create new classes and/or to dismantle and reassemble existing ones.

Sustaining vertical segmentation of society has proven itself a useful form of social organisation and, hitherto, an effective vehicle for rule. As shown during the oil boom years, the regime has effectively used the resources at its disposal to create new intermediaries, retire some old ones and revive others. Intermediaries are made up vertically along tribal, religious and confessional corporative lines – as well as according to wealth, kinship or residential areas. As local reserve sources for legitimacy of power, competing intermediaries reinforce the regime policies, including preserving segmentation of society.

Migration and Regime Stability

Following the phenomenal expansion in the labour markets of the Gulf countries, demand for migrant labour in the region took extraordinary leaps. Those leaps would have not been possible without abundant, accessible and reliable sources of manpower in the adjacent countries. Initially, Arab and non-Arab regional countries have, during the first years, competed as suppliers of both skilled and unskilled labour. Initially, too, the majority of migrants (80–85 per cent) were from other Arab countries. Migration flows to the Gulf region displayed five significant features (ESCWA, 2007):

- 1945–1973: migration of Arab labour to the region constituted some 85 per cent of all migrant labour.
- 1974–1975: in spite of the sudden and rapid increase in the number of migrants, Arabs represented 80 per cent of all foreign migrants in Gulf countries.
- 1976 onwards: a shift occurred, with a rapid increase in rates of migration from South Asia.
- 1980–1984: non-Arab migrants continued to increase following continued growth of the construction sector.
- 1990 onwards: the fall of Arab migrants' numbers accelerated following the second Gulf war (1990–1991).

According to the authors of the ESCWA report these shifts are the results of 'the policies adopted by GCC States [that] reduced the number of Arab migrants to those countries'. The percentage of Arab migrants fell from 72 per cent in 1975 to 56 per cent in 1985.

> That percentage continued to drop until, in 2002, such migrants represented 25–29 per cent of all foreigners. The highest decrease was in Kuwait and Saudi Arabia. In the latter, the relevant figure fell from 91 per cent in 1975 to 43–47 per cent in 2002. Over the past 20 years, the percentage of Arab migrants in Kuwait has dropped from 80 to 34 per cent, while, in 2002, that figure in Bahrain and the United Arab Emirates had fallen to 10 per cent. (ESCWA, 2007: 10–11)

Andrzej Kapiszewski suggests that a new phase was started with the post-1973 economic boom. While Arab migrants were particularly welcomed, their 'linguistic, cultural and religious compatibility with the local populations made them more attractive to nationals than other immigrants' (Kapiszewski, 2006). Soon, however, the situation changed in favour of migrants from Asian countries. Several factors have helped in making Asian migrants a better alternative.

That shift was not necessarily due to the inability of Arab labour exporters to meet the immediate needs of the expanding Gulf labour markets, but also carried economic, social and political advantages (Kapiszewski, 2006; Forstenlechner and Rutledge, 2011). For local employers, Asians were less expensive to employ and easier to lay off. They were also used to leaving their families at home, whereas Arab migrants usually brought their families to the Gulf with the hope of settling there for longer periods, if not permanently. Government authorities also appeared to have additional calculations. Historically, note Forstenlechner and Rutledge (2011: 30), 'political ideas "imported" by migrants in the 1950s and 1960s posed challenges to the ruling families of the Gulf, as Arab migrants – especially Palestinians, Egyptians and Yemenis – helped spread ideas of pan-Arabism, Nasserism, communism or socialism'. Asians, suggest Forstenlechner and Rutledge, were less likely to claim citizenship and were expected to remain disenfranchised.

The rise of the South and South East Asian region as the main supplier of labour to the GCC countries is problematic in the sense that it has produced a relationship of mutual dependency, a symbiosis as it were, between labour-sending countries and the GCC. From inception, this relationship has been both regulated and unequal. While the labour markets of the Gulf countries rely on labour supplies from South and South East Asian regions, they refrain from becoming dependent on any particular country. Attempts to negotiate bilateral and multilateral agreements regulating migrants' work conditions, wages and social benefits, have been futile (BNA, 2007). Unequal relations between the sending countries and the Gulf is exacerbated by the rising role that remittances play.[2] The estimated value of money officially transferred by migrants working in the GCC countries reached US$83 billion in 2012 (*Gulf News*, 2013). Informal channels for money transfer are utilised particularly, but not solely, by low-income migrants who are considered illegal because they have overstayed their visa permits. Business experts and business websites estimate that US$35 billion have been remitted through informal channels in Saudi Arabia alone (Soman, 2013).

As such, migration continues to generate unforeseen and undesirable consequences. Most of these are detrimental to the lives of individual migrants, and for some of them expatriate dreams of riches and happiness are cut tragically short. Almost every day there are small notices in the local media about 'an expatriate male worker' or 'a foreign maid' who has committed suicide. Details vary of course, but most of these personal tragedies are linked to the victims suffering from depression or despair because they saw themselves as unable to overcome their deprivation despite working 12 to 16 hours a day. Other press notices might describe a housemaid left paralysed after jumping from a building, or after burning herself in an unsuccessful suicide attempt. In their despair, and lack of legal protection, they discover that their meagre pay, despite hard work, cannot possibly sustain them, support their families back home or pay back the money they had already borrowed to pay for those who organised their migration to the Gulf. Some are driven to crime.

Citizenship As a Tool for Rent Allocation

Ruling families have gradually incorporated migration in their arsenal of tools to maintain the stability of their rule. Migration control and migration management policies provide the GCC states with several new tools to enable them to shape their societies at the micro level, and to control the activities of all inhabitants within their territories – whether citizens, *bidoons*[3] or foreign migrants. Foremost among the new tools of social control is the redefinition of citizenship and articulation of a new citizenship rhetoric. The GCC is not unique in this respect. The idea of citizenship was crucial to nation-building projects in other parts of the world. It has met with varying degrees of success, and has been instrumental in weakening ethnic, tribal, religious and class identities, and binding individuals to nation-state projects through the creation of common national ideals (Turner, 2006). Marshall (1965: 101–2) considers citizenship as a shared identity that would integrate previously excluded groups into a society and provide a source of national unity. This inclusion could be accomplished through integrating 'various ethnic, tribal, religious, and class components of the nation in a common culture and heritage'. With these characteristics, citizenship would threaten the dual position of the ruling Gulf monarchies as arbitrators and patrons among diverse ethnic, tribal, religious and class collectives within the territories they rule. Citizenship, as a shared identity, would require considerable changes in the ways the ruling families viewed their subjects. More gravely perhaps, it could challenge the founding myths of each ruling family's claims to authority and legitimacy.

In spite of their resilience and omnipotence, the oil monarchies have suffered from recurring crises of legitimacy and sovereignty. Both are, partly, related to the perception that they are artificial formations imposed in the nineteenth century by British imperial interests. At best, they have been viewed as transitional arrangements. Visions for the end of that transition vary considerably. Pan-Arab and pan-Islamist visions which have dominated political discourses since the 1940s, 1950s and 1960s have been augmented, but not replaced, by a pan-Gulf vision. Kinninmont notes that 'The legal, political and economic construction of citizenship by Gulf regimes has been designed partly to provide incentives for Gulf nationals to support the existing nations rather than being swayed by stronger pulls towards transnational Arab or Islamic identities' (2013: 49).

In this context, citizenship has been the key formal instrument to an intricate system of inclusion and exclusion in Gulf societies – between citizens and migrants as well as among diverse informal hierarchical categories within the two communities in the Gulf region. These forms of differentiations of rights, enforced by state authorities and jealously guarded by social norms, guarantee the redistribution of added value from the more vulnerable migrants to certain categories of citizens and privileged categories of migrants (Sater, 2013). Since the mid-1970s, the number of migrant communities living in the GCC countries has grown. They have lived side-by-side with citizens, thus becoming a potentially value-laden frame of reference not only affecting labour market efficiency, but also posing new socio-cultural threats. Indeed, the massive presence of a foreign population has deeply influenced, and even exacerbated, the distorted relationship between rulers and citizens. The widespread fear of culture loss has acted as a glue factor between rulers and citizens. (Fagotto, 2013: 5)

Citizens are entitled to rights and privileges that are not accessed by non-citizens. Among these is the right to sponsor and employ migrants. While citizenship signifies membership in the national community, as opposed to non-citizens, it has not, in practice, guaranteed equity among citizens themselves. Indeed, 'different degrees of privilege or exclusion, intersects with more subjective and contested identity politics' (Fagotto, 2013: 48). Citizenship in the Gulf States *does not* guarantee that all citizens can claim full and equal access to all the services provided by government, such as education, health care and social services. Preferential treatment is afforded for those who are members of tribal, religious, collectives. Whether acquired by birth or by naturalisation, citizenship status is linked to expectations of a set of social and economic privileges. Those expectations are not considered to be entitlements that can be claimed, but rather as forms of largesse from a benevolent ruling family.

Here one needs to recall Davis's distinction between the two modern Arabic synonyms for citizenship: *Jinsiyya* and *Muwatana* (Davis, 2000). In the case of the GCC countries the distinction is mostly based on informal practices of patronage that increase or decrease the access that individual citizens or communities have to their constitutionally stipulated equal rights. *Jinsiyya* denotes passport citizenship, and gives a person the right to reside, work and own property in the country as well as carry a passport to travel abroad. The latter, *Muwatana*, on the other hand is associated with equal entitlement to civil, political, social and economic rights. Gulf ruling families employ these de facto tiers of citizenship to determine 'who is entitled to which levels of economic benefits on the basis of ancestry, who is entitled to vote, whether women can pass citizenship on to their children, and in some cases, even stripping citizenship from dissidents perceived as being disloyal' (Kinninmont, 2013: 47). Barring a direct and specifically targeted intervention by a government authority, all tiers of citizens in the GCC countries are encouraged to benefit from the rent seeking opportunities opened by the migration policies of their governments.

Political Ramifications

There are two spheres where the ramifications of the past four decades of
purposive use of migration in reshaping the societies of the Gulf countries,
and consolidating the power of the ruling families, are clear. First, the
consolidation of the citizens/migrants segmentation of societies and labour
markets. Second, the emergence of the *kafala* system as an effective and
consensual tool to perpetuate social and economic segmentation.

Segmentation

Throughout the GCC, labour markets became segmented between nationals
and expatriates, as well as between the public and private sectors (Hertog,
2012). Rigid segmentation is sustained by differences in wages and benefits,
and by the preference of GCC nationals to work for government and other
public sector employers. The private sector does not attract nationals
due to its basic characteristics: low wages, unstable conditions and the
lack of reasonable prospects for mobility. By contrast, employees in the
government and public sector enjoy higher wages and more secure jobs,
and can look forward to improving their work status and pay. Another
form of segmentation is noticeable within the expatriate labour force.
Westerners are located at the top of the pyramid while Asians are at its
miserable bottom. Their different positions are visible in their wages and
living conditions, and in their legal status and the level of legal protection
they get.

The lowest tier within this segmentation of the labour market is allocated
to female workers from South and South East Asia, working mostly as maids
(Willoughby, 2008). Theirs is a particularly vulnerable situation, since
domestic services are specifically excluded from the stipulation of labour
legislations. Maids work for unspecified working hours, and are subjected
to the possibility of physical, psychological and sexual abuse.

South Asian countries have become reliable suppliers of cheap
labour, with the additional advantage of lacking any political rights. This
characteristic, in my view, is the strongest argument with which to explain
the GCC governments' ongoing reliance on South Asian supplies of labour.
It is also within this context that we may find explanations for the failure
of GCC governments to undertake the training programmes necessary to
improve the quality and skills of the local workforce. Here, too, we may find

explanations for governments' failure to encourage employment outside the already oversaturated government and public sector.

Altogether, these features of the GCC labour market help consolidate its segmentation. While government and public sector jobs are offered to locals, employment in the private sector is left to expatriates. Private employers, particularly in the construction sector and domestic services, offer mostly low-skill jobs with low wages. The consequences of this situation can be seen everywhere in the form of wage discrimination. The plight of foreign workers has been highlighted through media reports as well as through communiqués, petitions and appeals issued by various regional and international human rights groups. These have persistently noted the powerlessness, and at times unwillingness, of concerned embassies to provide victims of abuse with adequate support. The situation is exacerbated by the fact that until recently, and with the exception of Kuwait and Bahrain, the rest of the GCC countries do not allow trade unions or any form of free association for employees, foreign or local.

State-sponsored discourses have emerged to provide ideological frameworks that justify and legitimise social inequality and the ethnic hierarchisation of the labour market. One of the foundations of those discourses was easily accessible through the enforced segmentation of the labour market into migrants versus nationals. Governments have strongly benefitted from maintaining and expanding the segmentation of the workplace and other public spheres. The majority of the economically active population is excluded from politics, while citizens, who are a minority, would continue to rely on the ruling families to allocate the resources required to sustain citizenship privileges in highly competitive labour markets.

Kafala

The *kafala* system (see Chapter 4) is arguably one of the most important instruments for consolidating the system of patronage through various form of rent allocation in the Gulf countries. Its most important occurrence is evident in two widely different spheres – foreign labour migration and foreign investment ventures. The system has created a vast informal business niche, offering *kafalas* to foreign migrants or would-be investors. *Kafala* is generally perceived as a lucrative and easy way of making money: legally through business partnership, or illegally through sales of visas (Longva, 1997). In essence, the *kafala* system has created a market where income is derived from citizenship rather than merit. Citizenship is one's entry ticket to that market, where various forms of *kafala* become a source of income.

For foreign labour migrants, a *kafeel* is a local sponsor who may be one's employer or one's recruiting agent. The *kafala* system binds the migrant to a sponsor who is expected to provide authorities with a guarantee that workers under his or her sponsorship meet the necessary requirements to reside and work in the country. These include health certificates, medical insurance, a certificate of employment and residence. The *kafala* system has empowered individual citizens to participate in the 'privatized system of migration control' (Vora, 2013: 33).

Gradually, the *kafala* system has generated a variety of *kafeels*. Some, as is the case with most recruiting agents, simply charge for their services before handing the migrant to an employer. A second variety is made of local business people who import migrants on 'free visas'. Free visa migrants[4] are bound to their *kafeels* but not to any particular employer. This allows them to have unrestricted mobility in the labour market. For this service, a foreign worker, regardless of his or her occupational category and professional status, pays 'an appropriate' amount relative to their income. A third variety of *kafeels* act as a dormant partner in the migrant's business venture.[5] This category does not play the role of an employer per se, but rather facilitates the paperwork for foreigners needing the manpower. Such business arrangements, where the *kafeel* play a passive role, have introduced new complexities to an already complex system (Khan and Harrof-Tavel, 2011).

The substantial financial gains generated by the *kafala* system has entrenched its role as a business enterprise. GCC nationals can benefit substantially from selling visas they have acquired to others. This 'visa trading' has become 'a multimillion-dollar industry; there are high fees for the initial sponsorship, followed by two-year renewal fees' (Shah, 2008). Shah estimates that 70 per cent of visas issued by the Saudi government were sold in the black market. Various reports in the Gulf media claim that the visa-trading sector generates astronomical financial gains. In Saudi Arabia, according to the *Saudi Gazette* (2013), 'People who sell work visas have made millions of riyals – they recruit a foreigner on a work visa then free him to work in the market in exchange for a monthly fee. They can also sell visas to other brokers or merchants'. Saudi black marketeers, reports *Al Sharq,* charge between 10,000 and 15,000 Saudi riyals (US$2,700–4,000) for work visas, depending on the nationality of the migrants (*Al Sharq,* 2012). While they are likely to vary according to skill and nationality, visa prices fluctuate according to the seasons and the law of supply and demand. The following amounts were noted for free visas in Bahrain (US$2,500–5,000), the UAE (US$1,900), Qatar (US$2,550–5,500), Kuwait (US$1,780–5,300) and Oman (US$2,600) (LMRA, 2014; Shah, 2008; AlRaya, 2012; KNA, 2014; *Azamn Daily*, 2013).

Further, migrants are often left at the mercy of employers and recruiting agents who exaggerate the cost of their services. The *kafala* system provides employers with a significant market power derived from the fact that the employee is bound to work only for the employer that sponsors him or her. The absence of horizontal mobility, note Soto and Haouas (2012: 12), encourages 'employers to focus on labour-intensive techniques that, in addition to the normal profit obtained from selling goods, would allow them to extract the highest rents from the worker'. The system effectively prevents the migrant from negotiating his/her wages and work conditions (Fagotto, 2013).

For foreign businesses, regulations require that they have a local partner – an individual or a company – as a sponsor. While representing the joint venture publicly and in all legal matters, the local partner/sponsor role does not necessarily involve taking business decisions and risks. Whether an individual or a company, the local partner expects to be remunerated either with a fixed annual fee or a share of profits (Soto and Vásquez Alvarez, 2011). The amount of remuneration is linked to the social and business status of local partners, their level of influence and contacts with the ruling family, government officials and the local business community. Whether active or dormant, sponsorship provides the local partner with access to a sizable rent.

Concluding Remarks

In spite of political, economic and security turmoil in the region, the ruling families of the GCC countries have managed to survive and prosper. With the exception of Bahrain, the tumultuous events of the Arab Spring have only marginally troubled the internal affairs of the Gulf countries. On the surface, the ruling families of the GCC countries have managed to limit the ramifications of popular mobilisations elsewhere in the Arab region from reaching their hinterland. This achievement is only partly due to the extraordinary resources resulting from oil exports, together with the political capital resulting from long-term and stable alliances with the West.

Those resources and political alliances have improved their states' infrastructural and coercive capacities. State authorities have also been able to use those capacities to actually define the socio-political options available to all relevant domestic political actors, including traditional notables and various layers of modern elites (Khalaf, 2005).

In this chapter, I have sought to show how migration has been an integral tool in the ruling families' strategy to maintain the stability of their regimes. The growth of migrant communities has generated several spheres of shared interests between the rulers and the ruled. Hierarchies, and the segmentation and fragmentation of labour markets and societies, have provided the ruling families of the GCC countries with reliably efficient mechanisms for maintaining order among competing collectives, and between citizens and migrants. Continuing that remarkable success, however, is contingent on the inability or unwillingness of members of the different collectives to cooperate or build alliances (Fagotto, 2013).

Notes

1. Following Mahdavy (1970), Luciani (1987), Biblawi (1990) and Sadiki (1997), rent is simply defined as an income generated through ownership – of real estate, natural resources and 'all natural and differential endowments: location, climate, etc' (Biblawi, 1987: 383).
2. The importance of those migrants' remittances, according to a World Bank Report is noticeable in their support of the balance of payments of the receiving countries. 'In Bangladesh, Nepal, Pakistan and Sri Lanka, remittances are larger than the national foreign exchange reserves. All these countries (most notably, Pakistan) have instituted various incentives for attracting remittances. ... In India, remittances are larger than the earnings from IT exports. Remittances to India are expected to reach $71 billion in 2013' (2013: 5).
3. *Bidoon*, (an Arabic word for 'without') refers to stateless residents of GCC countries. Estimates of their number vary; Van Waas (2010) put their number at 'several hundred thousand'. Unlike migrants, the *bidoons* are not required to obtain work and residence. However, their labour market mobility is restricted. They cannot access the social and economic rights and privileges that citizens enjoy. As stateless residents, *bidoons* are denied basic services, they are unable to own property and their children cannot attend government schools.
4. While unofficial, the 'free visa' permits have become the most sought after work permit in the Gulf region. A 'free visa migrant' is a person whose sponsor does not provide him or her with specific employment, but allows them to seek employment elsewhere (see Harroff-Tavel and Nasrim, 2013). Migrants with 'free visas' have a certain level of mobility in the labour market, while they are required to maintain their juridical link with their sponsors. This

combination makes the allocation of 'free visas' an additional channel through which governments can dispense favours to members of the ruling families, as well as reward 'loyal' citizens.

5. Foreign sole proprietors or civil companies are exempted from this rule. Soto and Vásquez Alvarez (2011: 1) note that 'firms operated by professionals in particular vocations – ownership is 100% for the foreign investor [law firms, medical clinics, etc.]. However, it is compulsory to appoint a UAE national sponsor as "the local service agent". This local service agent is not involved in business operations and is paid an annual fixed fee or a share of profits. Nominally, the local service agent assists in obtaining licenses, visas and labor cards while ownership is 100% for the foreign investor'.

3

Overcoming Methodological Nationalism: Spatial Perspectives on Migration to the Gulf Arab States

Adam Hanieh

Flows of labour migration to the GCC constitute one of the most significant movements of human beings in today's world. In each of these states, the majority of the working population is made up of temporary, migrant workers who lack the political and civil rights held by the citizen population (Shamsi, 2006). For Kuwait, Qatar, the United Arab Emirates and Oman, the proportion of migrant workers exceeds 80 per cent of the entire labour force. Mostly found in the private sector, these workers carry out a vast array of manual work and provide construction, service and domestic labour. The majority of this migrant workforce originates from countries such as India, Bangladesh, Pakistan, Sri Lanka and the Philippines, and their remittances contribute to the survival of millions of people throughout these areas.

While there exists a wide set of insightful anthropological and sociological work on migrants in the Gulf, the political economy literature commonly treats the presence of these migrant workers as a minor adjunct to the main story of oil revenues and the machinations of the ruling monarchies in great power politics (cf. Mahdavy, 1970; Beblawi and Luciani, 1990; Crystal, 1995; Ross, 2001). Dominated by rentier state theory, much analysis of the Gulf's political economy focuses upon the interlinkages between the state, the ruling family and allied classes, and the ways in which oil revenues are redirected through these networks. Within this state-centric framework, labour migration is typically treated as a subsidiary question that is reduced to a potential 'demographic problem' rather than structurally embedded within the nature of the Gulf's political economy.

In those studies that do deal with the political economy of migration in the Gulf, an explanation of the region's reliance on these workers usually adopts the trope of neoclassical 'push–pull' factors: a lack of skills and population levels in the Gulf, and the prospect of higher wage levels, 'pulls' those who are simultaneously 'pushed' by the low wages in their country of origin (Birks and Sinclair, 1980; Kapiszewski, 2004). This approach often considers migrant labour flows as a 'positive sum game' for both the sending and receiving countries, thereby obfuscating the mechanisms of exploitation that underlie these movements of people. As a result, academic writing on the Gulf has a strong orientation towards 'technocratic' policy advice – what types of economic strategies the state should pursue, how to industrialise, how to deal with the question of non-citizen labour and so forth – that assumes the neutrality of the Gulf state and its dealings with migrant workers.

This chapter aims to present an alternative framework for thinking through labour migration to the Gulf States. It begins by outlining some of the dominant theoretical frameworks towards the political economy of migrant work in the Gulf, linking these to the wider migration literature. The key critique raised regarding this literature is its 'methodological nationalism' – a focus upon individual nation-states as self-contained, enclosed sets of social relations, separate from the wider region and world market (Wimmer and Glick Schiller, 2002). The chapter outlines an alternative perspective to this, drawing upon some recent thinking about space, class and region inspired by scholars of radical geography. Within this approach, migration to the Gulf can be understood as a process of class formation, demarcated by the institution of citizenship in the Gulf, and necessarily situated within the wider Middle East region and the political economy of the world market. The conclusion draws together some of the political and scholarly implications of this alternative framing.

Migration Theory and the Gulf

There are three broad strands of literature dealing with the political economy of migration to the Gulf. The first of these draws heavily upon neoclassical explanations that emphasise wage differentials as the driving force for migration (Castles and Miller, 2003). These approaches conceive society as a collection of rational, atomised individuals motivated by the desire to maximise self-interest. When faced by worsening conditions of income and employment at home, individuals make a self-interested choice to move to another location in search of better wages (Lewis, 1954; Harris and Todaro, 1970).[1] This process is often described by the terminology of 'push–pull' factors: migrants are pushed from a particular location, while simultaneously pulled by the lure of better conditions somewhere else. Migration is thus framed as a 'positive sum game', with all sides benefitting from the flows of labour. The policy challenge becomes one of matching labour surpluses with labour demand, and channelling remittances in such a way that they can be an aid to development.

Although the associated methodological assumptions often go unspoken, studies of migration to the Gulf frequently draw upon these neoclassical frameworks. The Gulf States are said to be 'capital rich' but facing 'a shortage of human capital [as] the major, even pre-eminent constraint upon development' (Birks and Sinclair, 1980: 2). Labour flows from other countries are thus a 'structural imperative ... as the oil-related development depends upon the importation of foreign technologies and requires knowledge and skills alien to the local Arab population' (Kapiszewski, 2001: 3). For labour-sending countries, outflows are caused by 'such push factors as the low per capita income, lack of job opportunities, low wage rates and/ or the prospects of slow growth in per capita income and wages' (Sherbiny, 1981: 42). In this context, the matching of labour demand in the Gulf with labour surpluses elsewhere can potentially provide a win-win situation. In some accounts from the 1970s and 1980s, when the majority of migrant workers in the Gulf came from the Arab world, the remittance flows that ensued from these labour flows were sometimes framed in Arab nationalist terms – a means through which the Gulf could redistribute its oil surpluses to the surrounding region.

The emphasis on wage differentials in these neoclassical approaches has, nonetheless, been widely critiqued. Numerous empirical studies have found that wage differences are not necessarily present in major migration corridors (Bilsborrow et al., 1984; Standing, 1985; de Haan, 1999). Moreover, a range of theorists have proposed that the methodological individualism inherent to the neoclassical models are mistaken for their lack of attention to the nature of decision makers – very often these are not individuals, but families who distribute risk depending upon particular circumstances. Families, or extended social groups, might decide on a variety of strategies to deal with this risk: sending individuals to pursue education opportunities, remaining on the land to assist in family labour or migrating to nearby urban areas. Within this perspective, migration becomes one among many options.

In response to these criticisms of the neoclassical model, a second approach to labour migration has refocused attention on the nature of decision-making in the migrant journey. This 'new economics of labour migration' (NELM) model emphasises that migration decisions are formulated within particular social networks and institutional arrangements, and thus cannot be reduced to wage differentials alone (Stark and Bloom, 1985; Stark, 1991). The NELM shares the same basic assumptions of neoclassical approaches (the utility-maximising rational agent operating in an environment of scarcity), but attempts to mediate these choices through particular institutional configurations. A related theme is the concept of 'relative depravation', the claim that migration decisions are also an attempt to improve the position of individuals or families compared to other relevant groups (Stark, 1984; 1991; Stark and Taylor, 1989). In this sense, the NELM approach has focused upon the nature of family structures in labour-sending countries; the question of power relations (including gender) in determining decisions; cultural and historical factors; as well as the networks established through the migration journey that help to shape its subsequent dynamics (Fields, 1975; Bhattacharya, 1993; Taylor, 1999). An important theme here is the question of path dependency, or, as it has become known in the migration literature, *cumulative causation* (Massey, 1990) – the notion that once a particular migration pathway is established it is more likely to continue in the same manner due to the networks that have been set up by earlier migrants.

This institutionalist approach is widely reflected in much scholarly writing on the Gulf, particularly in sociological and anthropological studies that look at the different mechanisms of decision making by migrant families, and the networks that are established through these movements. Some writers have examined the ways that institutional factors – such as recruitment structures, limited job mobility, gender and weaknesses of legal regimes – act to shape the patterns of labour flows to the Gulf (Baldwin-Edwards, 2011; Esim and Smith, 2004). The question of 'risk' is a prominent feature of this literature: i.e. migration carries an inherent gamble on future pay-off, and the ways that institutions are structured thus strongly impact the nature of this risk and hence the decisions to migrate (Rahman, 2011). The literature has also examined the ways in which the act of migration changes family structures, perhaps leading to a 'transnational split' as migrants who move to the Gulf are unable to bring their families with them and continue to maintain long-distance relationships (Boyle et al., 2003). Nonetheless, while this literature has contributed a rich array of insights into the mechanisms and specificities of migration to the Gulf (and the variations that exist between different areas as a result of institutional factors), it shares with the neoclassical approach the basic assumption of distinct and analytically separate 'push' and 'pull' factors as the principle framework through which to analyse the reasons behind migration (cf. Asfar, 2009: 11).

A third general strand of Gulf migration literature has concentrated upon the implications of migration for structures of power in the Gulf, bringing to the fore the significance of migratory movements for understanding the historical trajectories of these societies. These critical theories have thus helped to generate an important process of rethinking of Gulf histories, which foregrounds the ways in which migrant labour has constantly acted to challenge its subordinate position and, in constant interaction (and frequently tension) with the citizen population, helped to shape the nature of state power and its ability to maintain control over the wider population. Within this critical literature, some writers have emphasised the ways in which migration reinforced the position of traditional ruling classes by shifting citizens into non-productive activities that were dependent upon government employment (Beauge and Sader, 1981; Khalaf, 1985; Lackner, 1978; Halliday, 1984). In this manner, ruling elites could blunt any pressures for social change or democratisation. At the same time, migrant labour played a functional role for Gulf rulers, providing what was seen as a pliant and low-paid workforce. Disney, for example, has documented the role of South Korean labour in the Gulf's construction boom of the 1970s. Korean companies, organised through the *chaebol* conglomerates, would bring a 'semi-militarized labor force' of former soldiers who had been trained in specially converted military bases to work in construction, welding, truck driving and the operation of heavy equipment (Disney, 1977: 23). These migrants would be housed away from other workers, and were considered by the Gulf States as a low-wage, highly disciplined labour force that would be highly unlikely to engage in any subversive activity (although, in reality, a range of strikes and protests by these workers did challenge the fiction of political passivity) (Disney, 1977: 24). More recently, other writers have highlighted the fact that migrant labour in the Gulf needs to be seen as an active political agent, playing an important role in challenging the position of monarchies (Longva, 1997; Louër, 2008a; Russell, 1989; Vitalis, 2007; Chalcraft, 2010).

It is the contention of this chapter, however, that each of these three broad approaches tend to suffer from what can be described as *methodological nationalism*: a privileging of the national space as the vantage point from which to interpret social phenomena. As Wimmer and Glick Shiller have noted, this process has led to a 'territorialization of the social science imaginary and the reduction of the analytical focus to the boundaries of the nation-state. The social sciences have become obsessed with describing processes within nation-state boundaries as those contrasted with those outside, and have correspondingly lost sight of the connection between such nationally-defined territories' (Wimmer and Glick Schiller, 2002: 307). The problem with methodological nationalism is that social relations are not neatly bounded within national borders – flows of capital and labour, and the various policy frameworks that mediate them, act to tie different spaces to one another. Social relations are not demarcated by the borders of the nation-state but are internally-related (Ollman, 2003) – they are constituted in relation to the whole.[2] As Pradella has recently pointed out, at the roots of this methodological nationalism lie a particular view of the state, which affirms 'the same dualism between state and market, and between the national and international spheres, that is sustained by the neoliberal current'; i.e. the state is seen as an autonomous actor that is abstracted from social relations existing at both the national and international scales (Pradella, 2014: 181, 188). This particular conception of state theory – which also characterises both 'rentier' and 'developmental' approaches to the state – posits an analytical separation between so-called internal and external features of the state, providing primacy to the former (Pradella, 2014: 181).[3]

Bringing the Region Back In

Overcoming methodological nationalism thus implies an emphasis on the regional and world-market context, tracing the ways that social relations develop across and through borders within a single global structure. Seen from this perspective, an analysis of migration to the Gulf needs to begin with an understanding of the Gulf's place within the wider Middle East region. A full analysis of this is clearly beyond the scope of this chapter, but some essential features can be sketched here. Beginning in the 1970s

– and consolidating through the 1990s and 2000s – most countries in the Middle East and North Africa region have been profoundly transformed by neoliberal economic policies. These policies have included privatisation, labour market deregulation, opening up to foreign direct investment (FDI), increasing integration into global financial markets, reduction of tariffs and other barriers to trade, cutbacks to social spending (notably on food subsidies) and so forth (see Hanieh, 2013 for an account of neoliberalism in the region). The pace and form of these neoliberal measures has certainly varied from country to country, but all areas of the Middle East have been affected by their implementation. In particular, the countries of North Africa have been heralded as the 'model' of neoliberal reform – Egypt, for example, was frequently commended by the World Bank as a leading regional 'reformer' from 2005 to 2008.

These neoliberal processes engendered a range of important social trans-formations. Central to this was a major shift in rural conditions as land was privatised, caps on rents lifted, and prices liberalised for both inputs and marketed agricultural commodities. These changes produced an increasing insecurity of rural life, with farmers and their families finding it more difficult to survive on the land. Likewise, in urban areas privatisation and labour market deregulation generated escalating levels of unemployment, particularly among youth and university graduates. These processes hit young women the hardest, as the sector of the population most reliant upon jobs in the public sector. In general, these policies resulted in an increasing polarisation of wealth – mass impoverishment and precarity came to exist alongside a small layer of society that was enriched through neoliberal reform. Concomitant to these changes in the distribution of wealth was a realignment of state power, expressed most sharply in increasingly authoritarian regimes. Authoritarianism was the means through which neoliberalism was implemented in the Middle East (Hanieh, 2013).

The Gulf Arab States were central to promoting and facilitating this turn towards neoliberalism in the wider Middle East. This role began in the 1970s and 1980s, when Gulf States provided financial assistance to key Arab countries suffering from the debt crises of the time, while, in return, conditioning this support on reforms overseen by the World Bank, IMF and other international financial institutions. In Egypt, for example, the Gulf Organization for the Development of Egypt (GODE) – formed in 1976 by Saudi Arabia, Kuwait, United Arab Emirates and Qatar – provided loans to the Egyptian government in the context of a major debt crisis in the mid-1970s (Hanieh, 2013). The loans had both political and economic implications – they were a major part of Egypt's turn away from the Soviet Union and alliance with the US; they were also predicated on a series of economic reforms including cuts to food and energy subsidies and a devaluation of the Egyptian pound. These reforms were the initial phase of Egyptian President Anwar Sadat's *infitah* process, and were later deepened in structural adjustment packages (SAPs) that laid the basis for contemporary neoliberalism in the country (Bush, 1999; Mitchell, 2002; Wurzel, 2009). Similar policies were replicated throughout the region, with the Gulf States working closely with the international financial institutions to provide loans and aid linked to SAPs.

There are two important consequences of this deepening liberalisation as it relates to the question of labour migration in the Middle East. First, neoliberal reforms played a major role in generating the conditions in which migration became a principal mechanism of survival for millions of people across the Middle East and North Africa. Faced with the multiple socio-economic crises arising from the political economy of neoliberalism – including dispossession from land, political violence, rising land rents and growing precarity of labour in both urban and rural areas – migration acted as a mechanism of 'crisis management'. Remittances from those who migrated could help support families remaining at home. These flows of migration involved skilled and higher-paid workers such as teachers, engineers, medical personnel and veterinarians as well as lower-paid work in construction, agriculture and service sectors. They took place across international borders, as well as internally within individual countries (rural to urban migration). Migration was not only a means by which migrants and their families attempted to overcome the socio-economic problems they faced at home, it was also seen by governments as a way to ameliorate any potential social upheaval. In the case of Egypt, for example, the government 'welcomed the activities of emigrants who concentrated on making money instead of making revolution' (Marfleet, 2006: 92). Likewise, in Jordan migration was seen as a means of limiting political dissatisfaction among 'an influential sector of population' (Saif and el-Rayyes, 2009: 34).

In addition to this 'permanence of temporary migration' (Farrag, 1999: 55),[4] a second important consequence of the decades of neoliberalism in the Middle East has been the growing weight of the Gulf States in the regional political economy. This shift was particularly marked through the 2000s. Having amassed growing pools of surplus capital as a consequence of the rising price of oil in the first decade of the 2000s, the Gulf States were to become a primary beneficiary of neoliberal reform in states across the region. Gulf-based investors made major purchases of Arab companies involved in real estate, finance, industry, agribusiness and other key sectors. These sectors were not only economically significant; they were also strategically central to the broader neoliberal project. According to World Bank figures, the Gulf countries were the largest foreign investors in the Middle East in 2008, with total investments making up more than one-third of all investments in the region (World Bank, 2009: 56). From 2003 to 2009, projects in the Mediterranean countries announced by investors from the Gulf were greater than any other country or region.[5] Nearly two-thirds of investments from the Gulf went to Jordan, Lebanon, Egypt, Palestine and Syria. The predominance of Gulf investments in the region continued even after the 2008 economic crisis, with total FDI from the Gulf surpassing any other country in Egypt, Jordan, Lebanon, Libya, Palestine, and Tunisia, and ranking second in Morocco and Syria (ANIMA, 2011). These capital flows included both sovereign wealth funds as well as private companies based in the Gulf. They confirm that the liberalisation of markets in the Middle East was accompanied by the internationalisation of Gulf-based capital, with Gulf investors taking major (and often controlling) stakes in companies privatised by Arab governments. Neoliberalism, in other words, acted to simultaneously strengthen the position of national elites as well as the Gulf States within the regional order.

Viewed in their unity, these two concomitant processes of neoliberal reform – labour flows induced by the changing political economy and the growing weight of the Gulf States in the Middle East – are indicative of the unevenness of capitalist development in the region. They confirm, most significantly, that the 'push–pull' model is an inadequate one for understanding labour migration in the region. The social conditions that 'push' people to seek to migrate are bound up with the social conditions that 'pull' people towards a particular location. Both these factors are an outcome of the nature of capitalist accumulation in the Middle East, and thus the basic neoclassical assumption that they can be treated as distinct, separate phenomena is misplaced. Of course, not all of the migration in the Arab world is aimed at the Gulf States – indeed, increasingly these flows of people are directed at Europe or other states in the region.[6] But the Gulf remains a central destination point for many migrants, while simultaneously being a prime agent in generating the conditions for this movement. The uneven and combined development across the region as a whole means that the 'pull' is causally linked to the 'push' (and vice-versa) in a mutually reinforcing chain.

Spatial Structuring of Class

Moving beyond methodological nationalism means taking seriously the fact that class relations in the Gulf extend across the borders of the Gulf nation-state. In a related sense, the feminist geographer Doreen Massey has noted that capitalism is necessarily spatialised – the geographical arrangements by which capital organises its accumulation necessarily provides a spatial inflexion to the social relations that underlie it. Within this framework, class is not just an abstract category describing a certain relationship to the reproduction of society's needs; it is also marked by a particular spatial form in any concrete circumstance – it comes into being through the interlinking of geographical spaces (in addition, of course, to being racialised and gendered in particular ways). Viewed in this manner, migration to the Gulf can be understood as a process of *class formation* that is necessarily spatialised. The Gulf's class formation is – to employ a term used by Massey – a 'spatial structure'; one that involves the emergence of social relations intertwined across different geographical spaces (1984: 112).[7]

There are several useful insights that can be gained from approaching class formation in the Gulf States as a 'spatial structure' formed beyond the borders of any individual nation-state. First, it is through this spatial structure that Gulf States are able to institutionalise extremely high rates of exploitation. There are many well-documented accounts of the widespread abuse of workers in the Gulf and the systematically low levels of pay to which many of these workers are subject, but the key point is that this exploitation is *enabled* by the spatial structuring of class and the differential laws that demarcate citizenship rights.[8] The value of labour power in the Gulf is not measured by the cost of reproduction in the Gulf States themselves, but relative to the cost of labour power in the home country of the worker. If all workers in the Gulf had parity in terms of their labour and citizenship rights, then this difference would disappear.[9] There are no minimum wages in the private sector – where most migrant workers are found in the Gulf – and there are vastly different wage levels between citizen and non-citizen labour, which are even greater if non-wage costs are included (such as access to education, health, housing and other social rights for citizens).[10] Most strikingly, studies have documented differences in pay for the same work depending upon national origin of the workers (notably in domestic work). This observation has political and policy implications to which we shall return below.

These high rates of exploitation are not just a consequence of deteriorating social conditions in the home countries of migrant workers. They are also enabled by the enormous numbers of *potential* workers who constitute a labour pool for the Gulf. Once again, this illustrates the importance of understanding class in a spatial sense that breaks with methodological nationalism. Instead of seeing the Gulf's working class as being narrowly confined to those who happen to be inside its borders, we need to expand our notion of class to include the literally hundreds of millions of people who form a 'reserve army of labour' around the Gulf's periphery. These people may not be physically located in the Gulf, but they need to be seen as just as much part of the Gulf's potential labour force as anyone holding a work visa. The huge size of this potential pool, and the ability of the Gulf States to shift this spatial structure between different countries when necessary, acts to further depress wage levels that migrant workers receive in the Gulf itself. Most important to this spatial structuring of class is the institution of citizenship, which – through a highly complex system of border controls, work visas and sponsor systems – acts to mediate the spatialisation of class.

As well as enabling exploitation, the spatial structuring of class in the Gulf is a powerful disciplining instrument over labour. The ability of temporary migrant workers to be present in the Gulf is dependent upon a work visa and not determined by birth or citizenship rights. If a worker loses their job then it is very difficult for them to remain in the Gulf – even to search for alternative employment – and by law they must return home. Indeed, even children born to non-citizens who have been long-term residents in the Gulf lack any institutional route to citizenship or residency rights, and must depart if their parents lose their employment. This permanent precarity of status, fully dependent upon employment, means that any attempt to organise collectively can be met with the threat of deportation.

Moreover, the fact that a worker's spatial identity (their right to be present where they are) is constituted by and through their relationship with capital means that to engage in forms of struggle against capital is, to a large degree, to struggle against oneself (Hanieh, 2011: 63). The spatially and temporally precarious nature of working-class identity means that the nature of the class is continually being remade and reformed, divided across constantly shifting geographical boundaries. This places further obstacles in front of collective struggle and longer-term political organising. This should not be taken to mean that collective action by workers in the Gulf is impossible or unlikely (Chalcraft, 2010). Indeed, in recent years there have been sporadic examples of strikes, illegal demonstrations and other forms of protest by workers in the region. The point is, however, that the barriers to these types of actions – and their potential efficacy – are much greater because of the way that class is spatially constituted in the Gulf. This raises a series of important questions about forms of solidarity and the nature of struggle that will be discussed further below.

Spatial Fix

In addition to understanding migration as a spatial structuring of class that is constituted across national borders, a further useful theme of the geography literature is David Harvey's notion of a 'spatial fix' (Harvey, 1985; 1999). By this, Harvey attempts to describe the ways in which capitalism is continually acting to overcome barriers and moments of crisis through altering the spatial structures that underpin certain periods of accumulation. Many of Harvey's examples in this regard relate to a global expansion of capital (i.e. the seeking of new markets), or the restructuring and devaluation of fixed capital laid down through the course of accumulation in particular landscapes (e.g. transport lines, urban gentrification processes and factories) (Harvey, 1985). But, precisely because migration is an inherently spatial process, the concept of spatial fix can also be expanded to include these labour flows. Seen in this manner, the shifting of the dynamics and patterning of these flows becomes a potential means to facilitate and overcome potential barriers to accumulation.

In the case of the Gulf, the particular patterning of class formation through migration has enabled a 'spatial fix' for Gulf capital and the region's ruling elites. At moments of crisis, the Gulf is able to rework the spatial structures underpinning migration as a means of overcoming or displacing crisis away from the Gulf towards other surrounding zones. There are two examples of this spatial fix that are useful to highlight here – the shift away from Arab labour towards Asian labour in the 1990s and 2000s, and the response of some areas of the Gulf towards the 2008 global economic crisis.

The demographic balance of the Gulf's migrant labour workforce has been well noted in much of the literature on the region (Kapiszewski, 2004). In the initial phases of development in the Gulf through the 1970s, most of these workers were brought from neighbouring Arab countries. Over the subsequent decades, however, many of these workers began to challenge the types of differential rights that underpinned the second-class status of migrant work. Non-citizen Arab workers increasingly attempted to bring their families, expressed political aspirations and looked to settle for longer periods of time in the region (Louër, 2008a; Chalcraft, 2010). In response to the potential problems that this represented for a spatial structure dependent upon the predominant exploitation of Arab labour, Gulf States moved to adopt a spatial fix. This meant shifting migrant labour flows away from Arab countries towards South Asia and further afield. The 1990–1991 Gulf War presented an opportune moment to carry out this fix, with Arab migrant workers expelled en masse under the pretext that the Palestine Liberation Organization and Yemen had supported Iraq's invasion of Kuwait. In Kuwait, for example, the number of Palestinians fell from 400,000 in 1990 to about 50,000 by the mid-1990s (Fergany, 2001: 7). By 2002, the Arab proportion of migrant workers in the Gulf had fallen from 72 per cent in 1975 to around 25–29 per cent, replaced with cheaper labour from South and East Asia (Kapiszewski, 2004: 123).

The 2008 global economic crisis presented another example of the ways in which migration could act as a 'spatial fix' at moments of crisis. Through the initial phases of the crisis, particularly in areas such as Dubai that were hard hit by the withdrawal of financial flows and the puncturing of the city-state's real estate bubble, large state and private companies were able to reduce the hiring of workers and repatriate thousands as projects were postponed or cancelled (Hanieh, 2011: 169–73). The effect was felt most sharply in the construction industry and is shown in the decline of workers that left for the Gulf through 2009 and 2010. One construction company in Dubai noted that the numbers of workers it was employing in early 2010 had dropped from 50 to 100 a week down to one a month. While typically workers would stay for three years, 'some were now being sent home early due to the slowdown in the Dubai construction market'.[11] From 2008 to 2009, the outflow of Indian workers to the United Arab Emirates fell by 62.7 per cent, to Bahrain by 45 per cent and Qatar by 44 per cent (MOIA, 2012: 58). For Bangladesh, the number of workers travelling to Saudi Arabia and the UAE (the destinations of more than 60 per cent of all Bangladeshi overseas workers) fell by 89 per cent and 38 per cent respectively over 2008–2009.[12] This drop was reflected in figures for air travel from Bangladesh to the Gulf – with industry spokespeople claiming a greater than 50 per cent drop in the number of travellers per week from 2007 to 2009 (*Financial Express*, 2009). For Pakistan, the number of registered overseas workers in the Gulf also fell precipitously – for the UAE (the largest destination for overseas Pakistani workers) there was a

36 per cent drop, Qatar a 60 per cent drop and Kuwait a 75 per cent drop over 2008–2009.

These figures show the particular way in which the spatial structuring of class shaped the response of Gulf States to the crisis. Unlike many other countries that have had to deal with the severe social consequences of increased unemployment levels, the Gulf States were able to adopt a particular spatial fix to the crisis. This was a form of spatial displacement – pushing the worst effects of the crisis on to those surrounding countries that had formed the supply lines of the temporary workforce underpinning class formation in the Gulf. In the words of one analyst from the Saudi National Commercial Bank, the ability to repatriate workers in times of crisis and bring them back when needed was indicative of 'a positive externality of labor market flexibility' (Kotilaine, 2009: 21).

The Gulf and Global Capitalism

The final aspect to moving beyond methodological nationalist approaches to the Gulf is the need to situate migration flows within the overall hierarchies of the capitalist world market. As a range of authors have emphasised, US capitalism has taken a pre-eminent position in the world order since the Second World War. This position has both acted to strengthen the specific position of US capital vis-à-vis rival powers at the global scale, while simultaneously seeing the US play a lead role in 'superintending' capitalism globally. Competition between advanced capitalist states continued to be present, but, as Leo Panitch and Sam Gindin were to note, 'only the American state bore the burden – and had the accompanying capacity and autonomy – to take on the task of managing the system as a whole' (Panitch and Gindin 2003: 54–5).

Within this configuration of the world market, the countries of the Gulf region – most notably Saudi Arabia – have played a principal role. The region's enormous hydrocarbon supplies, coupled with the financial surpluses that accrue to the Gulf States as a result, have meant that the control of the Middle East confers an enormous source of strategic power (Bromley, 1991). In the post-war period the dominant position in this regard has been taken by the US, which has offered unwavering political and military support to the Gulf States, while ensuring that petrodollar flows are directed through US treasury bonds and its other financial markets (Gowan, 1999; Spiro, 1999; Hanieh, 2011). To be clear, this is not meant to imply that the US necessarily seeks direct ownership of the region's oil supplies (although this might be a feature of its strategic calculation in countries such as Iraq). Rather, the US aims to ensure that these oil supplies remain outside of the democratic and popular control of the peoples of the wider Arab region (Hanieh, 2013: chapter 2).

In this context, the spatial structuring of class discussed above takes on a particularly significant role. The hierarchies of the contemporary world market – and the position of US power within these – mean that the nature of class formation in the Gulf bears not only upon the position of local elites, but the entire architecture of global capitalism. Any challenge to this structure from labour within the Gulf – the likelihood of which would be greatly increased through the extension of equal rights to *all* workers regardless of origin – could profoundly shake this system. For this reason, the spatial structuring of class in the Gulf has underpinned the process of state formation itself – enabling the Gulf's ascension as a core zone within the global economy (Hanieh, 2011). A useful comparison can be drawn with the Gulf's oil-rich neighbours, Iraq and Iran, where working-class movements have historically played a central role in challenging both colonialism and domestic rulers. Contemporary global capitalism – and the particular location of the Gulf within it – would take a very different form if similar movements were present in the Gulf Arab monarchies.

Conclusion: Scholarly and Political Implications

In his sprawling counter-history of Western liberalism, the Italian philosopher Domenico Losurdo noted that many accounts of liberal thought tend to focus upon the beliefs, ideologies and interests of property owners, white settler populations and emerging middle classes in their struggles against representatives of the *ancien régime*. In so doing, this 'historiography tends to shade into hagiography ... a discourse completely focused on what, for the community of the free, was the restricted sacred space' (Losurdo, 2011: 299). Losurdo deemed this a process of discursive silencing, which ignored the 'profane space' of slavery, indigenous peoples and the various forms of indentured labour that accompanied the rise of Western liberal concerns with liberty, freedom and individual rights.

In many ways, a similar process of discursive silencing can be observed in studies of the political economy of the Gulf Arab States. The dominant approach to these societies tends to be concerned uppermost with the enormous wealth that accrues to ruling families and state elites as a result of the region's enormous oil supplies. Political economy analyses of the region are subsequently framed by how these revenues are distributed, and the concerns and attitudes of the citizen population who are tied to the ruling families in complex ways. In so doing, the kinds of questions asked, and the explanatory factors that are sought, act to sideline the most significant feature of these societies – the fact that they rest upon a profound exploitation of a temporary, right-less and easily deportable working class who form a majority of the labour force.

This chapter has argued that labour, class and migration needs to be placed at the centre of our understanding of the Gulf's political economy. In contrast to state-centric approaches that look at the Gulf's enormous petrodollar flows as the basis on which to develop a conception of these societies, we should begin with the nature of class formation and the ways in which this rests principally upon the inflows of millions of temporary, precarious and easily deportable workers from other countries. In doing so, we must break with a predominant perspective on these states that views migration through the lens of individual sending and receiving countries. Instead, migration is a 'spatial structure' that extends beyond the nation-state and reflects both the uneven and combined development of the region as a whole, and the nature of the Gulf's position within the wider world market. This particular spatial structure enables both a means of control and exploitation of workers in the Gulf, while allowing the Gulf States to displace potential crises through its migration corridors on to surrounding countries.

This framework raises a set of important political questions. Most importantly, human rights abuses arising from the institutions that mediate the spatial structuring of class in the Gulf – citizenship rights, restrictions on the movement of labour, the *kafala* system and so forth – are not simply failures of governance that result from a lack of awareness about international norms or a consequence of entrenched interests of individual Gulf rulers. Rather, these institutions are a reflection of the relations of power extant in the world market and the uneven development of the Middle East as a whole. A fundamental shift in the character of these institutions is not possible as long as this regional and international context remains in place. Thus the efforts of human rights organisations and activists to raise awareness of the conditions of these workers, while laudable, have little hope of success if they remain confined to a narrow focus on government legislation. Addressing the human rights abuses of migrant workers in the Gulf is inseparable from a challenge to the entire regional order.

Moreover, this approach also provides an insight into the very real contradictions that are developing in the Gulf as a consequence of the extreme reliance on a temporary workforce. Central to these contradictions is the growing level of youth unemployment faced by many citizens in many Gulf States, particularly in the context of a bulging youth demographic.[13] In response to this, Gulf States have attempted to implement a range of 'Gulfisation' programmes aimed at encouraging businesses to employ nationals rather than foreign workers. Once again, however, it is the opinion of this author that there is no resolution of these issues through government policies that leave intact the position of Gulf rulers within regional and global hierarchies. Precisely because the spatial structuring of class in the Gulf is a consequence of the uneven development of capitalism in the region – foundational to the way that Gulf rulers rule and pivotal to the arrangement of power in the global economy – there is unlikely to be any reversal of this structure without imperiling a range of systemic interests that depend upon the continued maintenance of this structure. Any significant level of proletarianisation of Gulf citizens would raise precisely the kinds of problems that the spatialisation of class serves to undercut – the spectre of indigenous labour movements with the potential to challenge the position of ruling regimes.

A rejection of methodological nationalism also raises the question of how migrant workers fit within the political project of Left, labour and other social movements in the Middle East. In recent decades, there has been a noticeable absence of any real solidarity with these workers from Arab political movements. Indeed, during the recent uprisings in Bahrain, migrant workers were often viewed as being antithetical to the interests of Bahraini protesters, consciously used by the Bahraini government to undermine the coherence of opposition to the monarchy. Nonetheless, because class formation in the Gulf is a process that envelops the region as a whole, acting to facilitate the central position of the Gulf within the Middle East, migrant workers are a key actor to any political change in the region. An effective challenge to the Gulf monarchies means fighting to extend equal social and political rights to workers from India, Pakistan, the Philippines and so forth, as an integral part of the region's working classes. Once again, this is bound up with a decentring of the nation-state as the exclusive frame of analysis; we need to challenge the assumption that those who are 'in the right place' have privileged access to rights or an ability to act politically.

Finally, while the Gulf States may demonstrate a unique reliance upon labour migration, it is important to recognise the similarities that do exist between the Gulf and other countries. Many of the features of the Gulf's labour markets have begun to be generalised across other areas. These include a systematic and structural system of differential and precarious rights granted to migrant workers; the phenomenon of 'containerisation' – where workers are brought to the region by a company, housed separately from the citizen population and returned home at the conclusion of the contract; and the widespread use of labour contractors and other agents in recruiting workers from the Global South. These phenomena mark what has been described as the 'tendential emergence of a global labour market' (Overbeek, 2002: 76). In this sense, many of the themes noted in this chapter bear wider significance for the study of other migration systems – an important laboratory and test case for the increasingly 'global factory' of labour (de Angelis, 2000; Chang, 2009).

Notes

1. The classic summation of this perspective is the Lewis Model, which was initially used to think through rural to urban migration in the developing world. According to this model, a two-sector labour market is made up of a rural sector (from which migrants are assumed to move) and an urban sector (to which they migrate). With the standard neoclassical assumptions of perfect information (i.e. knowledge of *all* available jobs, wage rates and conditions in the region of destination), surplus labour from the rural areas migrates to the urban sector in search of relatively higher wages. According to Lewis, as the modern sector expanded, these flows of labour would reduce labour surpluses in the rural sector and lead to increased wage levels in the areas of origin. Over time, wage levels between the rural and urban sectors would reach an equilibrium point and migration would halt (Massey et al., 1998: chapter 2). Lewis's model was developed in the mid-1950s and was aimed at laying out a model of industrialisation for newly independent European colonies (Canterbury, 2012: 41). The problem was that the model failed to adequately describe the ongoing reality of increasing migration flows to the urban areas despite increasing levels of unemployment. It was partly in response to this failure that the Harris–Todaro (H–T) model was developed. Within the H–T model, rural workers continue to migrate to urban areas despite the presence of unemployment because they are enticed by the *potential* to receive higher wages. What Harris and Todaro attempted to do was develop a theory that could integrate probabilistic

rational choice into the model – assessing factors such as likelihood of finding a job or being unemployed, and receiving a higher wage than that available in the rural area. The H–T model (with further refinements) has become the standard approach to understanding migration flows. Indeed, the original article published by Harris and Todaro was described by the *American Economic Review* in February 2011 as one of the 20 most important and influential articles the journal had published in 100 years of its history.

2. Ollman argues that we need to understand different social categories as 'internally related', i.e. the relations existing between things should not be considered external to the things themselves, but are part of what actually constitutes them. Any object needs to be seen as 'relations, containing in themselves, as integral elements of what they are, those parts with which we tend to see them externally tied' (Ollman, 2003: 25). The relationships in which all things are embedded do not exist 'outside' of these objects (or externally) but are internal to their very nature.

3. More generally, it is a view of the state that exhibits what Marx described as 'formal abstraction', in which particular categories are taken as natural and given (in this case state, class and nation) and treated independently from one another as separate spheres in abstraction from the totality of social relations. As Chang has emphasised in relation to theories of the Korean state – the other global example, alongside the Gulf states, where approaches positing the analytical separation of class and state are extremely prevalent in the literature – once these categories are presented 'as naturally independent of one another, without understanding of the inner-relations between those aspects through the *totality* of social relations, the only way to express the mysterious and complex relations between those aspects is to present the relations as externally mutual relations, such as relations between the "economic" class and "political" state' (Chang, 2009: 34). Chang's critique could be equally applied to many rentier state approaches to the Gulf.

4. Farrag used this phrase to describe the situation in Egypt, but it is applicable to most states in the region.

5. These figures are from ANIMA, an EU institution that monitors foreign direct investment in the Mediterranean region, which it defines as Algeria, Egypt, Israel, Jordan, Lebanon, Morocco, the Palestinian Authority, Syria, Tunisia and Turkey (ANIMA, 2009).

6. Moreover, these processes need to be viewed across the entire regional scale. Various examples of 'replacement migration' mean that outflows of people from one part of the Middle East to the Gulf are met with corresponding inflows from other countries in the region. A good example of this is shown by the situation in Jordan, where migration to the Gulf generated both a construction boom and a need for agricultural and other workers in the wake of rural-to-urban migration. Much of this demand was met by workers from Egypt, facilitated by the 'open-door' policy to migration adopted by the Jordanian government through the 1970s and 1980s. As a consequence, much of the agricultural labour in Jordan was performed by Egyptian workers.

7. Massey's empirical work examined the ways in which the political economy of Britain could be mapped through changes in the spatial location of different

classes and production networks (Massey, 1984). 'Different classes in society are defined in relation to each other and, in economic terms, to the overall division of labour. It is the overall structure of those sets of relationships which defines the structure of the economic aspect of society. One important element which any concept of uneven development must relate to, therefore, is the spatial structuring of those relationships – the relations of production – which are unequal relationships and which imply positions of dominance and subordination' (Massey, 1984: 87).

8. This is not to deny, of course, that individual workers in the Gulf may benefit from their employment, or may experience an improved standard of living vis-à-vis their compatriots who were unable to migrate. These benefits, though, are frequently overstated in the literature and often overlook the distributional effects that remittance flows may have on inequality levels in the country of origin. From the point of view of capital, however, the structural ability of companies in the Gulf to employ workers at a value that is vastly below the cost of reproduction of (citizen) labour power is indicative of extremely high levels of exploitation. In this sense, the Gulf States have a systemic interest in seeing widening levels of unevenness between themselves and the surrounding regions that supply its labour force.

9. Of course, this does not mean that exploitation per se would disappear, as the capital–labour relationship would still exist.

10. The exception to this trend is found in sectors such as high-level management, banking and finance, where a different type of migrant worker can be found (usually from Western countries).

11. Shane McGinley, 'Sharp Decline in Labourer Recruitment in Dubai', *Construction Weekly*, February 2011. www.constructionweekonline.com/article-7576-sharp-decline-in-labourer-recruitment-in-dubai/#.UWvj39GQfGs (accessed August 2014).

12. Figures from Bureau of Manpower, Employment and Training (BMET), Bangladesh.

13. Across the GCC, over 50 per cent of the population is now under the age of 25 (Malecki and Ewers, 2007).

Part II

Dimensions of Gulf Migration:
Law, Urban Space, Gender

4

Kafala: *Foundations of Migrant Exclusion in GCC Labour Markets*

Mohammed Dito

Introduction

Understanding the mechanisms of *kafala*, the work-permit sponsorship system in operation throughout the GCC, is essential to both explaining the conditions of migrant workers in the region as well as analysing the relationship between the Gulf state and its citizen population. Under this system, all migrant workers entering the GCC must have their entry and employment sponsored by a citizen. Citizens are granted the ability to issue these permits (subject to fulfilling certain requirements) by the state. Because residency and mobility rights of the worker are connected to the permit, employers come to wield significant power over labour market conditions.

As a word deeply rooted in both tribal and legal Islamic tradition, *kafala* possesses a distinctive duality within the Arabic language. Etymologically, it has two distinct meanings in classical Arabic: to guarantee (*daman*) and to take care of (*kafl*). In the former sense, *kafala* is often employed in commercial and business transactions. In the latter, it is used to express how one should behave towards a minor. Consequently, *kafala* expresses a sense of a 'good deed' while simultaneously implying asymmetric power relations. This duality can be seen in the origins of the system in the Bedouin tradition of 'granting strangers protection and temporary affiliation to the tribe for specific purposes' (Longva, 1997: 78). This fusion of different meanings plays a crucial role in framing how Gulf nationals conceive their relations with migrants.

Despite the fact that some Arab scholars have voiced sharp criticisms of *kafala* (Al Najar, 1983: 96), the system has not received adequate attention from either researchers or policymakers. Typically, *kafala* is analysed solely through an administrative lens, as a regulatory instrument that is often misused by employers. The ways in which *kafala* is constitutive of hierarchical social relations in the Gulf is rarely explored, although some anthropologists have been more attuned to this characteristic due to fieldwork experience with migrants in the region (Longva, 1997). It is only in the last decade or so that the problems arising from *kafala* have emerged as policy dilemmas for most GCC governments, partly as a consequence of increased international criticism. It is important to note, however, that studies of the *kafala* system have been hampered by the lack of credible data concerning the number of permits granted, the extent to which the system is abused and the rate of renewal of permits.

The aim of this chapter is to examine the different paths through which *kafala* comes to both reflect and constitute a power relation between employers/citizens and migrants in the Gulf. The chapter begins by analysing the origins of *kafala* in the state–citizen relationship of the Gulf States, and the transformation of a work-permit system into a control mechanism founded upon the exclusion of migrants. The employer–migrant relationship is constructed along four different paths, the totality of which gives *kafala* a multidimensional character that goes far beyond a simple permit system. Each path contributes to the overall impact *kafala* has on both labour markets and the broader society. The chapter concludes with a discussion of the impact that this system has on both migrants and citizens in the Gulf.

Origins of Kafala: Rentier State and Citizenry

The origins of *kafala* can be found in the specific Gulf version of the rentier state, particularly in the feature of wealth redistribution that constitutes the core of the state–citizen relationship. By employing nationals in the public sector, a mechanism was created 'through which GCC governments transfer a portion of rents to their people' (Kamrava and Babar, 2012: 9). At the same time, state expenditure on infrastructure and construction projects enabled the redistribution of oil revenues to the private sector. This spending reached a massive scale during oil booms, such as those experienced in the mid-1970s. The labour-intensive nature of many of these projects meant that huge numbers of workers were required to facilitate the state-led support of the private sector.

Two factors need to be considered in explaining why exclusion became so important to the way migrants were employed in the Gulf. First, the tribal nature of the Gulf's ruling families meant that ruling elites tended to 'view the nation as a "natural" and ethnically "pure" community, as opposed to a community based on equal rights and duties' (Longva, 2005: 119). Exclusion was thus built intrinsically into the tribal nature of the Gulf regimes. Second, 'rentier arrangements shape and inform – and in turn restrict – the policy choices and options open to state elites' (Kamrava, 2012: 6). In the context of redistributional strategies, the number of beneficiaries of the state largesse was not open-ended. This quantitative factor is often underestimated in the literature on the rentier state. Exclusion remains an essential requirement for maintaining wealth redistribution to the citizen population, something that would become impossible if migrants were integrated as equals into the society.

The link between wealth redistribution and exclusion is critical to understanding the evolution of *kafala*. As a power relationship between migrants and their Gulf employers, *kafala* evolved from being a consequence of rentier state policies to become a principal enabler of this system in later years. In order to comprehend the evolution of this power relation, it is essential to differentiate between two spheres: the state domain (authority over who is allowed entry to the country for the purpose of work), and the labour market domain (business enterprises or private households). The unique characteristic of *kafala* is that the state 'delegates' the authority needed for a migrant to enter the country to the local employer, who thus becomes the owner of the work permit. This delegation acts to fuse the power of both the state and employers, with both spheres controlling the right of entry of the migrant into the Gulf.

Why does the state engage in this delegation of authority? Researchers have pointed to the inadequate capacities of the state to deal with the substantial expatriate presence on its territory, which could be solved by outsourcing 'the responsibility of alien surveillance to the citizens which can be considered as a kind of "civic duty"' (Longva, 1997: 100–1). Three issues are combined in this respect: state capacity, the nature of civil duties and security concerns. Among these factors, the question of civic duties is key and reveals the crucial non-economic function of *kafala*. As Longva has pointed out in her case study of Kuwait, by 'shifting the state's power of control over the migrants on to Kuwaiti civil society', dominance was no longer merely a property of macro relations between the state and the migrant population, but a central component in the relationship between individual citizens and individual migrants (Longva, 1997: 100). After four decades of successive and increased waves of migration to the Gulf, this delegation of power continues to play a central role in rentier state redistributive policies, contributing towards reproducing and maintaining the existing socio-political power structures.

In many ways, the state's ultimate ability to delegate these rights is similar to the role of patron traditionally played by the ruling tribe towards its 'subjects'. It has led to a stronger dependency of the private sector and households on the state for their labour needs. Moreover, there is an essential link between the state authorising the employment of migrants, and the exclusion of the latter from society. Wealth redistribution in the Gulf rentier states would be impossible if it was not restricted to a limited number of the native population. For this reason, the exclusion of migrants is embedded within the very nature of this system – it is foundational to the hierarchical power relations of all Gulf States.

Work Permits

Despite the fact that work-permit systems are in place in many countries throughout the world, they function very differently within GCC societies. Rather than simply an admission tool for migrants, the state's delegation of its power to the employer is complemented, as Longva notes, by 'the restriction imposed on the migrant worker's right to act as a judicial person and the delegation of this right to his or her sponsor' (1997: 101). According to Longva (1997: 101), the final outcome of this gives the employer three distinct powers:

> (1) his own, qua employer; (2) the one delegated to him by the state to use on the migrant; and (3) the one the migrant workers had to surrender to him to allow him to act on their behalf. Before the law, therefore, the sponsor represented not only himself but also the state (vis-à-vis the migrant worker) and the migrant worker (vis-à-vis the state).

In addition to the employer powers mentioned above, the employer has authority over four critical factors: entry–exit of the migrant to the country via work permit, renewal of stay in the country, cancellation of the work permit and control of the migrant's ability to move to another employer. These four factors span the entire life cycle of a migrant's residence in the Gulf. Periodic attempts to reform any aspect of this cycle have been met with significant resistance from employers. The Bahraini government, for example, attempted to improve the mobility of migrant workers in 2009 by allowing them to change employment without their employer's consent after a notice period set in the worker's employment contract. Employers strongly opposed this move, and by mid-2011 a new regulation (Article 25 of Law 19, 2006) was passed by which migrant workers were obliged to stay with their employers for one full year before they could change jobs without employer consent.

This case confirms the priority of the state–employer relationship over the employer–migrant one. The situation of the migrant workers (in this case their abilities to change employers) is strongly affected by the nature of alliance between employers (sponsors) and the state. The employer's power over the migrant can be 'adjusted' by the state through the work-permit regulations that deal with the four factors mentioned above. Because the state deals only with the employer as the sole owner of the work permit, the migrant is therefore excluded from any possibility of having a say in these four factors. A migrant's position in the power relation (employer–migrant) is defined exclusively through what the state and employers agree between themselves.

There are different degrees and a variety of forms of migrant exploitation in the Gulf, but it is precisely these extreme cases that indicate the social logic of *kafala*. Moreover, *kafala* also strengthens the existing power relations between the ruling families and the citizen population. As is discussed further below, this inflated authority is decisive in enabling the employer to extract additional benefits from employing the migrant – benefits that cannot be obtained from employing a national in their place.

Four Paths of *Kafala*

The four key paths of *kafala* currently present in the Gulf demonstrate the variety of routes followed by the sponsor and migrant in establishing the *kafala* relationship (see Figure 4.1). They are affected by complex socio-economic factors in both the host and sending countries. The motives and interests of migrant and sponsor are different on each path, yet this does not exclude similarities between them, and in certain cases

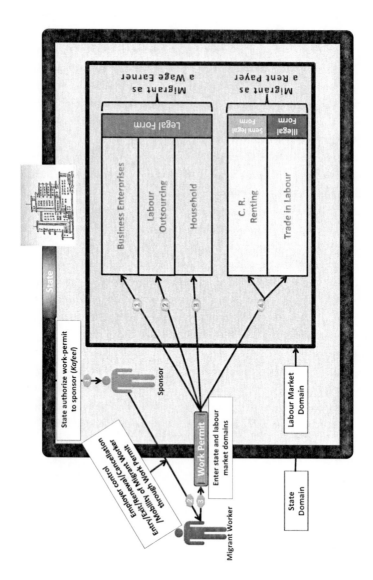

Figure 4.1   The four paths of *kafala*

they can be intertwined with each other. The variety of these paths also illustrates how the sponsor–migrant relationship extends beyond the traditional employer–employee relationship, combining legal, semi-legal and illegal practices. Moreover, these paths reveal the rent and non-rent seeking activities within the *kafala* relationship, thus situating the role and functions of the GCC labour market within the overall mechanism of the rentier state in the Gulf. Because of the complexities of elements defining each path, it will be extremely difficult to quantify them based on work-permit or visa categories; after all, there are only two main types of work-permit categories used in all GCC countries: worker and domestic worker permits. The four paths are therefore a theoretical construction of what cannot be captured clearly using only administrative data. Finally, it should be noted that the realisation of these paths is closely linked with the operation of a vast network of private recruitment agencies in both the sending and receiving countries working together with the social network of migrants and sponsors.

Path 1: Kafala *in Private Sector Employment*

This is the oldest path used by the private sector to employ migrants in the Gulf. It can be considered a classic example of the typical legal route used to employ the vast majority of migrants in the region. It consists of an employer getting approval for a work-permit application from the Ministry of Labour, which allows entry of the migrant to the country and their employment by the sponsor. Despite some slight variations in procedural requirements between GCC countries, the general outline is the same for all of them.

Both the ownership of the work permit and its regulations give the employer the right to cancel the work permit or request its renewal. Employer obligations and responsibilities to the concerned state body (usually the Ministry of Labour), which are set down in the rules of the work permit, are ultimately transformed into greater authority over the migrant, thus making the relationship between employer and employee much more asymmetrical than a normal labour market situation. This has led to a condition where the hidden authority derived from work-permit ownership overrides the authority of the employer in their labour contract with the migrant. In Bahrain, for example, out of the twelve conditions for the sponsor to be granted a work permit to employ a migrant, nine are directly related to the employer and only four are concerned with the migrant (Article 2, Decision No. 76, 2008). It is noteworthy that it is the employer who is granted the work visa, not the worker. Articles 7 and 8 of the law governing the permit define the 'duties' of both the employer and migrant in the context of the work-permit provisions (see Box 4.1).

Within this path, the definitions of responsibilities and duties are a mixture of procedural elements (e.g. finger prints), financial obligations (e.g. payment of fees) and issues directly related to labour law provisions (Point 5, Article 7 and Point 3, Article 8). Precisely because labour laws are subsumed within broader residency requirements – over which employers hold ultimate say – migrants are faced with a deep structural imbalance in power. An example can be found in Article 37 of the Saudi Labour Law of 2005, which states: 'The work contract for non-Saudis shall be written and of a specified period. If the contract does not specify the duration, the duration of the work permit shall be deemed as the duration of the contract.' In this case, the power of the employer to set the duration of the residency permit gives them control over the length of a work contract. As researchers have noted: 'Kafala is a system only partly codified in law' (Gardner, 2010: 59); it is precisely this latitude embedded within the work-permit regulations that open up the space for deeper exploitation.

Occasional migrant surveys and field studies conducted in recent years reveal the exploitation of migrants whose work permits are obtained by this route. There can be economic, social, psychological and health consequences as a result of the unequal power relations. The most negative effects are those relating to the living and working conditions of migrants, although official evidence is scant in this regard. Beside of periodic reports published by human rights organisations, there is no attempt by the governments of the region to assess the conditions of workers. One study prepared by the ILO in collaboration with the Kuwait Economic Society (Kuwait) and The University of Sharjah (UAE) has revealed the following critical issues (Khan, 2010: 15):[1]

- *Debt bondage*: 'More than three quarters of expatriate workers accumulated debt prior to traveling and hiring; a third (Kuwait) to half of them (UAE) have not finished paying off this debt' (Khan, 2010: 15). The survey also noted that the debt bondage limits workers' bargaining power over the terms of the official work contract.
- *Confiscation of the migrant's passport by the sponsor*: 'In the UAE no expatriate worker has his passport in his own possession. In Kuwait only 20% are in possession of their passports, 43% of domestic workers

Box 4.1   Employer versus migrant obligations as per work-permit regulations (example from Bahrain)

Decision No. (76) (2008) with regard to regulations of work visas of foreign employees except the category of domestic servants*

Article (2)

The employer shall be granted a work visa to employ a foreign employee, as stipulated below:-

1. The employer should be registered in the commercial register or equivalent and should have obtained a unit number from the Central Information Organization.
2. The employer should have settled all due fees in favour of the Authority with regard to work visas.
3. There should be an actual necessity to employ one or more foreign employees, taking into consideration, the size of the establishment, the nature of activity and the conditions of the conduct of business.
4. The employer should not have a proven record of violation of any of the substantial obligations imposed by the Labour Market Regulation Act and the regulations, orders and decisions implementing thereof.
5. The employer should not have a proven record of cessation of conducting the licensed activity or had closed or changed the place of work in violation to laws and regulations in force.
6. The employer should have settled the fines issued by final decrees in accordance with provisions of Labour Market Regulatory Act.
7. The employer should have fulfilled his obligations of providing insurance for his employees with Social Insurance General Organization.
8. The employer should not have a proven record of failure to meet the obligations towards workers' rights.
9. The worker should be medically fit and free from contagious diseases.
10. The profession of the foreign worker should not be one of the professions reserved exclusively for national employees in accordance with decisions of relevant authorities.
11. The foreign employee should have obtained the license necessary for the practice of certain professions in accordance with decisions of relevant authorities.
12. The foreign employee should not have been repatriated or deported out of the Kingdom on criminal grounds or due to his violation of the Labour Regulatory Act and decisions implementing thereof.

Article (7)

The employer who is licensed to employ a foreign employee shall fulfill the following requirements:

1. To employ the foreign employee in the same work stated in the work visa.
2. To ascertain that the worker had captured the finger prints together with his photo and signature and provided the Authority with same within the specified period.
3. To employ the foreign employee in the location indicated in the work visa or in the employer's branch conducting the same activity.
4. To settle the work permit prescribed fees.
5. To immediately notify the Authority, in case the worker abandoned work in violation of the work visa.
6. To immediately notify the Authority, in case the worker ceased to have one or more of the conditions for the grant of the work permit as stated in Article (2) of this decision.
7. To immediately notify the Authority in case the worker caught one of the contagious diseases that require transport to the location specified by the Minister of Health.
8. To immediately notify the Authority in case of the employer's liquidation of activities, declared bankrupt, cancellation of the commercial register, or cancellation of the license to conduct activities.

Article (8)

The foreign employee for whom a work visa was issued shall fulfill the following requirements:

1. Shall not conduct any work not stated in the work visa.
2. Provide the Authority with finger prints, photo and signature upon arrival to the Kingdom for the first time within a period not exceeding one month.
3. Shall not abandon work except as provided by law or without the permission or consent of the employer for a period exceeding fifteen consecutive days.
4. Shall not work with an unauthorized employer.
5. Shall conduct work in the location indicated in the work visa or in the employer's branch conducting the same activity.
6. Shall notify the Authority and the employer of his intention to transfer to another employer within the period specified in the decision with regard to the mobility of a foreign employee to anther employer.

---

* Decision No. (76) (2008) with regard to regulations of work visas of foreign employees except the category of domestic servants, Labour Market Regulatory Authority (LMRA), Kingdom of Bahrain, http://portal.lmra.bh/english/legal/show/14

and 41% of service workers are not in possession of their passports. Half of these workers did not consent to the sponsor keeping their passports.' Longva points out that this act of passport confiscation 'had an important symbolic significance as well. As an event occurring at the outset of the interaction between sponsor and employee, namely upon the employee's arrival in Kuwait, it set the premises for the dyadic relationship of power and dependency that was to characterize the interaction between the two parties' (Longva, 1997: 97).

- *Migrant harassments and mental abuse*: real concerns were expressed in the survey results: '17% of the Kuwaiti sample, mainly in domestic sector and services industries, have been harassed or mentally abused in the last 12 months. 43% of these victims want to leave their jobs. They cannot do so without the consent of the employer who is retaining their passports' (Khan, 2010: 19).

- *Long workings hours*: 'In the UAE, the survey showed that the majority of workers surveyed work more than 10 hours a day. These workers are not paid additional money for their extra working hours. Three-quarters of respondents (51% and 25% in services and domestic sectors respectively) say they work more than eight and up to 16 hours a day. 62% of respondents are required to work on holidays with no compensation (including 90% of domestic and service sector workers)' (Khan, 2010: 22).

- *Problems of wage payments*: this issue is one of the most recurring problems facing migrant workers in the Gulf and it takes many forms: 'unlawful salary deductions, delayed payment, partial payment, and nonpayment of salary or the overtime due' (Khan, 2010: 8). This situation leads many migrant workers to choose leaving their employers in search for other work opportunities even if it means becoming 'illegal workers'. One worker noted, 'I came to Bahrain as a welder in a car carriage repair shop. For four and a half months, I received no salary, so I filed a case. Then I finally left the company. My case is now in the courts. I filed a case against my sponsor. The case states that he did not pay me four and a half months' salary. I filed the case in the beginning of 1998, and there has been no progress [as of July 2003] ... As an illegal worker, I do have worries. I have a paper that I received from the court, and now I am afraid to go the police about this paper. I don't want to have to go to jail for being an illegal worker and that is why I can't go to the courts anymore or ask the police for help. I will wait for amnesty. If amnesty came tomorrow, I would go' (Gardner, 2010: 53).

Moreover, the fragmented institutional framework for dealing with migrants – often divided between different government departments, such as the ministries of the interior, labour, health and so forth – acts to weaken the ability of workers to contest any violation of rights. Consider, for example, a situation in which a migrant worker is faced with the withholding of their passport, forced to work long hours beyond the legal norm, and without basic safety and health conditions at work or in their housing conditions. In this situation, it is very difficult to pursue any complaints procedure because of the segmented institutional bodies that have authority over each of these different spheres (residence in the country, labour, occupational health and safety, housing and so forth). The migrant worker is faced with the choice of either accepting these conditions or pursuing a complaints system that is confusing, institutionally fragmented and heavily stacked against them. Given these odds, it is much more likely that the worker will simply endure the substandard conditions. Some of these problems echo the characteristics of slavery and feudal-like relationships: extreme control over the worker's freedom of movement, using coercion as a means of enforcing long working hours and debt bondage as a means of chaining the migrant to the *kafeel*.

Another important factor affecting a migrant worker's ability to contest the employer is the wider responsibilities they often hold beyond their individual interests. In his work on Indian migrants in Bahrain, Gardner observes:

> The overall portrait emerging from my interviews suggests that the individual laborer is deeply enmeshed in a complex web of household relations and dependencies: he arrives in Bahrain as an emissary of a household-level strategy that places the well-being of the extended family before the transmigrant's individual interests. ... these typical aspects of Gulf migration forge unequal relations between foreign workers and their sponsors, for in their actions foreign workers risk not only their own lives, well-being, and future, but also those of their families in India. (Gardner, 2010: 61)

Path 2: Kafala in Outsourced Labour Activities

This path is exactly the same path as the first in terms of both procedural and legal aspects. The difference lies in the fact that the migrant worker has two employers, one who employs him through the work permit, and the second who benefits from his labour as an end user. The proliferation of labour outsourcing firms in the Gulf reflects changes to business structures over recent years, and this route has become a major driving force for migrant employment in the GCC. The combination of using labour outsourcing within a labour market that is heavily dependent on *kafala* can lead to a further blurring of employment relationships. A 2005 report by SwedWatch illustrates these issues:

> The Swedish-Saudi companies have made different choices as regards sponsorship. Danya Foods and Saudi Crawford Doors Factory have chosen to become an employer and consequently sponsor to all their foreign employees. In contrast, Al-Rashid Abetong uses some agency staff where both employer and sponsorship responsibility lies with the staffing agency instead. This company estimates that approximately one-third of its production workers are agency staff ... ABB Saudi Arabia also hires agency staff, primarily Asian workers to work in production ... SwedWatch has requested more information from ABB regarding this agency staff but has received no answer. The necessity of making demands on staffing agencies becomes clear in the Tetra Pak Saudi Arabia example. The company uses agency staff if it receives a large order with a short deadline. In these cases the company does not bear employer or sponsorship responsibility. 'Initially this caused problems' says the company's HR Manager Faisal Ghulam. 'Sometimes their employers did not pay their salaries at the proper time, which of course affected the employees' performance. They could see that Tetra Pak employees got their payment on time, but not them. I have now talked to their employers and said that we will cancel our contract if they do not pay out salaries properly in the future'. (SwedWatch, 2005: 25)

The size and significance of this path cannot be traced through traditional labour market data available in the Gulf. The only statistical indicator is the magnitude of state contracts awarded to firms that specialise in labour outsourcing. Data published by Bahrain Tender Board on the tenders awarded to private sector enterprises during the period from 2008 to 2011, reveals that there were 78 contracts for labour outsourcing with a total value of 67 million Bahraini dinar. In Kuwait, during the period from January to mid-September 2012, there were some 27 contracts for labour outsourcing awarded to private sector companies with a total value of 24 million Kuwaiti dinar (approximately US$84 million). This is a significant amount for labour outsourcing activities within a period of only nine months. It should be emphasised that these data only concern workers contracted to the public sector through a private sector company; the size of the labour outsourcing market within the private sector itself remains unknown.

Path 3: Kafala *in Migrant Domestic Services*

In terms of administrative procedures, this route appears to resemble Path 1. There are, however, two major differences. The first relates to the nature and place of work, with migrants (mostly female) employed in the private household. The second concerns the absence of a legal framework regulating the relationship between the employer and domestic worker. In the GCC, labour law does not cover domestic workers. With no framework for any type of protection, and the fact that the place of work is the same as the place of accommodation, migrants in this category are among the most vulnerable of all. Moreover, this path has the most direct impact on the citizen perception of migrants outside the scope of private sector employment.

The extent and magnitude of dependency on foreign domestic workers in the GCC is a phenomenon that cannot be fully explained by the labour market participation rates of female citizens. There are more crucial factors rooted in the socio-cultural values that shaped the Gulf societies after the mid-1970s oil boom. Extending the provision of employing foreign cheap labour to address 'household needs' was a logical consequence of the changes in the Gulf society's value systems and culture. The link between effort and reward has been weakened through the wealth redistribution strategies applied by the Gulf rentier states; a situation has emerged where Gulf citizens could live beyond their means and could compensate for any shortages of local labour supply through easy access to the global labour market. *Kafala* played a crucial role here, as it encouraged the 'commodification' of migrant labour, and the scope of this process has been extended far beyond private sector labour needs.

By mid-2012, according to data published in Kuwait, there were 607,465 non-Kuwaitis working in households (foreign domestic workers), equivalent to 16 per cent of the total population living in Kuwait (3,806,643).[2] In the UAE, according to one estimate, 'each household in the United Arab Emirates employs, on average, three domestic workers' (ILO, 2013a: 33). In Bahrain the share of domestic foreign workers to total foreigners employed in the country reached 18 per cent by the end of 2011. Nowhere else in the world is there such a high percentage. According to the ILO figures, the highest percentage of domestic workers to total employment elsewhere in the world reached approximately 9 per cent in South Africa, and the lowest was in Switzerland (1.24 per cent), both in year 2006 (ILO, 2010: 6).

The domestic work *kafala* path is one of the most complicated in the GCC because of a range of socio-political problems associated with it. It is also the path where cases of forced labour are found, despite their hidden character. Antoinette Vlieger, for example, who has conducted fieldwork in Saudi Arabia and the UAE, states that forced labour in domestic services is the norm and not the exception (Vlieger, 2012). In one case, an Indian female migrant was deprived from returning to her home country for almost 21 years, and despite the expiry of her resident permit and passport she was 'kept in an irregular, un-documented status by her employer for 17 years' (MWPS, 2012). Cases such as these are important precisely because they reveal all the moral, legal and institutional flaws in *kafala*.

Path 4: Kafala As Rent Seeking Activity

The fourth path is one of most peculiar and unique forms of migrant employment. Its main driving force, as the ILO has noted, is the extraction of rent through an ambiguous and disguised form of employment (ILO, 2005: 11). According to the definitions of the ILO, an *ambiguous employment relationship* exists where the main factors that characterise it are not apparent: 'This may occur as a result of the specific, complex form of the relationship between workers and the persons to whom they provide their labour, or the evolution of that relationship over time. Such situations may occur with persons who are normally self-employed' (ILO, 2005: 11). On the other hand, 'a *disguised employment relationship* is one which is lent an appearance that is different from the underlying reality, with the intention of nullifying or attenuating the protection afforded by the law' (ILO, 2005: 12).

The combination of ambiguous and disguised employment is what makes the task of estimating the size of this path of *kafala* extremely difficult. From a procedural point of view it is the same as the paths described earlier. Its uniqueness lies in the fact that workers become rent payers to the sponsor, rather than wage earners as in the other three paths. Rent seeking is the primary motive of the sponsor, and the traditional employer–employee relationship is transformed into rent payer (migrant) and rent collector (sponsor).

This path takes two typical forms. The first can be termed CR (commercial registration), in which a sponsor will bring a migrant to the country in order to operate and run a commercial activity, such as a small grocery shop. According to GCC laws, migrants cannot be self-employed or act as an employer except in very limited spheres of activity (mostly related to businesses aimed at attracting FDI). In order to circumvent these rules, the sponsor will arrange an unofficial agreement with the migrant to operate the business and the migrant will, in turn, agree to pay rent (typically on a monthly basis) to the sponsor. Although these types of arrangements are illegal, they are nonetheless extremely common among small businesses in the Gulf (although statistical data are almost non-existent). The combination of the legal form of employing the migrant, and the illegal agreement between both the sponsor and migrant, gives this path a semi-legal form. It is an ambiguous employment relationship because the migrant is legally registered as a formal employee, whereas in reality he is self-employed or even an employer. The disguised, rentier arrangement between the migrant and the sponsor is hidden behind the apparent formal and traditional employer–employee relationship. Both the ease of starting a business for local citizens, and the surplus benefit provided through the ownership of a work permit, has strongly encouraged this rentier business mindset among a wide circle of Gulf society.

The second form of this fourth *kafala* path is trade in work permits. Longva describes this as the 'Backdoor' of the sponsorship system 'where the two groups (natives and migrants) met and dealt with each other' (Longva, 1997: 108). It begins legally with the sponsor applying for a work permit for a newly opened business (a valid CR is the main condition). Following approval by the respective authority he will send it to the migrant who enters the country under two possible agreements: either he pays his sponsor a regular amount of money in exchange for maintaining his legal work-permit status, or he pays a one-time lump sum in exchange for allowing him to enter the country. This differs from CR in that the migrant is not bound to work in the sponsor's own business enterprise; he can pursue any activity within the labour market as long as he regularly pays the agreed rent. The sponsors in this path resemble landowners who receive regular rents from the users of their land. If the respective migrant fails to pay the rent, the sponsor will lodge a complaint against him as a 'runaway' case and the migrant's status in the country becomes illegal. Steffen Hertog called these types of sponsor 'labour brokers' (Hertog, 2010: 16). He notes that 'many sponsors also demand money for visa cancellations when workers want to return home, and ask for extortionate sums if workers want to officially transfer their sponsorship to their real employer. During autumn 2007 amnesties for illegal laborers in the UAE and Bahrain, many sponsors refused to return passports to workers unless they paid them back a year's wage or more' (Hertog, 2010: 16–17). Overall, this mechanism exists in all GCC labour markets. However, there are variations in the procedural details from one country to another.

In this manner, the *kafala* system has encouraged additional hidden driving forces for the Gulf's reliance on migrant workers. It has created what some researchers called 'minor rentiers', mostly acting as small establishment owners or work-permit owners. The size of this path of *kafala* is very large: in Saudi Arabia, for example, the number of small establishments employing (1–4 workers) formed 84 per cent of the total establishments operating in Saudi Arabia, while the medium-size establishments employing (5–19 workers) reached 13 per cent, the remaining 3 per cent went to the large establishments which employed (20 workers or more) (CDSI, 2010). The demand for work permits in these small establishments constitutes a substantial share of the overall new permits issued each year. In Bahrain, for example, the share of new visas issued to establishments employing less than ten workers was 40 per cent of the total new work permits issues in 2010 (BLMN, 2013).

In both forms of this path the migrant is paying rent to the sponsor, and as such the demand for work permits becomes increasingly detached from local economic conditions and determined by the nature of the migrant labour supply in sending countries. Some countries proved to be more attractive than others in supplying workers in this manner. A combination of extreme poverty in heavily populated rural areas, and the persistence of bonded labour across much of South Asia, makes countries such as Pakistan, India, Sri Lanka and Bangladesh a common source of labour for these rent-extracting circuits. As such, 'many workers will be willing to pay the difference between the income they need to induce them to immigrate to the Gulf and the income they expect to receive' (Willoughby, 2006: 239).

There have been several attempts by scholars to estimate the approximate size and value of the market generated by this path of *kafala* (Willoughby, 2006; Hertog, 2010). Regardless of its economic value, however, it has brought devastating social consequences to Gulf societies. Its prevalence is a partial explanation for the rise of the so-called *nouveau riche* in the Gulf, with ordinary citizens becoming deeply enmeshed in the extraction of rent through the mechanism of *kafala*.

Kafala *and Irregular Workers*

The significance of the work permit as a control mechanism defining the status of migrant workers in the Gulf can be illustrated in the way these workers become irregular (usually described in GCC law as 'illegal' – workers whose actual status is not in line with what it should be according to the regulations). Three major categories of irregular workers can be described: (1) migrant workers who have remained in the country despite the expiration or cancellation of their work-permit; (2) migrant workers who hold a valid work permit but have absconded from their work and been reported by their employer as a 'runaway worker'; (3) migrant workers who are working for an employer other than their original employer without adhering to the legal procedures governing their labour mobility in the country. This third category of irregularity appears legal according to all administrative records of the state, yet the migrant's real status can only be determined through labour inspection visits. This category may include migrant domestic workers who have entered the country through an appropriate work permit but then take up work in a private sector enterprise. It also includes migrants classified as dependent family members, but who work in the private sector. Finally, this third category includes foreigners who entered the country under a tourist visa but later take up work without applying for a proper work permit.

Two important issues can be highlighted in this regard. The first concerns the reasons for irregularity under the *kafala* system. In most other countries, illegal status results from an infringement of existing laws. Under *kafala*, however, irregularity is a direct *consequence* of the structure of the legal system. The sponsor's extremely powerful position over the migrant, one that is codified in law and arises precisely because of the *kafala* regulations, means that many migrants have no other solution to the difficult and exploitative conditions they face except to become irregular. In some cases, the strength of social networks among certain migrant communities can encourage or discourage this act.

The fact that the state has delegated the task of managing the migrant's legal status to individual citizens means that the borders between labour and residency issues are blurred. As a consequence, the migrant can be criminalised due to the negligence of their employer, such as when the sponsor fails to renew a work-permit or fails to pays the necessary fees. The migrant is thus categorised as 'illegal' and subject to deportation – the victim is criminalised because of the act of their sponsor.

The case of Sushila Jayathilaka in Bahrain illustrates this process. Jayathilaka was a 49-year-old Sri Lankan woman who fled her employer's home in Hamad Town following ten months of mistreatment. According to a local news story,

> She later filed a case against her employer with the help of the Migrant Workers Protection Society (MWPS). But the Urgent Matters Court, which took more than a year to issue a verdict, ruled against her after her sponsor filed a counter case demanding BD600 for breach of contract. Judges ordered Ms Jayathilaka to pay him BD580 as compensation and BD10 court costs. (Grewal, 2013)

Moreover, this tendency towards criminalisation can also be seen within the law enforcement process. Most of the labour inspector's time is consumed with chasing irregular migrant workers during inspection visits. Instead of focusing attention on core labour inspection functions such as observing the adherence of employers to labour standards, these inspectors act as labour market police. In addition, the institutional fragmentation between various state organs dealing with migrants (ministry of interior, justice and so forth), and the poor levels of coordination that exist between them, ultimately leads to very weak law enforcement. Many cases get stuck in the courts waiting to be solved. This atmosphere encourages both employers and migrants to break the law, as the law itself has become irrelevant. In many cases, labour problems that start within arrangements that are legal, subsequently encourage illegality. Irregularity is not simply a breach of the legal framework governing migrant workers, but a logical consequence of it.

Summary of the Four Paths

The true magnitude of problems resulting from *kafala* can only be understood by taking into account the specificities of the four paths of *kafala* and the three categories of irregularity. *Kafala* resembles a conglomeration of power relationships that manifest in different ways; its overall affect is to regulate the interaction between migrants and citizens of the Gulf. This system also carries implications for interpreting official data and statistics regarding labour markets in the Gulf. Restrictions on certain occupations for migrants within the so-called 'nationalisation programmes' have led employers to circumvent these rules by choosing different occupational titles when applying for work permits. The result is occupational information that does not reflect actual realities on the ground, and makes accurate analysis extremely difficult. A migrant labourer might be an employee, one of the categories of irregular worker, or a self-employed person who pays rent to a local citizen, yet in official statistics they will be simply be classified as 'wage earner employed'.

The significance of the wide scope and varieties of *kafala* means, in practice, that it encompasses almost all employers and households who employ a migrant. The lengthy period of time over which these practices have developed has had a very significant impact not only upon labour market realities, but also on the psychological traits of both Gulf citizens and migrants. The most important of these is the *kafala* system's exclusionary effect. As a labour relation it contains all elements of pre-capitalist labour relations (slavery and feudal) no matter how they may be disguised by modern terminologies. This exclusion is an essential feature of how Gulf States operate in the contemporary period. Migrant exclusion is not simply confined to the labour market; it extends throughout the whole complex of social realities that migrants in the Gulf encounter on a daily basis.

In a famous letter addressed to Lafargue, Marx wrote: 'Workers in the North have at last fully understood that white labour will never be emancipated so long as black labour is still stigmatized' (Marx, 1866). To some extent, this sentiment can also be seen in the impact of migrant exploitation on the employment of nationals in the Gulf. The poor conditions and structural exclusion of migrants in the Gulf constitute the 'invisible hand' that guides employers in their employment choices, with the *kafala* system becoming the undeclared standard upon which Gulf employers base their labour market preferences. Levels of skill, labour cost, educational attainment, years of experience and attitudes, etc., are all reprocessed through the lens of this standard. The severe deterioration of labour conditions that underpins this system acts as a firewall against the employment of nationals. The 'active' exclusion of migrants thus leads to the 'passive' exclusion of citizens, with *kafala* playing an instrumental role in this process (Sen, 2000: 14–15). A recent report by the ILO and UNDP has clearly described the 'vicious circle' that ensues (ILO, 2012: 38):

1. Immigration policies that allow the payment of lower wages to migrant workers than those paid to national workers encourage the use of labour-intensive techniques in the private sector.
2. Labour-intensive techniques lead to low labour productivity.

3. Low labour productivity leads to low wages also being offered to nationals in the private sector.
4. Low private sector wages increase the incentives for nationals to seek employment in the public sector.
5. The government tries to accommodate the concerns of nationals and increases employment, and with it the expectation of employment in the public sector.
6. In such an environment, there are few incentives for nationals to really invest in human capital – beyond credentialism.
7. This results in low productivity in the public sector, too, because of low skills, oversupply and underemployment.
8. As a result, the economy is locked into a low productivity equilibrium.
9. Low productivity means that low wages prevail, the attractions of immigration increases and the vicious circle continues.

At the macro level, *kafala* in the GCC has proved to be an important tool in the 'persistence of temporariness' of migrant populations, which means they are neither temporary in reality nor permanent in status. This has a profound impact on the functioning of the rentier state in these countries. It is a form of double exclusion, in which the political exclusion of migrants complements the exclusion of citizens from the labour market. Instead of one society, we have two societies within each country; one for the citizens, the second for the migrants. Between the two exists a spatial socio-political and cultural segregation, with a mutual economic dependency, founded on the dominance of the first upon the second. As Philippe Fargues has noted, 'oil-generated wealth could support high rates of growth among both nationals (through high fertility) and foreign nationals (through high immigration) while the lack of naturalization and intermarriages makes the two populations reproduce in isolation' (2011b: 274).

One of the crucial outcomes of this situation can be seen in so-called 'second generation migrants', a phenomenon that can be observed in many countries in the Gulf. In Kuwait, for example, government data indicate that among the 2,610,837 non-Kuwaitis residing in the country, there are 463,203 who were born in Kuwait. Of these, 39 per cent (180,705) are aged 20 years and above. Approximately 79 per cent of those non-Kuwaitis, who were born inside Kuwait, are of Arab nationality (367,440) (PACI, 2012). In Bahrain, the 2010 census indicated that approximately (266,469) 40 per cent of non-Bahrainis have lived in the country for six years or more (Bahrain CIO, 2010).

The large-scale presence of long-term migrants raises a fundamental question often ignored in literature dealing with migration in the GCC: why are questions of migrant integration and naturalisation absent from the public discourse? Discussion often focuses on reducing the number of migrants or seeking only high-skilled workers; very few analysts or policymakers are willing to publicly discuss the necessity of migrant integration. One explanation of this lacuna is the core role that exclusion of migrants has played in restricting the numbers of citizens and further reinforcing citizen allegiance to the ruler. In this context, the alternative option of including migrants as equal citizens in the Gulf raises a whole set of fundamental questions about the ways in which these societies are structured. Rather than framing inclusion through the lens of scaremongering around the loss of Gulf identity (as it is typically approached), it should be considered as a potentially enriching element both demographically and culturally. In contrast to other states where migrants form a primary source of new citizens, Gulf States have consciously excluded the settlement of foreigners or non-citizens while they continue to struggle with making immigrants unnecessary (Fargues, 2011b: 275). As Fargues concludes: 'The exceptional demography of the Gulf States is not explained by an exceptional level of immigration as much as by an exceptional closure of local societies' (2011b: 275).

In sum, we note that *kafala* as a power relation between citizens and migrants was an outcome of specific relations between the rentier state and citizens of the Gulf countries. Over the years, it has helped shape the perception of citizenship and the relations to migrants. Being 'ruled' by other power structures (political, economic and social), Gulf citizens find themselves 'ruling' over migrants in the same society by becoming *kafeels*. This duality leads to the compartmentalisation of thinking and a process of depersonalisation. Both can underpin racist sentiments and a lack of concern towards the suffering of others, reflected in the weak engagement of citizens with migrant workers' rights (with the exception of the work done by a small number of civil society and human rights organisations). Addressing *kafala* as an exclusion mechanism is not simply a managerial or institutional task. Because of its foundational roots within the rentier state mechanism, any substantive change requires the redefinition of citizenship and the subsequent reshaping of the relation between the state and its citizens – a new emphasis based upon rights and duties and not privileges and patronage. Only then can the attitudes and approach towards migrants rest upon an appreciation of diversity and inclusion.

Notes

1. The workers surveyed for this study were 75 per cent male and around half of them were Indian (Khan, 2010: 15).
2. Data from The Public Authority for Civil Information: www.paci.gov.kw/index.php/2011-03-06-18-21-09

5

Rootless Hubs: Migration, Urban Commodification and the 'Right to the City' in the GCC

Omar AlShehabi

Discussion of migration in the GCC has traditionally exclusively focused on labour. This chapter focuses on other dimensions of migration which have started emerging over the first decade of the twenty-first century in the Gulf Arab States.[1] These other aspects of migration will be highlighted through the lens of 'international mega-real estate projects' (IMREPs). I will argue that these newly emergent mega-real estate projects highlight a marked shift in citizen-state-expatriate dynamics within the region. This is evident in two central ways. Firstly, expatriates are not only workers and a source of labour, but increasingly they are also consumers, investors, owners of property and users of the urban space – indeed, they are persons involved in diverse activities which I summarise using the phrase 'agents that animate the city'.[2]

Second, such mega-real estate projects point to an underlying vision that has been guiding the establishment and development of the cities under consideration, which I call 'rootless urbanism'. The guiding principles of rootless urbanism are defined by two features: (1) the increasingly important role of IMREPs aimed at expatriates as a final consumer within the local economic and spatial frontiers, making them new urban 'centres' in a unique form of urban segmentation and commodification; and (2) although a host of enticements and benefits are placed on offer to attract expatriates as the primary targets for such projects, expatriates are ultimately denied *de jure* the possibility to live and settle within GCC societies permanently. Thus, rootless urbanism is a vision that gears urban space production towards a predominantly expatriate population, but where this population is conceived as being permanently temporary: one that is expected to spend a significant amount of time in these cities, but is formally not allowed to establish permanent roots in them.

Such a vision, I argue, is inherently unstable, partly because of its transitory nature, and partly because of the tensions it creates with 'citizens' within society. The consequences of 'rootless urbanism' will increasingly play a more significant role in power and social relationships between the state, business, citizens and expatriates, with a complex web of stratifications emerging that is mainly segmented across citizenship and economic class. Questions regarding the distribution and usage of urban space and the 'right to the city' will increasingly become contestable and more important in defining the relationship between these different groups within the smaller states of the GCC.

Critical urban studies is a largely virgin field within the academic literature focusing on the Gulf,[3] particularly in relation to migration. To our knowledge, this is one of the first attempts to analyse the relationship between migration and the new mega cities that have emerged across the GCC in the twenty-first century. The focus in this chapter will not be on the political economy of the production of such mega-real estate projects (a topic that I have tried to address elsewhere in AlShehabi, 2012), but instead we cater the discussion to the spatial and demographic transformations that have accompanied them.

The consequences of such projects for migration in the region could be potentially immense, raising several avenues of important and relevant research. These new cities are also part of a process that is still in development and in its nascent phase. Hence the large scope of issues involved, the dearth of previous material on the topic and the relatively new and ever-changing nature of the dynamics at play necessarily limits the depth that the chapter delves into. Instead, we focus more on providing an overview of the phenomenon and its ramifications.

We begin by outlining the phenomenon of IMREPs in the four countries (Bahrain, Qatar, UAE and to a lesser extent Oman) who have adopted such IMREPs as a central platform of their economic visions, followed by a discussion of their implications for migration. We then turn to examining the new urban reality that is being formed as a consequence of these new real estate projects. Finally, we focus on what these new cities imply for power relationships in the GCC between citizens, expatriates, the business community and the state, and what they might indicate for the future of the region. We conclude by looking at the case study of Bahrain for the consequences of such cities.

The International Mega-Real Estate Projects

The real estate boom and bust over the first decade of the new millennium has come to be seen as a symbol of the global excesses of the period, with Dubai becoming the international icon of this phenomenon. The extent of the real estate boom in the GCC cannot be understated, constituting the bulk of economic activity in the region after the oil and gas sector. At the height of the oil boom in 2008, 57 per cent of the value of all announced projects in the GCC – US\$1.2 trillion out of a total of US\$2.1 trillion – were directed towards these mega-real estate projects (*AMEinfo*, 2008). The ten biggest projects in the GCC were of the mega-real estate variety, worth about US\$393 billion (MEED, 2010). The infrastructure needed to make such projects a reality included planned energy projects worth US\$134 billion, and water and sewage infrastructural spending worth another US\$40 billion. It was estimated that demand for desalinated water and electricity was to increase at an annual rate of 8 per cent and 10 per cent consecutively (EDC, 2007; Das Augustine, 2009). The scale of these projects was so immense that a third of global project finance flowed to the region in 2006 (Hanieh, 2011: 110).

As a consequence of these investments, the growth in the real estate sector was staggering. In Bahrain, the sector grew by a compound annual growth rate of 7.1 per cent between 2003 and 2007, while in Kuwait the annual rate reached 8.7 per cent between 2002 and 2007. In Oman it grew by 10 per cent between 2003 and 2007, while in Qatar it reached 39.2 per cent during the same period, with the UAE registering 24.5 per cent. Overall, revenues grew by more than 37 per cent annually between 2002 and 2008, for the overall revenues growth to reach more than 500 per cent in this period (Ellaboudy, 2010).

These real estate projects were in large part a state-driven and shaped process in conjunction with the 'private' sector. The policies, energies and legislation of these four countries have not only enabled such projects, but they have focused on propelling them and putting them at the centre of their economies. Indeed, many of the real estate companies driving these projects, such as Emaar or Dubai World, were state-owned enterprises or controlled by ruling family members. Nothing highlights the central role played by the state in driving the real estate growth more than the most important economic documents produced by the GCC states, the so-called 'economic visions'.

Officially, the economic visions focused on the goals and aspirations of these countries over the next few decades, outlining the economic and social strategies that would be employed to reach them. These economic visions were written primarily by Western consultancy firms employed by local rulers. The extent of the phenomenon of hiring non-local firms to write, shape and outline the whole economic vision and strategy for a county represents to my knowledge a unique and unprecedented situation of entrusting a nation's economic future to outsiders.[4]

The Bahrain Economic Development Board announced its 2030 vision, and Abu Dhabi followed suit with its own 2030 vision. Not to be outdone, Qatar also laid out its own 2030 vision, while Dubai outlined a 'Strategic Plan 2015'. The first stand-out characteristic of these visions is the remarkable similarity in the language and terms used. Furthermore, very similar strategies are outlined within them, as if they were written by the same hands.

What emerges from reading these economic visions is the almost compulsive obsession with increasing global business competitiveness and openness towards FDI. Terms such as 'ease of doing business', 'property rights', 'competitiveness', 'investor perception' and 'international hub' pop up regularly. At the centre of these visions lie the mega-real estate projects. A detailed exposition is not possible here, but some excerpts are sufficient to illustrate the above points:

> Bahrain is conveniently located at the heart of the GCC, and provides a gateway to Asia, Europe and Africa. In addition to the region's standard economic incentives – zero taxation for private companies, few indirect taxes for private enterprises and individuals, and free movement of capital – Bahrain offers one hundred percent foreign ownership of business assets and real estate in most sectors of the economy. (Bahrain Economic Development Board, 2008: 8)

> Bahrainis welcome foreigners into their country, integrating them into their community in the true Islamic tradition of tolerance and hospitality. As a result, the population is diverse, living and working together peacefully. (Bahrain Economic Development Board, 2008: 8)

When it comes to property rights, the passing of recent legislation formalising the right of foreigners to own real estate has shown that Abu Dhabi is actively seeking to protect the property rights of all in the Emirate. Foreign nationals are now permitted to own real estate in the Emirate within specially designated zones. The Government intends to expand property rights further for foreign investors. (Government of Abu Dhabi, 2008: 50)

The level of foreign ownership remains low within the Emirate, thus indicating an opportunity to boost FDI and speed-up the roll-out of leading edge technologies, business processes and management practice to the rest of the economy. (Government of Abu Dhabi, 2008: 49)

Thus, such projects were not only facilitated by the state, but indeed they constituted a central part of their economic strategies. Governments rolled out supportive visions and provided the general environment and the material means to make these mega-real estate projects a reality.

New Forms of Migration?

The question that necessarily arises is to whom are these projects, which have become a central plank of the countries' visions, destined? Given the small national population of these countries, it quickly becomes clear that such projects cannot be targeted towards citizens as final users, but they would necessarily have to be geared towards expatriates as end users. Otherwise, such projects necessarily will end up being ghost towns.

By the start of the new millennium, a batch of real estate laws in four out of the six GCC countries were introduced that explicitly opened the door for the purchase of real estate by non-citizens for the first time in the region. In 2001 Bahrain announced that it would allow expatriates to buy real estate, Dubai quickly followed suit in 2002, and four of the remaining six UAE emirates consequently joined the bandwagon. Qatar and Oman incorporated such laws in 2004 and 2006 respectively. Saudi Arabia and Kuwait hesitated regarding adopting similar laws, but in 2010 Saudi Arabia announced that King Abdullah Economic City will be the first place where foreigners are allowed to buy real estate. Thus Kuwait remains the sole country that is yet to announce the introduction of similar laws,[5] although there have been growing calls by the business community to adopt them.

In tandem, legislation that linked the purchase of real estate to the right to obtain residency permits was passed in the four countries that opened up to international real estate markets. Bahrain legislated for five-year residency visas that are automatically renewed with the continued ownership of the property, while the UAE announced the introduction of three-year renewable visas after first limiting them to six months. Qatar and Oman followed Bahrain in opting for five-year renewable residency visas.

These laws paved the way for a huge boom in the construction of such IMREPs. At the height of the boom in 2008, extremely conservative estimates show that there were plans to build more than 1.3 million units that allow for foreign ownership within these four countries (see Table 5.1). If one conservatively assumes three individuals per unit, that implies a capacity to house more than 4.3 million individuals. The total combined number of citizens of these four countries in 2008 was 3.8 million. If these projects were to materialise in their totality,[6] they would have the potential to house more individuals than the total of all the citizens of these four countries. Thus, for these projects to have any viability, they necessarily must be geared towards expatriates.

Table 5.1   Announced number of international real estate units in 2008 that are completed or planned to be built by 2020 (thousands)

Country	Number of Units	Total Capacity	Number of Citizens
UAE	1104	3544	892
Abu Dhabi	180	759	–
Dubai	690	2070	–
Ajman	28	83	–
Um Al Quwain	183	548	–
Ras Al Khaimah	28	84	–
Bahrain	60	180	538
Oman	94	282	1967
Qatar	67	324	220
Total	1329	4330	3617

* The huge number in Um Al Quwain is due to the White Bay project which was eventually cancelled

Source: author calculations from various resources. For in-depth calculations see AlShehabi (2012).

But who are the expatriates that must be attracted to these real estate projects? Data on this issue are limited. The real estate boom was still in the speculative phase when the financial crisis hit the region in 2009, as laid bare by the fact that the main buyers in some of these countries were GCC speculators who were aiming to resell the properties for a higher profit. Furthermore, data on such issues are notoriously difficult to come across within the region.

There are some indirect indications, however. In Bahrain, the authorities announced in the 2010 municipality elections (where GCC residents and expatriates who own real estate were allowed to vote) that there were 8,150 registered voters who were not citizens (*Al-Wasat*, 2010a). Given that the 2010 population census data show there are about 3,400 resident GCC citizens in Bahrain that are of the eligible voting age (Bahrain 2010 Census, 2010), this implies that there are several thousand non-GCC expatriates who own property (with this figure not including their families and dependants), a small but not insignificant proportion of the population.

The value of all real estate property bought in Bahrain by non-GCC expatriates was 43.1 million Bahraini dinar (BD) in the first half of 2012. This made up approximately 13.5 per cent of total property dealings in Bahrain (whether IMREPs or not), with GCC citizens making up another 10 per cent and Bahrainis making up the remaining 76.5 per cent (Bahrain Survey and Land Registration Bureau, 2012).

Data from within these newly established international gated communities support such numbers. In an interview with a senior employee in a district of Amwaj, one of the most established gated communities in Bahrain, they indicated that roughly 40 per cent of owners are expatriates from outside the GCC, while the other 60 per cent are owned by Bahrainis and other GCC members (with the proportion of Bahraini owners outnumbering those from the GCC). In terms of renting, the proportion is closer to 70 per cent expatriates and 30 per cent Bahrainis and GCC citizens, indicating that quite a few Bahrainis and GCC citizens are purchasing to rent to expatriates.[7]

According to the same employee, most of the expatriate buyers of property are British, followed by Americans, with a few from India and Pakistan. Most are usually working in Bahrain, and either looking for a long-term investment or a home to live in. Thus, most are long-term buyers. The situation has changed since the onset of the political crisis in Bahrain in 2011, as some expatriates have become nervous. Their selling rate has increased, with Bahrainis purchasing more of these units.

Dubai, the most advanced market for IMREPs and the city that has become the envy and role model for many of the others, provides the most relevant data on the extent of the phenomenon. The first glaring difference in comparison to Bahrain is that of scale, with the size of trade in mega-real estate in Bahrain completely dwarfed by Dubai.

The 2006 Dubai data reveal that the number of Arab buyers (including GCC citizens) constituted 28 per cent of all real estate transactions, with 72 per cent coming from non-Arabs (Futurebrand, 2006: 12). The highest proportion of buyers by purchase value came from India (24 per cent), followed by the United Kingdom (21 per cent), Pakistan (12 per cent) and Iran (10 per cent) (Futurebrand, 2009: 70). This trend within purchasers seems to recur yearly, with Indians again topping the 2011 figures, spending 2.1 billion dirhams, thus making up 16 per cent of total expenditure on real estate in the emirate (*India Real Estate Monitor*, 2012). The new money flowing into the Dubai property market in 2011 from abroad totalled 13.13 billion dirhams.

In the first half of 2012, the total value of direct foreign investment in the real estate sector shot up to 22.1 billion United Arab Emirates dirham (AED) (Dubai Land Department, 2012), with 12,875 properties bought. Indians once again came top of the pile, buying 2,153 properties valued at 3.751 billion AED, closely followed by Pakistanis with 1,841 properties at 1.713 billion AED and British investors coming third with 1,564 properties worth 2,529 billion AED.

Table 5.2   Real estate transactions in Dubai in the first half of 2012 by nationality

Nationality	Value (AED)	Number of Investors	Average Value per Investor
India	3,751,846,026	2,153	1,742,613
Pakistan	1,713,837,907	1,814	944,784
Britain	2,529,944,501	1,564	1,617,612
Iran	1,515,712,994	1,057	1,433,976
Russia	1,438,760,857	694	2,073,142
Saudi Arabia	1,059,886,515	416	2,547,804
America	694,529,969	415	1,673,566
Canada	754,015,467	329	2,291,840
Jordan	460,188,771	268	1,717,122
Other	8,234,221,965	4,165	1,977,004
Total	22,152,944,972	12,875	1,720,617

Source: Dubai Land Department (2012).

The data in Table 5.2 show that there are at least tens of thousands of expatriate property owners in Dubai. Informal evidence supports such data.

Regardless of the owners of the real estate projects, any stroll through the streets of Dubai – the Marina district being a potent example – confirms that the majority of dwellers in these newly completed projects are expatriates, generally from non-Arab countries. This corroborates information obtained from interviews with employees in such projects, who identify that the vast majority of buyers are non-Arab expatriates.

An employee in one of these projects, for example, contends that there were a significant number of Iranian buyers during the initial phases of the real estate boom, since real estate ownership entitled them to a visa. Increasingly, Russians and Chinese started entering the market after the financial crisis, their main concern centring on investment and profit making. Thus, in Dubai the main motivations for buying were flipping, investment or a visa. Some buyers were also living in the country, with many combining working with real estate ownership.[8]

What can also be assumed is that the price of buying and renting real estate in these projects necessarily entails that buyers and dwellers are from the middle- to upper-class strata of society. The average value of a real estate purchase in the first half of 2012, for example, was 1.7 million AED.

X[9] is a typical example of such property owners. She is a married mother of two from South Africa in her late thirties, who bought a one-bedroom flat in Dubai while working there at the height of the real estate boom in 2007. The flat is located in one of the newly built high-rise developments in Jebel Ali Dubai. Although she no longer lives there, she still owns the flat. The primary reason for buying the apartment was as an investment. By 2012, when the interview was conducted, she had no choice but to hold on to the flat, as the price did not allow for a significant return on sale. Rental prices have dropped form 11,000 AED per month to nearly 3,000 AED, and she had to make do with renting the flat to other expatriates living in Dubai.

It is not unusual for individuals from the above listed countries, particularly within Asia, to make up the bulk of the market in Dubai and indeed possibly the rest of the GCC. India, Pakistan and Iran have long historical, geographic, migratory and cultural links with the region, with a population bloc of more than 1.5 billion between them. They also constitute the biggest proportion of migrant labour in the region. Figures show that there is between three and five million Indians alone working and living in the region. For Pakistan, the figure hovers around one to two million, while Iran has more than 200,000 individuals (Kapiszewski, 2006). 'Asians' overall constituted 92 per cent, 59 per cent, 46 per cent, 65 per cent, 80 per cent and 87 per cent of the expatriate labour market in Oman, Saudi Arabia,

Qatar, Kuwait, Bahrain and UAE respectively (ILO, 2009b). Furthermore, by the twenty-first century these countries were no longer simply exporters of unskilled cheap labour to the region, with many of the middle-class professionals in the Gulf originating from them.

They have also witnessed a significant widening in their middle-class base over the past few decades, providing a significant potential supply that can afford such real estate projects. In India, for example, the middle class was estimated at 50 million individuals in 2011, and it was expected to reach 580 million individuals by the year 2025 (Pilling, 2011).

The four GCC states studied here have made no secret of their wish to tap into this emerging globally affluent class. Indeed IMREPs were not the only outward-oriented ventures witnessed during the last decade. A plethora of new museums have emerged in the past decade (e.g. the Guggenheim in Abu Dhabi), as well as universities (e.g. Qatar Educational City) and cultural institutions and events (e.g. Oman's Royal Opera House) that cater mostly to an affluent foreign clientele.

Furthermore, there has been a concerted drive by all GCC countries to increase the global flow of goods and people passing through their air and sea ports, with the logistics, transportation and tourism sectors becoming increasingly big drivers of their economies. By the beginning of 2014, there were ten fully-fledged international airports within the GCC.[10] The six countries saw more than 1.5 million flights pass through their airports in 2010,[11] carrying well in excess of 100 million passengers. Dubai International Airport on its own carried more than 66 million passengers in 2013 at an annually increasing rate of 15 per cent, becoming the seventh busiest airport in the world (Dubai Airports, 2014). The national airlines of the GCC have increasingly become major players on the global level, frequently competing with and even buying out more established companies in Europe and the US. This boom in passenger movement was complemented with a huge increase in goods movement via an expansive shipping and air cargo sector. Thus, becoming a 'hub' for the global movement of goods and people has become a central part of the visions and economies of the GCC. This was complemented by a concerted effort to become serious 'international cities', moving beyond the 'standard' image of oil sheikhdoms and indeed even becoming tourist destinations. Naturally, a large flow of people, the vast majority of whom are not citizens of the GCC, became a central pillar to this model of 'transit states'. What happens once a significant proportion of these individuals are no longer simply passing through the region, and are actually spending a substantial part of their lives in it? In other words, what about migrants to the Gulf?

Expatriates: Beyond Labour

It is beyond doubt that one of the defining dichotomies of inhabitants of the GCC is between citizens and non-citizens: i.e. migrants. There are a host of legal, economic and (as is discussed below) geographic distinctions between the two, starting from the *kafala* law that controls everything from the legal nature of expatriates' presence in the GCC to the exclusive social benefits that citizens obtain. Furthermore, the ability for expatriates to become nationals is severely restricted and for all intents and purposes impossible,[12] leading Longva to describe the situation as that of an 'ethnocracy', where 'the acquisition of the defining feature of the ruling elite (citizenship) lies beyond the dominated groups (expatriates)' (Longva, 2005: 125).

This distinction between nationals and expatriates is inherent in nearly all academic discussions of migration in the modern era of the GCC. Nearly equally ingrained is viewing the sole economic role of expatriates as exclusively based on labour provision. Expatriate workers are seen as a necessary input for economic growth, in essence a productive factor that is needed for the crucial supply of labour. However, as the GCC economies have continually expanded to become global hubs for the movement of goods and people, this chapter argues that migrants' economic roles within the region increasingly transcend pure labour considerations. Expatriates are increasingly ingrained as people that play multiple roles within GCC societies, and very often the same individual plays more than one role within this mesh.

No longer are expatriates simply needed as a source of 'manpower', but they are enticed to the region as travellers, consumers, investors and indeed inhabitants of the urban space of the region. They are a source of purchasing power that actively need to be marketed to, attracted and recruited in order to travel through, buy, invest and even live in the region. The vision is for them to become 'agents that animate the cities' of the Gulf, a phrase that signifies the multiple roles that people play in creating and interacting with the physical space of the cities in the Gulf, whether through consuming in them, working in them, renting or buying real estate, and indeed living in them.

One obvious way is through consumption. Although private consumption as a percentage of GDP is notoriously low in the Gulf (hovering between 20 and 35 per cent in comparison to roughly 60 per cent in the OECD), expatriates increasingly make up a large bulk of consumption expenditure in the GCC, particularly in the smaller states.

Data from the 2009 household census (Dubai Statistics Center, 2009) in Dubai, for example, show that out of a total annual expenditure of 47.7 billion AED, only 8.4 billion AED (17.6 per cent) came from national households, while expatriates constituted 82.4 per cent of expenditure. Even expatriate subgroups' expenditure exceeded that of nationals. What is classified as 'Asian households', for example, had double the expenditure (16.2 billion AED) of nationals (9.2 billion AED). 'Collective labourers' had about the same level at 8.9 billion AED, while 'European households and the like' stood at more than half at 5.0 billion AED.

In Bahrain, average annual per capita expenditure in the 2005–2006 survey was 2,255.66 BD for citizens (table 3.90 in the Bahrain 2010 Census), while average per capita expenditure of expatriates registered higher at 2,729.4 BD (table 3.91). Given that expatriates outnumbered citizens in 2012, this means that overall expenditure (assuming the same expenditure patterns) would be higher for expatriates than citizens. Similarly in Qatar, the average Qatari's monthly individual expenditure from the 2008 household is 4,335.55 Qatari riyal (QR), while the expatriate's average monthly expenditure is 2,903.84 QR. Given that Qatar's expatriate population outranks the local population by a ratio of nearly 9:1, it becomes increasingly clear that the expenditure of expatriates is quite important in driving total private demand. Thus, expatriates play at least an equally important role in private demand, if not more so, than local households in the smaller GCC states. This of course generates an economic role for a particular segment of expatriates as engines of private demand (however limited the overall role of the latter) within the GCC economies that goes beyond their role as providers of labour.

My main focus within this chapter, however, is specifically on the IMREPs that have been targeted towards an expatriate clientele as an illustration of the multiple roles played by expatriates that transcend labour. It is well known that real estate represents one of the greatest rent and income generators (after oil) in the region, whether through renting or sale of property. Prior to the new millennium, expatriates living in the region were not allowed to own real estate, and hence they were confined to renting and living in properties owned by nationals. Hence, local households have traditionally derived a significant proportion of income from real estate. A large proportion of such rented real estate is targeted towards expatriate tenants, making the latter a significant source of rent income for locals. For example, local households in Bahrain indicate that they generate 21 per cent of their income from real estate possessions (table 4.43 from the Bahrain 2010 Census), while in Dubai citizens indicate that 16 per cent of income is derived from real estate (table 02–03 in the Bahrain 2010 Census). In Qatar, the proportion of citizens' income from entrepreneurial and business activities, including real estate, reached 33 per cent in 2006–2007 (Qatar Statistical Authority, 2010).

With the advent of these new mega-real estate projects, possession of real estate on a freehold or 99-year leasehold basis for expatriates was allowed, and as we outlined above was marketed as a primary engine of growth in the economy. The advent of these IMREPs provides a prime example of the qualitative and quantitative shifts in the economic roles played by expatriates in the region. The most hitherto discussed migration phenomenon in relation to these real estate projects focuses on the plight of construction workers brought in to build these projects. Poorly paid, inadequately housed and with an extremely precarious short-term stay in the country, there were more than 1.5 million expatriate construction workers in the GCC at the height of the real estate boom in 2008 (Baldwin-Edwards, 2011). Our focus here, however, is not on the workers involved in constructing these cities but their envisaged inhabitants.

Firstly, expatriates are increasingly becoming asset (and capital) owners within the region. Asset ownership obviously involves a different set of social relations when compared to labour providers and wage earners. Part of this is certainly the social standing and influence that the purchase of real estate affords to its buyer, but it also entails radical changes in the legal and economic relationships with the rest of society's actors.

One way this manifests itself is the legal status of expatriate real estate owners vis-à-vis local businesses, citizens and the state. Since local legislation in all four countries that have enacted freehold ownership for foreigners directly link real estate ownership to the right to obtain visas, owners are no longer tied to local sponsors for their residency, as is the case within the *kafala* system. The link between a local sponsor, whether a citizen or business enterprise, and the expatriate is broken, with the sponsor now becoming the state directly. Expatriates are no longer dependent, theoretically at least, on any single individual or company for their stay. This breaks the traditional link that has characterised all previous expatriate relations and marks a milestone in the state–citizen–expatriate relationship.

There are also important ramifications on sovereignty in terms of the legal ownership of the real estate projects and its infrastructure between the state, the real estate owner and the real estate project developer. For example, these new mega-real estate projects are very often closed gated communities, where the individual unit owners jointly own all the common facilities, and where the estate is managed by a private contractor. Commonly owned facilities could include roads, pavements and infrastructure. Tala, for example, is a closed gated community within the artificially constructed island of Amwaj in Bahrain, the latter also being a closed gated community itself. Residents jointly own many of the common spaces within Tala, which is managed by an appointed maintenance company (Tala Island, 2007: 3).

On paper at least, the state has no ownership, claims or jurisdiction within these communities and their common facilities, which are in the domain of the homeowners' associations and project developers. In an interview with an employee in a leading Bahrain closed gated community, for example, he indicated that the only interaction with the local municipality and the state revolved around collecting refuse and paying the municipality tax and the electricity and water bills. It seems that there were a host of legal complexities inherent in the relationship between these new cities, the state and the wider community, regarding ownership and usage of resources, which were not completely resolved.

This phenomenon of independent 'enclaves' has its precedents in the early gated communities of the international oil companies in the region (e.g. Bapco's Awali in Bahrain or Aramco in Saudi Arabia), and has resonance with the advent of various financial[13] and free zones[14] across the GCC, each with their separate jurisdictions, labour laws and licensing rules. Such fragmentation of sovereignty has fundamental implications on the applicability and interactions of laws and regulations between these different jurisdictions and enclaves, and indeed the state at large.

Furthermore, such real estate projects could entail a potentially fundamental shift in the way (a certain segment of) expatriates are able to mobilise and group. This is highlighted by the advent of residents' associations springing up within these new mega-real estate projects. These residents' associations legally allow real estate owners to group together and form a lobbying organisation that jointly manages the affairs of the community, as well as jointly owning all the common properties. This allows real estate owners to act in an organised and sustained formation that is legally recognised, in a manner akin to unions (Tala Island, 2007: 1–5). Unions, as is well known however, are an option currently not afforded to expatriate workers in the GCC.

X, the South African apartment owner in Dubai whom we met before, is a member of the homeowners' association of Nakheel, the developer of the gated community project where she owns a property. The homeowner association is extremely large and has thousands of members, which potentially allows for lobbying and concerted action. Indeed, such concerted action has already been witnessed. For example, most of the maintenance in such real estate projects used to be run by the developers themselves as a monopoly, charging high rates in the process. Home owners' associations started a strong campaign directed towards the authorities against such practices, which eventually helped in introducing new legislation that allowed home owners to choose their maintenance providers (*The National*, 2010).

Transit States and Rootless Urbanism

The phenomenon of mega-real estate projects was not only a GCC phenomenon. Indeed, it was in many respects a global phenomenon typical of the financial boom at the dawn of twenty-first century, with the urban expansion craze in condominiums witnessed in India, China and Spain being only the most glaring examples.

Two factors, when combined, make the situation in the GCC countries under consideration unique in my opinion. The first is the lopsided concentration of the local non-oil economic and spatial activity on these 'international' real estate projects, with the resources geared to such projects reaching science-fictional proportions. Indeed, these projects have a dominant presence within the physical landscape of the cities in the four countries that allowed for such projects, constituting new urban 'centres' that exist in parallel to other urban spaces in an increasingly segmented city. The second is the fact that the GCC does not have the national population to support such real estate projects, which would necessarily mean catering them towards expatriates if these projects are to be in any realistic way viable. The catch, however, is that such non-citizen buyers are not allowed to permanently settle and integrate into the local society. These two factors, when combined, create what I call the phenomenon of 'rootless urbanism'.

Let us start by understanding the extent of these projects. A good starting point is to look at the newly laid-out master plans for the GCC cities. These master plans outlined the new urban landscapes these city-states were to take, and as with the previously discussed economic visions, they were designed in their entirety by Western consultancy firms. Bahrain's master plan was entrusted to Skidmore, Owings and Merrill, while in Qatar Oriental Consultants, a Japanese firm, was charged with drawing up its master plan. Abu Dhabi's 2030 urban plan outlines its vision that by 2020 the emirates' inhabitants would reach two million residents living in 411,000 residential units, further increasing to 3.1 million residents by 2020 in 686,000 units, the vast majority of this increase being through a rise in expatriate numbers, with the percentage of nationals projected to decrease even further (Abu Dhabi Urban Planning Council, 2007). The IMREPs are destined to make up a significant chunk of the new projects in these master plans.

Since their conception, such projects were driven by a high degree of a top-down management regarding the design and development of IMREPs. Indeed, they frequently entail building entire cities along with their infrastructure completely from scratch. This top-down planning, however, is frequently privatised. Although the state, as we saw, played a central role creating the overall economic environment that propelled these projects and made them prosper through its economic visions and spending on supporting infrastructure, the involvement of formal state institutions in the concrete planning and design of such projects varies. No longer are the configurations of the GCC cities in question dominated exclusively by the central planning of an omnipresent 'petro-modernist state',[15] as was the case in the 1950s–1990s, when the layout and planning of neighbourhoods, roads and the urban environment was an exclusively state-driven process. Instead, the planning process for these new cities and projects has frequently been carried out by private firms and companies. Interviews with several architects and planners in private firms have indicated that plans and designs for new projects were often formulated, approved and put into practice by the companies involved in the project, with input by the relevant state and municipal authorities being a formality that was little more than an afterthought. This is an extremely unusual and relatively recent development in the Gulf, which any person who has gone through the heavily bureaucratised and state-regulated process of building a privately owned dwelling will attest to.

The scale of such projects is also immense, often covering an area of several kilometres squared and encompassing thousands of housing units. Such real estate projects usually manifest themselves in one of two ways. They are either built as urban high-rise towers in commercial areas of the city, or they are gated communities of luxurious villas and apartments, usually by the seafront or in the desert.

Amwaj, a man-made island on four kilometres squared of reclaimed sea in northern Bahrain, is a typical example of these projects. It is a closed gated community, with several closed gated communities within the bigger project itself. An example of these projects is Tala, made of 90 villas and 585 apartments on the sea. Not far is the 'Floating City', inspired by Venice, where water canals hug the 213 housing units in the project, allowing residents to moor their yachts (TEN Real Estate, 2011). Within the wider Amwaj project there is a school, several shopping malls, supermarkets, hotels and facilities that make it a closed gated community totally independent of the surrounding environment. Currently, Amwaj is one of the most expensive areas in Bahrain, and the most favoured residential area for well-to-do expatriates and professionals.

Dubai, the city that symbolised real estate drive more than any other, needed more than one master plan to keep up with all the projects under construction. The now-suspended Waterfront project, for example, is projected to span an area of 1.5 billion square feet, surpassing the size of Washington, DC three times and accommodating up to 1.3 million residents. Its master plan was designed by the famous Dutch designer Rem Koolhaas (Ouroussoff, 2008).

Upon reflection, the first thesis we propose should be obvious, but has so far received quite limited attention: the urban space of the cities of the smaller GCC states are significantly reconfigured by these 'international' mega-real estate projects. Although such real estate projects are a work in progress, and although the numbers occupying them by the end of 2013 were still not at their peak, they had already generated a huge transformation in the physical space of the cities themselves. This transformation has had a profound impact on the natural environment, the habitation patterns across the city and the relationship between locals, expatriates, the state, the business community and the built-up area where they interact. To use the literature jargon, these projects represent new areas and forms of 'centrality' in the city (as opposed to the periphery), at least in geo-economic terms, increasingly using up and having some of the best access to the resources the city has to offer.

Figure 5.1 presents an aerial view of Dubai. Parts highlighted in the darker shade represent areas allocated to IMREPs. By its very nature this is an incomplete list, and does not include projects that were yet to commence, which by the end of 2013 were many. The tag pin represents the location of the old city centre of Dubai.

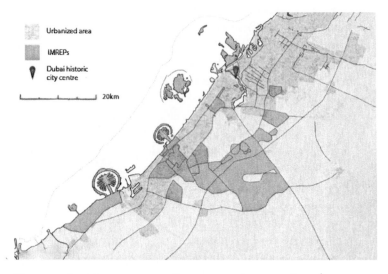

Figure 5.1   Spatial representation of IMREPs in Dubai, December 2013
The author would like to thank M. Aziz for his assistance in preparing this illustration.

'Build it and they will come', went the famous adage in Dubai. It is still a matter of debate regarding whether they indeed will come, but regardless of the numbers already inhabiting these cities, and regardless of whether all of the projects materialise or whether many end up as ghost towns, it immediately becomes obvious that these IMREPs already form a significant part of the urban landscape, occupying large swaths of real estate that is adjacent to the sea (in addition to newly reclaimed land). They also constitute some of the most easily identifiable, largest and most iconic landmarks of the city. If we follow Schmid (2012: 42–64) and take urban space to mean the built-up environment that constitutes the place of material interaction and physical encounter, it is obvious that these real estate projects constitute a large part of Dubai's urban space: i.e. they constitute significant parts of the city's 'centres'. This phenomenon is repeated to varying degrees across the Gulf cities where the IMREPs phenomenon has taken hold. To take another example that is not as well

known as Dubai but is probably more extreme, we next turn our attention
to Bahrain.

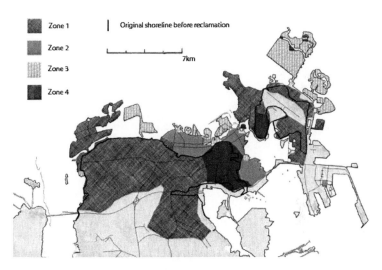

Figure 5.2   Spatial representation of IMREPs in Bahrain, December 2013
The author would like to thank M. Aziz for his assistance in preparing this illustration.

Figure 5.2 presents an aerial view of the northern third of Bahrain,
where more than three-quarters of the total population (expatriates
and citizens) live. Zone 3 represents IMREPs that take the form of gated
communities (where entrance and access is monitored), while Zone 2
represents international real estate in newly built urban high-rise areas
that are commercial centres of the cities. Both are areas where freehold is
allowed for non-citizens. Zone 4 represents the historic city centres of the
capital Manama (to the left) and the second city of Muharraq, while Zone
1 signifies residential areas, where only local (GCC) ownership of land is
allowed and where the vast majority of citizens live. The dark line highlights
the original shoreline of Bahrain before the reclamation of the sea over the
past four decades.

Focusing particularly on the IMREPs in Bahrain (whether closed gated
community in Zone 3 or urban high-rise areas in Zone 2), it becomes
obvious that just like in the case of Dubai, they occupy a large chunk of the
urban landscape and constitute many of its 'centres'. They occupy some of
the most valuable and central locations, being situated close to the historic
cities of Manama and Muharraq and to the Northern seashore. They also
constitute some of the most iconic buildings and the most expensive areas.

Once again, regardless of the numbers inhabiting them, it is clear that these projects play a dominant role in defining the physical geographic landscape of Bahrain, which in turn interacts with and has repercussions for the demographic dynamics on the island.

Just as important as the emergence of these new 'centres' in parallel to the older established areas is the urban segmentation witnessed between them. The appearance of new enclaves with different socio-economic functions and classes of inhabitants points to a deepened parallelism between very different spheres, operating within a mixture of private-public zones of influence. Indeed, it is worthwhile asking whether it makes sense to talk of multiple 'centres' anymore, rather than congeries of parallel hubs, deepening existing socio-economic and regulatory segmentation and indeed in many cases creating new ones.

Although no concrete data exist on the distribution of people according to specific areas in Bahrain, first-hand observation and field visits reveal quite strong and undisputed characteristics regarding the geographic habitation of the island: IMREPs (those that have already been completed) are mostly populated by well-to-do expatriates, with a few of these projects separately catering to affluent citizens too.[16] This corresponds to the numbers detailed above for one of these projects (see p. 106). The same applies to the newer urban high-rise areas, which are either composed of commercial spaces or residential apartments whose occupants (but not necessarily owners) are overwhelmingly expatriates. All of these areas have been built on reclaimed land. Increasingly historic areas, highlighted in Zone 4, are also nearly completely composed of expatriates, but of the lower- to middle-income class, as locals have increasingly vacated these areas. Nationals are almost exclusively housed within the suburban areas (Zone 1), with some expatriates also renting and living in such areas.

What is striking is that the physical geography of the city is nearly completely determined and segmented based on two criteria: citizenship and economic class. Expatriates of upper-income status are housed in the mega-real estate projects, those of upper- to middle-income in the newer urban high-rise areas, while those of middle to lower income are housed in the historic city centres (increasingly vacated by nationals). Finally, some 'labourers', those that work in the construction business and factories, are housed in labour camps far away from the city centres, and which barely register in Figure 5.2. Locals, on the other hand, live almost exclusively within the suburban areas (Zone 1), where expatriate domestic workers live in the same houses.

This phenomenon is not unique to Bahrain, and indeed is replicated and much more accentuated in the other cities where such real estate projects have been witnessed (Abu Dhabi, Doha, Dubai and Muscat). Increasingly, living areas are segmented, with each class and citizen group living within their own area, with interaction mainly occurring in the urban high-rise areas and historic city centres, when individuals attend work or go shopping.

Talk of expatriates in the Gulf typically conjures up images of construction workers in overcrowded labour camps. This is certainly one (ugly) side to the situation of expatriates in the region. It is indeed worth noting the extreme poles that expatriates occupy geographically, ranging from the most squalid conditions in labour camps right through to those living in the places most representative of luxury, opulence and mass consumerism in the Gulf found in IMREPs. Although many more expatriates experience the former, it is the latter that occupy 'the centres' of the urban space and have a much more disproportionate impact on the physical landscape of the cities under consideration.

This brings us to the second important point on the conception of the 'rootless city'. To have any viability, these international projects have to be geared towards expatriates. Within the local population alone, these 'international' projects simply have no use value, and consequently cannot generate an exchange value. In other words, without an expatriate population to live in them, they ultimately have no end user or purpose, and would end up being worthless in the long run. A new non-local population is needed that can generate a use value from inhabiting such cities, thus creating an exchange value and a trading price for these real estate units.

There is a catch, however. Although these 'international projects' are geared and marketed towards expatriates, permanent integration and settlement within these countries is still ultimately not allowed, whether for holders of real estate or expatriate workers. Although the four countries under consideration have enacted legislation that allows for property ownership, and linked such property ownership with renewable residency visas, and indeed embarked on an unprecedented marketing campaign to attract international buyers to these projects, the fact remains that no state explicitly allows for the integration of expatriate individuals into society on a permanent basis. Indeed, as X from South Africa put it when asked what would be the best incentive to generate demand for these real estate projects: 'At the end of the day you can never belong here, no matter how long you stay. You feel like it can never be your home, and that there is always somewhere else you must go back to. We are not even allowed to work in the region.'

This is a curious combination, where a state and a significant proportion of its politically and economically influential class focuses such a huge part of its resources and energy on building projects that its current demographic base is unable to support, thus needing a new population base to inhabit and buy units in such projects while also explicitly preventing them from integrating permanently.

This phenomenon has strong resonance with what has come to be seen in the literature as the commodification of the city, a process by which the urban space and the city itself becomes a commodity and is thus systematically exploited simply to generate exchange value. In the words of Schmid:

> This process encompasses not only the sale of parcels of land, and the reservation of exclusive locations for certain population groups. At stake, more generally, is the process by which urban space as such is exploited. The entire space is sold – including the people living in it, as well as the social resources and the economic effects produced by them ... The people, residents and visitors alike, are reduced to mere 'extras' in the great urban spectacle. (Schmid, 2012: 55)

Rem Koolhaas famously expounded the idea of the 'generic city' in his 1995 essay of the same name (Koolhaas and Mau, 1995). For Koolhaas, the generic city is one which sheds its identity and history, which relieves itself with the obsession with the 'historical centre'. It is multiracial and multicultural, and it is based on people always on the move, global nomads with few local loyalties. Its most defining structure is the airport, a concentrate of the hyper-local and the hyper-global, and around which the activities of the city are concentrated. The 'in-transit' condition is the norm. Supremely inorganic and planned, the city is populated by skyscrapers and highways built specifically for cars, which connect its diverse buildings in an aesthetic that can be best described as 'freestyle'.

Although such a description has strong resonance in the Gulf, it does not adequately describe the unique situation that lies at the heart of its cities. I prefer to use the term 'rootless hubs', where the majority of agents that animate these cities are not allowed to establish roots. Rootless here does not refer to the fact that these individuals have no historical roots in the city, or that they spend a relatively short time in the city before moving on (transient), although both these things are possible and are probably true for the majority of the cities' inhabitants. It instead refers to the fact that they are not allowed *de jure* to settle in the city permanently and establish roots. Their presence in the country is always precarious, always conditioned and can never be made permanent. They are in a state of permanent temporariness. Integration and settlement is simply not an option. They are present as transient agents in the grander scheme of the commodification of urban space as an object of exchange value, explicitly prevented by law from establishing any permanent roots within the commodified urban space.[17]

Power Relations and the Right to the City

What does rootless urbanism that is dominated by these IMREPs mean for the unfolding dynamics between the state, businesses, citizens and expatriates? I would like to end this chapter by looking at the power relationships unfolding between these divergent groups, and offer a tentative outlook for the future. My main assertion is that such rootless hubs have an inherent instability at their core, and that ultimately they are untenable in their pure envisioned form. There are two sources for this inherent disequilibrium. First is the instability in the proposition of trying to incentivise expatriates to rent, buy and live in such cities, while at the same time excluding outright the possibility of permanent settlement and integration. The second, and equally important, factor relates to a group that already has a legal right to establish roots, settle permanently and integrate in the city: citizens.

Let us begin with the latter point. Historically, labour migrants to the region were a source of rent either for businesses or citizens. Expatriates who buy in IMREPs, on the other hand, are only a source of rent for the businesses who sell the real estate, as well as a source of consumption for local retail outlets. They, however, have very few shared interests in common with the rest of citizenry. The lack of a common form of nationalism is compounded by the lack of any form of common material interests. In fact, they are increasingly a source of competition, both for resources (land, utilities and infrastructure) and in being a key constituency whose needs and desires have to be taken into account by both the state and local businesses. Thus, questions over distribution and access to resources and privileges, and consequently questions regarding being at the centre versus periphery of the city, will increasingly become important issues.

These tensions have already started surfacing. Nationals are outnumbered by expatriates in four out of the six GCC countries, and frequently form a small minority of the inhabitants of cities. They increasingly live in specific quarters that have often become tangential and peripheral to the overall dynamic within the city. A discourse of a general sense of alienation and discord with their urban surrounding is increasing, with talk of a demographic 'tsunami' becoming louder.[18] Issues of the erosion of the Arabic language, preserving local culture and the rise of the so-called chicken nuggets or 'nido' generation[19] have become hotly debated topics within national circles.

In essence, by the end of the first decade of the twenty-first century there was a growing perception among citizens that they are marginalised from the overall dynamics of the city. They are not important productively, increasingly less influential as consumers and form a minority within these cities. Hence, they increasingly find themselves at the periphery of urban dynamics.

It is beyond doubt that ultimate power in the GCC, whether economic, security or political, is still largely dominated by local rulers and the state apparatus they control. The state still plays the role of the omnipresent decider and arbitrator within society. Its actions, however, are increasingly constrained by having to take into account the different constituencies that it needs to cater to. An increasingly important but often neglected constituency is expatriates. This takes us to our second point, regarding the inherent instability in the concept of 'rootless urbanism' that is held as a guiding vision for these cities.

Let us take a quick summary view of the trajectory of events over the first decade of the twenty-first century. Faced with an oversupply of capital, the state and the private sector of the four GCC countries under consideration embarked on a programme of building new real estate projects of vast proportions. For these new cities to have a use value and hence be a source of exchange value, it entails the need to import a whole new population to inhabit these new cities, as nationals neither have the numbers or the interest to live in such cities. Hence, these countries have embarked on a series of legislative and administrative reforms to attract such new investors and inhabitants to the region, including offering the right to buy real estate and tying this right to long-term residency.

This is quite a development in countries that barely a decade ago refused flat out to sell any real estate to foreigners, ensuring a steady stream of income rent to property owners and not allowing permanent settlement that would create competition on benefits and resources with locals, in addition to deterring any perceived 'security' concerns. However, it seems that decision makers in the GCC countries – and with different gradations between them – were still keen to limit and avoid any sort of political power that might be entailed by such ownership, and were certainly not yet considering permanent integration. Abu Dhabi, for example, has limited land transactions involving foreigners to 99-year leases and *musataha* deals, where investors are able to buy the built-up area of a building but not the land beneath it. Bahrain on the other hand has allowed freehold ownership, and went the extra mile in allowing property holders to vote in its municipality elections since 2006. This illustrates the inherent tension that lies at the heart of the rootless urbanism vision, to create a hub society populated by people who are expected to work, consume and indeed live, but who are not allowed to permanently settle or integrate.

It became increasingly obvious that for the IMREPs to have any viability, the state was under growing pressure to offer further incentives and to cater for the inhabitants of such cities. Otherwise a real danger emerges, in that the huge amounts of invested capital will turn into ghost towns of incomplete and abandoned projects, with significant repercussions for international debts and claims outstanding from such projects, which amount to tens of billions of dollars.

For example, the UAE announced in 2011 the extensions of residency visas associated with ownership of real estate from six months to three years in order to resuscitate sagging demand in the aftermath of the financial crisis (John, 2011). Furthermore, an escrow law was passed to regulate the amounts of money going into projects that are yet to be completed. A strata law was further enacted, and RERA, the real estate regulating authority, was set up to regulate the sector in 2007 (Dubai Land Department, 2007). Hence, a significant investment has been made not only in terms of money and infrastructure, but also in terms of laws and institutions put in place for IMREPs. In Bahrain, and in light of the political ramifications of the February 14 Movement, expatriates officially demanded inclusion in the appointed legislative Shura Council, as well as in the chamber of commerce (*Al-Wasat*, 2011). Such demands for greater participation are likely to increase with time.

Hence it seems that that the ideal of 'rootless hubs' is increasingly unstable, with the dynamics of capital, migration, politics of the state and international considerations all possibly playing an increasingly important role in how such a vision unfolds. Legislation, as we saw, is extremely vague in the case of IMREPs, with local laws not keeping up with the advent of such projects, raising important issues around sovereignty. There is considerable uncertainty over the laws applicable in disputes with regards to the roads and public ways in such projects. Are they the property of the developers, as the developers stipulate in their contracts, or are they commonly owned by the tenants, as the latter would like to claim based on similar laws applicable elsewhere in the world, or are they the property of the state? Most of the contracts involved in these real estate projects are based on international law, particularly English common law, whereas the local law is yet to be developed enough to deal with such issues.[20]

Such sovereignty and judicial issues have indeed started surfacing in the aftermath of the financial crisis. For example, Arcapita, a Bahrain-based investment bank with considerable involvement in some of the biggest real estate projects in Bahrain and beyond, filed for Chapter 11 bankruptcy under US law in 2012, raising questions regarding the claims of ownership over such projects. Given that many of the main lenders and financiers of these projects are international financial institutions, the dictates of international capital have also increasingly entered into the equation.

Thus, the question that will be of ultimate importance in the GCC, to use an often-abused term from Lefebvre, is who has 'the right to the city'? This, as Mark Purcell succinctly point out (Purcell, 2002), involves issues of scalability and identity. Increasingly, there is competition over space between expatriates, citizens, businesses and the state. In terms of scale, questions arise around the scope of parties and agents who should be involved in the shaping of the urban space and the usage of resources. In terms of identity, the fact that there is such a marked distinction in terms of the use of space based on nationality certainly has social and political ramifications. Furthermore, it increasingly becomes obvious that expatriates, just as in the case of citizens, cannot be treated as one cohesive block. It is unlikely, for example, that real estate-owning expatriates of the upper middle class have similar interests to the construction workers who build their properties.

The Right to the City in Bahrain

Questions of class, space, resource usage, nationalities and the diverse discourses emerging around these issues make for an extremely complex landscape within the cities of the GCC. Events in Bahrain give a pertinent example. Much ink has been spilled on events in Bahrain since the explosion of 14 February 2011, but very little has been written on the role of IMREPs and the changing urban and demographic landscape within the ensuing events, although such factors had an extremely important role to play.[21]

Between 2000 and 2010, more than 50 kilometres of sea (or nearly 10 per cent of the country's landmass) has been reconstituted into reclaimed land. Most of the reclaimed land, mainly located on prime real estate property by the northern shore, has been allocated to creating new IMREPs. By 2008 there were more than 20 of these mega-projects that have been or were being built in Bahrain, with the aim of creating more than 60,000 new residential units with corresponding commercial and office spaces (DTZ, 2008).

On the demographic front, Bahrain has faced a unique issue centring on what has become known as political naturalisation. Since the middle of the twentieth century, and increasingly in the first decade of the twenty-first century, the opposition in Bahrain has accused the government of fast tracking the arrival of carefully selected foreigners in order to change the demographic makeup of the country for political purposes. Citizens regularly complain that such groups were given houses and other benefits that are already in severe shortage. There are no official numbers regarding the extent of political naturalisation, with the only existing estimate putting the number at 62,000 between the years 2001 and 2007 (Marzooq, 2011), or approximately 15 per cent of the citizen population (for more, see Chapter 7).

These two issues, political naturalisation and the land appropriated for mega-real estate projects, were the two major political points of contention in the country in the run-up to February 2011, in addition to grievances surrounding the structure of the local political system. A strong grassroots movement developed around these two issues that cut across citizen groups and threatened to build a national opposition to the government on common, non-sectarian grounds.

When the political situation exploded on 14 February 2011, the issues played a vitally important role in the opposition's discourse. The importance of the 'appropriated public land' discourse was exemplified when Sheikh Ali Salman, the head of the opposition society al-Wefaq, held up a deed in a press conference showing that the land for the Financial Harbour, a flagship IMREP, was sold to the Prime Minister for 1 BD (US$2.5). Protesters subsequently held up 1 BD notes in demonstrations to highlight the issue (Al Hussaini, 2011).

The importance of the role of the demographic currents surfaced on the first day, when graphic videos of the attacks by security forces against protesters showed actions that involved some foreign or politically naturalised security forces. They would reappear once again when fights allegedly broke out between Shia locals and their naturalised counterparts at schools (Al Slaise, 2011). Scuffles also allegedly occurred between local and politically naturalised youth in a suburban town of mixed composition, Hamad Town, leaving several injured (*Reuters*, 2011).

Some expatriates on the island were also involved in the ensuing events. Groups of expatriates have attended pro-regime demonstrations, whether willingly or not, helping to swell the size of the demonstrations. There have also been reports of attacks on working-class expatriates in Manama by anti-government demonstrators (BBC, 2011). The main local English newspaper, *The Gulf Daily News*, also carried several comments and letters by expatriates showing their frustration with the anti-government demonstrators and highlighting support for the government. Indeed, the state actively used expatriates as a weapon for popular legitimacy. For example, when the Bahraini Doctors' Society was perceived to be under the influence of figures sympathetic to the opposition, the ministry of social affairs decreed that expatriate doctors should be allowed to register in the society and vote in the elections of its management board, hence more than doubling the society's membership and ensuring that a board sympathetic to the government was elected (Abdulla, 2012). Representatives of the diverse expatriate communities were also included in the government-sanctioned National Accord Talks, where they officially demanded inclusion in the appointed legislative Shura Council, as well as in the chamber of commerce. The secretary-general of the Federation of Expatriate Associations, a largely pro-government organisation of expatriates that regularly comments on political developments in the country, caused a storm in 2012 when she commented that 'we make up 51 per cent of the population', and 'the majority do not support terrorism, but they end up victims of it' (AlGhatta, 2013).

On the other side, holding protests in the historic city of Manama has become a primary goal of the opposition, with weekly attempts at occupying the narrow alleyways of the city which are usually violently dispersed by the police force (*Reuters*, 2012). These protests are never sanctioned by the regime, which instead prefers to give official authorisation for protests in villages far way from the central districts of the capital. A contest over the use of urban space has arisen. As previously mentioned, the historic centre of Manama has been largely deserted by locals since the beginning of the new millennium, becoming instead mainly inhabited by low- to middle-income expatriates. The insistence of parts of the opposition to hold demonstrations in these quarters is an attempt to reclaim the urban space of these historical cities and to impose their presence in the 'centre' of the city. The government, of course, would prefer that they remain in the periphery of the urban space, away from the most strategic urban locations.

At the time of writing this chapter, the developments in Bahrain were still in a state of flux, but events there already showed that the power relations and the discourses surrounding the 'right to the city' in the GCC are not a straightforward matter, with the interplay between expatriates, citizens, the state and even groups within and across such categories making for a constantly evolving and dynamic environment. Issues of the centre and the periphery are already being discussed, raising questions as to who has access to increasingly scarce resources in the region and 'the right to the city'.

Conclusion: Rethinking Migration and the City in the Gulf

Migration in the Gulf has traditionally been analysed in academic circles through the lens of labour, with the discourse usually focusing on the 'structural violence' that expatriates experience in the region, particularly under the vagaries of the *kafala* system. This is further augmented by a burgeoning literature on the 'transnational' character of migration and the associated network of middlemen, family members, remit paths and support networks that characterises such migration. Our hope in this chapter is to provide a first attempt at analysing the presence of expatriates in the region within a wider geographic framework, one that looks at the urban dynamics that transcend labour relations.

As an important development, we have focused our discussion particularly on the phenomenon of IMREPs. An examination of the spatial manifestation of these mega-real estate projects necessarily entails seeing expatriates as more than simply a productive source of manpower, but should instead be seen as people with diverse lives and actions, who increasingly are a source of consumption and purchasing power, and are part of the production and usage of the urban space in the GCC's cities. We have used the term 'agents that animate the city' to describe the multiple interactions and socio-economic relations that people, whether expatriates or citizens, play within the city, including being consumers, producers and inhabitants.

We then argued that there are two features that make such IMREPs in the GCC unique. The first was that they have increasingly come to constitute new urban 'centres' and enclaves in progressively segmented city spaces. Furthermore, we contend that one of the defining 'ideals' of this new phase of urban reality is its 'rootless urbanism' vision, where the primary intended targets of this urban expansion – expatriates – are encouraged to come to the region, while explicitly being denied the possibility of permanent settlement or integration. This creates an inherent instability and tension, both vis-à-vis expatriates and with respects to citizens. Increasingly, 'the right to the city' and the power relations arising within and between the different social groups will play an important role in the dynamics within the cities of the GCC.

A critical urban view of the cities of the GCC opens up more questions than it answers. For example, how is one to approach the spatial interactions between the historic city centres (increasingly inhabited exclusively by expatriates), the mega-real estate projects, the suburban areas inhabited by nationals and the labour camps for migrants in unskilled jobs? Taking a more international view, what are the different circuits and networks of capital and individuals – both local and international – that the different groups of expatriates with interests in the region (e.g. those who own real estate), are able to utilise and tap into? The increasing importance of international capital in the GCC, particularly in IMREPs, will also necessarily imply a transnational dimension to the question, particularly with regards to the ramifications of the financial crisis and legal complexities involved in the cancellation of many of these real estate projects. Such issues highlight the importance of a critical examination of the urban geography in the GCC with respect to migration, upon which hopefully we have been able to shed an initial light in this chapter.

Notes

1. The author would like to thank Steffen Hertog for his comments on an earlier draft. This research was partly carried out with the support of the Arab Council for the Social Sciences – 'Inequality, Mobility and Development in the Arab Region' Program 2013–2014.
2. I would like to thank Michelle Buckley for providing the inspiration for this phrase.
3. Notable exceptions include Elsheshtawy (2010) and Fuccaro (2001).

4. The huge expansion of these western consultancies was a phenomenon unique to the region, where their growth was to encompass all areas in the economy, including security and legal matters. It is probably unsurprising in the GCC, however, where the vast majority of the labour force is composed of expatriates, and where importation of everything from labour to consumer commodities is the norm.

5. Which is unsurprising considering that Kuwait has the strongest national democratic tradition in the region.

6. The 2009 financial crisis cancelled or put on hold many of these projects, while new ones have emerged.

7. Interview with a manager of a IMREP facilities management company, 14 October 2012.

8. Interview with a manager of a IMREP facilities management company, 14 October 2012.

9. The name has been changed to to protect the interviewee's anonymity, 14 October 2012.

10. These exclude regional-oriented only airports, including one airport in Bahrain, two in Dubai, one in Abu Dhabi, one in Qatar, three in Saudi Arabia, one in Oman and one in Kuwait.

11. Author calculations from officially released statistics.

12. With the (possible) exception of Bahrain.

13. For example, Doha Financial Centre and Dubai International Financial Centre.

14. For example, Jebel Ali Free Zone.

15. See Chapter 1.

16. For example, Phase 1 of Durrat Al Bahrain is almost exclusively owned by GCC citizens.

17. The flipside of this has been the construction of an historical 'Gulf image' – with 'folk' museums and 'traditional' housing aimed at attracting tourists and locals alike.

18. For example, the comments of the former Bahraini labour minister on a demographic tsunami (Al Alawi, 2011).

19. Local youths who, although having spent the majority of their lives in their own country, nevertheless speak English as a first language and present strong identification with 'Western' culture.

20. Interview with Dr Hassan Radhi, leading corporate lawyer in Bahrain, 15 December 2011.

21. I have written a more detailed study on Bahrain's spatial and demographic changes in (AlShehabi, 2014).

6

Construction Work, 'Bachelor' Builders and the Intersectional Politics of Urbanisation in Dubai

Michelle Buckley

As the financial crisis of 2008 enveloped the global economy, media reports broadly pronounced the beginning of a 'male recession' (Burns, 2009), in which sectors typically dominated by men such as heavy manufacturing and finance were at the forefront of lay-offs internationally. Leading the retrenchments in these sectors were beleaguered construction sectors both in North America and across the globe; in the wake of tightening global credit markets, once-booming real estate and construction markets from Dublin to Dubai were going bust, leading to cancelled development projects, speculator retreat and severe retrenchments in construction labour markets. This contraction in the construction sector was particularly devastating for migrant workers, who tended to be over-represented in the most casualised, informal and insecure occupational segments of the industry (Awad, 2009; Martin, 2009). As the global credit crunch spread outward from Western banks to the Gulf Arab region and beyond, plummeting real estate prices in key Gulf cities such as Dubai, Doha and Kuwait City were prompting forecasts of the mass outflow of predominantly South Asian migrant construction workers from metropolitan centres across the region (ILO, 2009a; Martin, 2009; Krings et al., 2009; Awad, 2009).

For the most part, however, recent research has yet to substantively explore the gendered political economies underpinning male migration in GCC states. This is a significant lacuna considering that Gulf migration since the mid-twentieth century has been to a very great degree characterised by the mobility of men from the Middle East, North Africa, Britain, Australia and in more recent decades by men from South and East Asia (Kapiszewski, 2006; Arnold and Shah, 1986).[1] At the same time, research on urbanisation in the Gulf region, which has expanded dramatically over the past decade, has yet to contend substantively with the distinctly gendered, embodied and non-citizen relations of work and employment through which capitalist urbanisation has been taking place in GCC states.

Over the last 15 years, GCC states have made marketised and neoliberalised forms of mega-project urbanisation a cornerstone of their economic diversification and liberalisation agendas. The day-to-day task of Gulf city-building associated with these agendas, meanwhile, has fallen almost entirely to the work of foreign architects, engineers and planning consultants, and most sizably, to the daily labours of an immense migrant construction workforce mainly comprising men from India, Pakistan, Nepal, Bangladesh and other South and East Asian countries.

Through a case study of the city of Dubai, in this chapter I explore how the imperative of large-scale, market-led urbanisation adopted by the emirate has led to new forms of socio-spatial regulation aimed at migrant men employed in the construction trades. Examinations of the ways that urbanisation incorporates migrant builders, and how their lives in the city are circumscribed by an array of employer- and state-based forms of control, serve to incorporate and foreground the role of migration flows and migrant labour markets in understandings of contemporary capitalist restructuring processes across the Gulf region. Specifically, I argue here in favour of the need for intersectional perspectives (McCall, 2005; Browne and Misra, 2003; McDowell, 2008) on the regulation of lower-waged migrants in the construction trades in exploring the social, cultural and spatial politics surrounding construction migrants in the city.

I begin by briefly outlining the Dubai state's adoption of an immense urban construction programme since the late 1990s, and explore how a feminist political economy lens serves to highlight the major impact that large-scale construction programmes across the GCC have had in gendering contemporary migration flows to the region. Following this, through interviews with local developers, construction contractors and labour-sending consular officials undertaken in 2008 and 2009 in Dubai and Abu Dhabi, I build on previous work (Buckley, 2013; 2014) to explore how lower-waged construction labour has been re-regulated by the state and other actors in the city, and to illuminate how the contemporary political economies of urbanisation have entailed the production of complex inequalities comprising ethnicity, gender and sexuality.

Specifically, I argue that predominantly working-class and South Asian construction migrants have been at the centre of three distinct but entangled projects of 'securitisation' underpinning recent practices of city-building in Dubai. The first concerns the state's efforts to inscribe highly constrained forms of sexual citizenship on migrant builders following the influx of large numbers of construction workers into the city in the mid-2000s. The second relates to discursive constructions about 'safe' and 'suitable' construction migrants produced by consular officials and employers in the sector. The final, meanwhile, has revolved around the state's efforts to respond to the perceived geopolitical threat that migrant builders posed to national security, in which increasingly militant labour actions by construction migrants in the city have become key targets of the state's anti-terror agenda. I point to the ways in which this trifecta of securitisation initiatives have overlapped both spatially and practically, leading to contradictory practices relating to the ways that different arms of the state produce and manage 'single', South Asian migrant men in the city.

Urbanising Migration: Connecting Male Migration Flows to GCC City-building Agendas

As Mohammad and Sidaway (2012: 608) note, over the last decade and a half, Gulf cities have pursued 'a development path that requires and is expressed via fast urbanization' (see also Hvidt, 2011). The restructuring of Gulf political economies since the beginning of the twenty-first century has entailed the concerted urbanisation of both capital and labour, as post-oil liberalisation agendas across the GCC have come to focus heavily on the production of spectacularised, sovereign gestures of urban hyper-building (Ong, 2011) as well as diverse experiments with affluent enclave developments undergirded by consumer-oriented forms of urbanism (Elsheshtawy, 2010; see also Chapter 5). Similarly, the ongoing tertiarisation of contemporary Gulf economies – which have been marked by efforts to foster the growth of liberalised, service sector local economies focused on services like regional and global financial services, telecommunications and retailing – has resulted in Gulf cities becoming crucial sites in which processes of regional integration and national economic diversification are playing out (Hanieh, 2010a; Buckley and Hanieh, 2014).

The vast urbanisation of both private and sovereign capital has been partly a response to processes of GCC market integration and harmonisation, in which recent post-oil diversification programmes adopted by states in the region have been modelled in part after Dubai's real estate growth strategies, intended to encourage greater foreign direct and indirect investment into new specially designated urban mega-projects. As a result, construction activity has contributed significantly to GDP growth in most GCC states over the past decade (Hanieh, 2011: 112–15; Buckley, 2012a). Hanieh (2011) notes that this trend has been most prominent in the UAE and Saudi Arabia, in which mega-project urbanisation has characterised the circulation of oil and investor capital into the built environments of a number of cities in these countries including, and particularly, Dubai.

While the state-led push to develop urban mega-project markets across the region has been especially lucrative for Gulf-based construction conglomerates (Hanieh, 2011; Buckley and Hanieh, 2014), the construction industry more generally has been particularly resistant to national programmes aimed at nationalising the private sector workforce. Particularly at the lower end of the industry's occupational segments, construction work is comprised of a diverse range of jobs that are often dirty, dangerous, low status and poorly paid. The professional occupational segments in the industry in Dubai, meanwhile, are also almost overwhelmingly comprised of professional migrants, whose jobs are better remunerated but often involve working extremely long hours. Thus construction has long been, and remains, a key industry for migrant work and employment in Dubai and across the region.

The growth of construction activity across the Gulf region, meanwhile, has necessitated the vast importation of construction labour at both the top and the bottom of the industry's occupational segments. The ethno-national background of workers in the lower tiers of the industry varies; workers from southern India have been among the most common, while Pakistani, Bangladeshi, Nepalese, Filipino and Sri Lankan workers also comprise significant numbers in the lower-waged ends of the industry. As the search for lower labour costs intensified in the mid-2000s in response to rising material costs, in recent years Vietnamese and Cambodian workers have also been recruited for predominantly lower-waged jobs as steel fitters, water carriers, masons and painters. Similarly, the growing prevalence of state-affiliated Chinese firms winning contracts to build large subdivisions in Dubai resulted in many cases in these firms recruiting Chinese labourers already employed by the firm (Buckley, 2011).

Such seismic political-economic reforms are never gender neutral. In Dubai, the demographic impacts of these new accumulation strategies have been stark; at the end of 2008, an estimated 80 per cent of the population was composed of young men between the ages of 20 and 45 (Hanieh, 2011; Renaud, 2010; Smith, 2010).[2] This figure is inextricably linked to Dubai's rapid urbanisation agenda; as Hanieh (2011) notes, the city's demographics were due in large part to the presence of an estimated 700,000 foreign construction workers in a city with a population of 1.4 million (see also Khalil, 2007; Buckley, 2011).

A fuller understanding of the gendered impacts of these economic transformations on migration, however, cannot be relegated to simply quantifying the men and women who have emigrated to Dubai; gender is not an ontologically given or stable personal attribute that happens to be deemed useful or problematic to economic change, but is always actively (re)produced, transformed and contested through day-to-day social practices and institutional relations. In recent years, feminist scholars have made some of the most important insights into the ways political-economic change in the Gulf region has been reliant upon the production and maintenance of intersectional forms of complex inequality comprising gender, nationality, class and race. First and foremost, this work has served to challenge the gender-neutrality of overarching theoretical frameworks that have often dominated Gulf migration research in recent decades. In doing so, this research has drawn attention to the growing feminisation of migration flows to the Gulf region in recent decades (Fernandez, 2011; Robinson, 2000), and redressed a major lack of focus on female Gulf migration in a literature that had to date overwhelmingly documented male migration (e.g. Kapiszewski, 2006; Willoughby, 2006; Arnold and Shah, 1986). By understanding gender, race, ethnicity and class in the GCC as mutually constitutive elements of capitalist state power and process, this scholarship has both broadened and complicated dominant portrayals of the hierarchical 'ethnocratic' social relations that structure GCC labour markets (e.g. Willoughby, 2006).

Second, while building on intersectional feminist scholarship exploring how constructions of gender and ethnicity have been important to the segmentation of migrant labour markets (Pratt, 1999; Ehrenreich and Hochschild, 2002; Yeoh and Willis, 2004; Perrons, 2004; McDowell et al., 2007), feminist research on GCC labour migration has also elucidated how labour market regulation is a deeply spatialised process – one that both shapes and is shaped by social norms that encode scales and sites such as the body, the home, the city or the nation-state. This scholarship has demonstrated how women migrants' incorporation into Gulf labour markets is regulated through the relations of embodiment; for example, regarding the care work needed for children or others inside a family home, migrant women's gender is crucial to their perceived suitability to work in these spaces and segments of the labour market (Silvey, 2004).[3]

By focusing on the particular policies, practices and responses of labour- and host-country governments in regulating these sites, these studies have demonstrated how 'micro-scales' of the home and the body are constructed and mediated transnationally between nation-states in ways that have major impacts on migrants' prospects for good, fair and decent work. For example, in her work on Indonesian domestic migrants working in Saudi Arabia, Silvey (2004) seeks to 'gender the state' by highlighting how patriarchal categorisations of the home as a 'private' space by both labour-sending and GCC country governments serve to exclude migrant domestic workers from the rights, protections and entitlements afforded to foreign workers employed in so-called 'public' spaces. As Silvey (2004: 246; cf. Cravey, 1998) rightly points out, 'gender is a key modality through which states aim to construct particular social orders and maintain legitimacy, and states' particular manipulations of "gender contracts" shift and retrench in complex, contested manners along with economic internationalization'.

If we want to consider the possibilities, constraints and potential for decent and fair work for lower-waged construction migrants in Dubai, then, we must equally consider how power between state actors, employers and workers is constructed through more than just the relations of class or ethno-nationality. An intersectional focus on how the state has sought to regulate and discipline migrant builders over the last decade demonstrates how the imperatives of capitalist marketisation collide and interlink with state agendas of geopolitical securitisation and planning and urban policing practices. This requires a shift to an understanding of these various state agendas of securitisation not as discrete projects that simply run alongside each other in Dubai, but as ones that are intricately enmeshed because they often target the same populations in the city.

Following Hanieh (2010b; 2011), we might now broaden the gendered sites and scales of feminist political-economic research on the Gulf by exploring how recent processes of political-economic restructuring have entailed the pan-GCC adoption of policy agendas and regulatory reforms that carry gendered implications for migrant male workers employed in the construction trades. A focus on the contemporary politics surrounding construction migrants requires a reorientation of focus: first around how the physical construction of Gulf cities in the region is deeply reliant on a variety of migration networks, and second on how gender and sexuality are two important political dimensions in Dubai shaping state and employer efforts to control and regulate the lower-waged construction workforce. In the next section, I explore the contradictory and multi-scalar state strategies through which sexual citizenship among migrant builders in Dubai has been produced in recent years.

Constructing 'Bachelor' Subjectivities

As in most other GCC states, in the UAE citizenship is very rarely granted to foreigners. The vast majority of transnational workers emigrate to Dubai under the federal *kafala* rules, which require every emigrant to have a *kafeel*, or sponsor, who is a UAE citizen and who assumes both legal and economic responsibility for the worker throughout the length of their contract. Under this system, foreign workers' employment visas have in recent years almost exclusively been characterised by a three-year, renewable work visa[4] that requires workers to remain with their original employer for a minimum of two years; to leave their job without the written consent of their employer in some cases[5] amounts to a breach of contract, rendering one's immigration status illegal. Debates about social polarisation and inequality in Dubai often set the restrictions imposed on foreign workers by the *kafala* regime against the host of extensive entitlements that the state grants to Emirati nationals, such as the provision of free medical care, high-paid government jobs, free higher education, subsidised supplies of energy and free land (see, for example, Davis, 2008; Hari, 2009).

Debates about citizenship in Dubai which hinge summarily on arguments around these *de jure* forms of belonging and entitlement, however, reflect only the federal policies and practices through which citizenship is formulated in the UAE. They address only one part of a rights regime in which a host of other practical, day-to-day and institutional strategies have been mobilised to rule different segments of the expatriate population. In particular, key to an understanding of the political landscape for construction migrants are the 'bachelorised' politics that transect construction workers' daily lives. The label of the 'bachelor' is a popular term for both expatriate men and women in Dubai who do not have their families with them in the city. It contrasts sharply with other ethno-nationally and class-inflected terms for foreigners such as 'expatriates', which is a term often used to describe professional and often white and Anglo-American migrants in the city, or with the 'entrepreneurial' masculine identities self-narrated by members of Dubai's largely affluent and well-established Indian merchant class (Vora, 2011). With respect to many lower-waged men employed in the construction trades, I conceptualise these bachelor subjectivities as an array of gendered, ethno-national and embodied class arrangements – which operate in the workplace but also the city – for 'single', blue-collar migrants. In Dubai, bachelordom does not define the actual marital state for many lower-waged construction migrants, but rather a specific set of institution-alised and quasi-legal conditions of both employment and residency status for low-waged and predominantly South Asian men.

Similar to guest and contractual worker schemes in other countries, most low-waged foreign workers are not permitted to bring their wives, husbands or children with them because their salaries are not high enough under UAE law to allow dependents to accompany them. Thus broadly speaking, whether married or single, the migrant category of the 'bachelor' in Dubai refers not to one's familial status generally but to their familial status *in Dubai*, which acts in many cases to delineate a subordinate class position for many lower-waged foreign workers. It should be noted, however, that the institutional production of 'singleness' is not solely restricted to lower-waged migrant men; not only do lower-waged female workers face similar restrictions, but, as Vora (2008) points out, Emirati immigration laws that regulate professional, middle-class migration also construct particularly gendered subjectivities, since the rights to spousal and family immigration granted to professional male migrants under UAE law are not granted to most foreign female professionals. As a result, she argues, most foreign families in the UAE are nuclear, affluent and patriarchal, while foreign female professionals are similarly rendered 'single' in the city.

Beyond the federal institutional policies and laws governing immigration and residency for construction migrants, the day-to-day reproduction of working-class singleness takes place through a distinctly urban set of relations that hinge on the practices of state-affiliated actors such as the police, Ministry of Labour officials and labour-sending governments. In particular, labour-sending country consular staff in Dubai tend to play a particularly important role in both supplying and regulating labour flows to the building trades. As one senior official from one labour-sending country consulate explained: '[w]e [the consulate] attest to the validity of both firms and contracts that want to advertise back home for jobs.

They have to come through us [...] Then what happens is that we OK one contract here, and then the company goes through a recruiter back home [to source the labour]'.[6]

While these practices vary significantly between consulates, in many cases consular staff in the UAE are intimately involved in day-to-day sourcing of migrant workers for the local construction labour market. Consular offices based in Dubai and Abu Dhabi often provide crucial information to recruiters back home about changing labour market needs in the city, vet the credentials of prospective employers and employees, and communicate job opportunities via their home-country networks.

In recent years, however, growing competition among labour country states has also shaped the practices by which consular agents have sought to incorporate migrant workers into the labour market. For example, in an attempt to address concerns that the construction labour market may become dominated by a single country during the building boom, the Dubai government instituted new rules in 2005 requiring all contractors to source their labour from no fewer than three different countries. As a result, many consulates intensified efforts to 'market' their own workers for construction jobs. This in part involved conferring advantage to their workers through allusions to a host of desirable embodied attributes; as one staff member at a labour-sending country consulate in Dubai suggested, '[our] workers have been appealing to the employers here because they are ... heat-resistant, used to very hot climates, and they don't fall apart in the weather here like others'.[7] As another member of the same consulate suggested, workers of other ethnic backgrounds, such as East Asians for example, just 'aren't built for [the heat]' in the way that their workers were.[8]

As McDowell (2009: 132) points out, depictions of strength and stamina are common ways of ascribing value to masculine working-class subjects. Pointing to class differences between particular constructions of masculinity in the workplace, she suggests that '[f]or working class men, masculinity and masculine advantage in the labour market are based on bodily norms of strength and virility, on the ability to endure hard labour, even an insensitive toughness that permits bodily labour to be undertaken day after day' (McDowell 2009: 132). Consular narratives of desirable labour delineate an embodied form of urban citizenship; suitable candidates for construction jobs must not only be physically strong enough to endure conditions on the construction site, but tough enough to 'take' punishing working conditions that are a facet of the city and its climate.

Following the onset of Dubai's construction boom, these consular agents also became increasingly implicated in mitigating growing concerns by the Dubai government about the social implications of hundreds of thousands of lower-waged South Asian men migrating to the city. Consular officials whose citizens formed a significant part of the city's construction workforce narrated state concerns about the influx of large numbers of lower-waged South Asian men in the city as a key dimension affecting their work in sourcing workers from their home country. As one labour-sending consular official in Dubai suggested, paramount to his and his staff's efforts to maintain good relations with the Dubai government and the Emirati federal state was the ability to ensure that those workers who came to the Gulf adhered to particular ethno-national constructions of sexual and moral propriety. As he explained, his work in part involved working with recruiters back home to ensure that workers coming over to work in lower-waged construction jobs in Dubai 'embody certain values that the locals [Emirati citizens] here do. They are, for the most part faithful, they don't cheat on their spouses back home by going to brothels here. They are disciplined workers. They don't really drink. There are a few that stray of course, but the majority have the same character as the people here'.[9]

In the mid-2000s, these discourses were paralleled by the marked intensification of state practices of socio-spatial segregation that were heavily (though certainly not exclusively) aimed at working-class construction migrants. Actions included municipal permissions to construct a host of new employer-run labour camps to house workers in industrial areas or on the far outskirts of the city – an effort seen by some as reflecting the local rulers' agenda to '[sanitise] the city ... by displacing its poor, who should be kept out of sight for fear of spoiling the carefully crafted ultra-luxurious cityscape' (Elsheshtawy, 2010: 125). Other practices included systematic efforts by state officials to evict or prevent migrant bachelors from living in villas or other more affluent, 'family'-designated neighbourhoods. For example, in seeking to prevent construction migrants from living in these subdivisions instead of commercially run labour camps in industrial areas, municipal inspectors in the neighbouring emirate of Sharjah banned company buses from entering residential neighbourhoods, thus forcing migrant builders to walk miles back to their homes (Al Jandaly, 2009). Meanwhile, ongoing forms of aggressive policing by both Dubai police and private sector actors have also sought to discourage working-class South Asian men from occupying affluent spaces such as beaches, night clubs and café boulevards or ogling female tourists (Ahmed, 2007; see also Kanna, 2007; Smith, 2010).

While the classed dimensions of these state tactics of segregation are well documented, less acknowledged has been the ways in which these practices of spatial exclusion are also distinctly sexualised and gendered. In particular, migrant construction workers have been deeply entangled in the growth of what Lori (2011) has called the rise of 'family social security' as a relatively new national security discourse that has arisen in conjunction with increased immigration over the past decade. Through the detailed documentation of police reports since 1994, Lori notes that the police's identification of a range of 'security threats' to nationals has been specifically linked with concerns over the large presence of male 'bachelor' construction workers (2011: 322). These identified threats, moreover, were often explicitly sexual; while police reports voiced concerns about crimes like theft and drug trafficking, they particularly emphasised the concern that the bachelor workforce might harbour the threat of rape or child abuse, or fuel the city's illegal prostitution sector. In response, Lori notes that the last decade has given rise to a 'preemptive' policing regime in which the police and security forces seek to identify potential criminals through various means of surveillance to deem which populations are worthy of increased surveillance, an effort to 'control' heterogeneity by 'disaggregating the mass of "expats" into manageable units by national origin, and governing and preemtping the expatriate impact by making those units legible' (Lori, 2011: 325). These delineations of sexual citizenship have thus been enacted through ethno-nationally focused forms of surveillance targeting specific groups of men in the city.

These discursive and material practices demarcate a variety of embodied and sexualised forms of belonging, discipline and entitlement for migrant builders that are in some ways contradictory. In placing formal immigration policy next to everyday state practices towards low-waged builders, for example, one can see how different factions of the state at once produce yet pathologise 'singleness' among working-class, South Asian migrant men. These consular and policing practices also illuminate the fact that citizenship formation has been shaped in part via a range of actors and institutional frameworks that are both internal and external to the governing state, including the federal immigration law, labour-sending country consular activities, urban policing practices and the ad hoc actions of municipal inspectors. These relations shed empirical light on Vora's (2011) contention that citizenship in Dubai is thus a far more unstable social position, characterised by multiple forms of belonging and freedom, and whose dynamism is very much shaped by recent political-economic transformations in Dubai. In the penultimate section I turn to explore how the state's recent efforts to manage and mitigate diverse forms of militant politics among migrant builders have also shaped the gendered regulation of the city's construction workforce.

Illegible Militancy and the Construction Workforce

Running parallel with embodied narratives of sexual propriety and physical endurance were another set of discourses revolving around the ethno-national temperament and political inclinations of the migrant construction workforce. One labour subcontractor interviewed suggested that his workers, who were largely sourced from one particular state in India, 'don't make much trouble. They have brains. They aren't rash [...] they don't make undue demands, they do what they are told. It's not like if you had the Chinese working in these companies. They would cause problems.'[10] A site supervisor and architect working for another construction firm also felt that 'national disposition' mattered in the making of a 'manageable' construction workforce, claiming for example that 'Pakistanis are too fiery – they are prone to fly off the handle'.[11]

Stereotypes about the passivity of some South Asian workers have long been key to their appeal in some GCC member states. For example, it was in no small part due to the spread of left-wing labour and anti-monarchist movements among Egyptian, Syrian and Palestinian migrants working in the Gulf during the construction boom of the 1970s that a number of GCC states, including the UAE, sought to replace foreign Arab workers with migrants from South and East Asia (Kapiszewski, 2001). South Asian workers were not only willing to work for cheaper wages, they were considered more 'politically tractable' (Foad, 2009) as well as more obedient and efficient (Ghobash, 1986) than their counterparts from Arab states.

Efforts to construct a politically docile workforce has been paramount to smaller labour-sending states such as Pakistan and Bangladesh, whose transnational capital accumulation strategies have come to depend particularly heavily on remittances from construction labour markets across the Gulf region. As the senior officer in charge of labour welfare issues at one consulate put it in no uncertain terms: 'we are very, very conscious to entreat our workers here to follow the rules. We are very concerned that our image as a calm workforce, as a law-abiding workforce, as a good workforce is kept up. These remittances are very important to [our country's] economy. You understand?'[12]

These statements point to a fundamental conflict of interest that labour-sending countries confront in their participation in the day-to-day operation of the construction labour market, since in the absence of an empowered civil society in Dubai consular offices are frequently tasked with championing workers' rights on one hand, yet they also actively construct workers' desirability through depictions of political docility while working to ensure their trouble-free insertion into local labour markets. Together with earlier depictions of morally upstanding workers in the previous section, the concerns of the labour welfare officer above reflect what Gibson and Graham (1986: 132) note as the increasingly inseparable connection between the role that labour-sending governments have come to play in 'guaranteeing not only a supply of cheap labour on an international market but also its "controllability" in the international workplace'.

Not unlike the political upheavals of the 1970s, perceptions about the political passivity of South Asian blue-collar workers took on a new dimension in the mid-2000s as state concerns about political unrest among construction migrants became increasingly imbricated with discourses of geopolitical security in Dubai and the rest of the country. As the construction market grew exponentially, dozens of labour strikes and public demonstrations by migrant construction workers swept across Dubai as well as other cities in the GCC. A number of intersecting factors motivated the strikes, including the chronic non-payment of wages by employers and overcrowded and poorly maintained labour camp accommodations, where most lower-waged construction workers are obliged to live. Coupled with these conditions, rampant inflation across the UAE and rising domestic currency rates across South Asia had severely eroded the remittance value of dirham-based salaries that had remained stagnant for many workers in Dubai (Bowman, 2008). Together, these conditions led workers to risk incarceration and deportation to challenge both employers and the local state. This rising labour insurgency proved difficult to quell, and at the height of the construction boom in 2006 and 2007, labour strikes eliciting costly work stoppages posed a real and immediate risk of bursting the speculative property bubble that had been driving the city's economic growth.

Beyond the immediate economic interests that the state and employers might have in maintaining a docile and 'reasonable' workforce, it is important to recognise how state efforts to curb labour militancy among blue-collar migrant builders became imbricated with state concerns about religious extremism. As explained by a senior embassy official from one labour-sending country, the state's preference for acquiescent workers from some countries over others was not simply that workers from his country tended not to be prone to unpredictable behaviour or get involved in immoral or criminal activity, but 'our workers don't get involved in local politics. They love to stay involved in the politics back home, but they are happy to have nothing to do with UAE politics. So unofficially ... what is not said is that [workers from my country] are not generally jihadists.'[13]

The possibility that sectarian tensions between Shia and Sunni Muslims might erupt in the city, or that terrorist factions might launch an attack in Dubai as the most Westernised city in the Gulf, have long been acute concerns of the Dubai government and UAE officials (Davis, 2006; 2008). However, less remarked upon in 'threat' narratives that permeate some of the literature on Dubai are the ways in which such discourses have been mobilised by state actors towards other political ends. At the height of these strike actions, state rhetoric about 'security' was deployed by government officials to legitimise the state's efforts to repress the growth of collective labour action, which included mass arrests, deportations and working bans on those considered strike instigators. As the then Minister of Labour, Ali bin Abdullah Al Ka'abi, ominously suggested at one point, the state's responses to the strikes were justified not simply because workers' actions were illegal under UAE law, but because they constituted a direct threat to 'the security of the state and safety of residents' (Rahimi, 2007). These notions were roundly dismissed by both labour-sending country officials and international labour rights groups; as one labour-sending country ambassador recounted:

in one of the recent strikes, it was totally linked with wages, and I think it was Egyptian and Pakistani workers, and their protest turned into 'Allahu Akbar!' ... And then the MoL [Ministry of Labour] started to get very scared and paranoid that this level of organisation was some indication that there was an 'outside' organiser – that this was the work of Al Qaeda or some terrorist group. And I said [...] don't be silly! Think about it – these guys' wages used to translate into 7,200 rupees to send home. Now it is only 6,000 [due to rapidly rising international exchange rates]. This is a problem. There is no big bad Al-Qaeda behind the scenes here. Get real. It's not complicated.[14]

As Lori notes, since 9/11 national security systems in the UAE have adapted to increasingly focus their attention on non-state networks. In his words, '[i]n addition to greater border controls and efforts to standardize identification and travel documents, the private security industry and national security systems are constantly developing new technologies in surveillance and internal policing strategies to track [...] threats' to local and national sovereignty (Lori, 2011: 316). While Lori identifies the ways that security forces manage expatriates' impacts on the emirate and rest of the UAE through their surveillance of 'illegal' migrants and cultural infringements by foreigners, or managing the naturalisation of long-term expatriates, a third objective has arguably been to mitigate and pre-empt the politicisation of working-class migrants. Whether simply rhetoric or something more, the state's security narrative provided an effective rationale by which the state justified the ongoing arrest and deportation of those identified as labour leaders.

These events reflect the growing imbrication – discursive, spatial and practical – of the state's anti-terror and anti-union agendas. Moreover, it shows how political-economic change in Dubai has been reliant upon the construction of subjects and circumstances that are exceptional to 'ordinary' state governance (Ong, 2006). These events reflect how urban security measures targeting particular populations have been legitimised through the discursive mapping of public fears about ethno-nationality and class on to urban space; they build on a long legacy of work charting the racialised, gendered and classed subtexts that have typically transected state strategies of what Amar (2009: 7) has called 'governance through panic'.

Ironically, despite the state's adoption of an increasingly sophisticated and pre-emptive policing regime towards construction migrants, these politics also demonstrate the *illegibility* of construction worker militancy to the state. As Lori (2011: 316) suggests, it is precisely 'the nebulous nature of non-state threats to national security' that 'has prompted these governments to dissolve the distinctions between "external" and "internal" security'. In some sense the jihadist and the labour militant are similarly illegible masculine figures in these scenarios – foreign, rogue subjects mounting radical challenges to sovereign powers, neither is dissuaded or disciplined by the autocratic state's significant arsenal of disciplinary force such as summary deportations or incarceration, nor is their organisation and operation predictable or particularly visible to the state. Neither, in their own way, has access to legitimate channels of autonomous bargaining, negotiation or governance in the city; the illegibility of the strike actions thus stemmed in part from the state's exclusion of this group of men to any institutional channels that might have granted state actors either coercive or co-optive power over them.

Conclusions

Through a focus on the politics surrounding lower-waged migrant construction workers, I have argued here for a consideration of the ways that urbanisation in Dubai has been a process fundamentally moderated by and through the production of multiple and interlocking subjectivities such as gender/sexuality, ethno-nationality and class. In particular, a focus on the gendered and embodied discourses surrounding migrant builders in the city highlights how the state-led securitisation of urban space over the past decade has comprised an overlapping set of agendas to safeguard capitalist accumulation, enhance national security and redefine the splintered contours of sexual citizenship in the city in response to the influx of large numbers of construction migrants to the city in the twenty-first century.

Rapid urbanisation and post-9/11 securitisation agendas have been entwined through their focus on construction workers in the city. The production of 'good' workers suited to both life in the city and the labour market that have hinged significantly on the successful production of an array of masculine identities – and which simultaneously mobilised stereotypes about ethno-nationality, gender/sexuality and class – have comprised a set of practices through which sending country officials, the Dubai government and private employers have sought to place strict limits around the political, sexual and spatial entitlements of the construction workforce. A focus on the place-specific politics of urbanisation reflects an effort to illuminate some of the gendered dimensions of everyday employer and state practices of segregation and control of lower-waged construction migrants in Dubai, and to raise questions about the ways that regional urbanisation is 'gendering' GCC political economies in new and important ways. However, I want to caution against any simplistic framing of Dubai's experience as emblematic of the kinds of urbanising gender contracts struck in other GCC cities. Meanwhile, research emanating from locales outside of the Gulf region has elucidated similar kinds of intersectional politics that are increasingly blurring the distinctions between sexual, geopolitical and capitalist security (Puar, 2007) or has connected working class, racialised masculinities to the twin projects of capitalist accumulation and the securitisation of urban space (Cowen and Siciliano, 2011).

Beyond offering an intersectional reading of the politics of urbanisation in Dubai, then, we can also consider the relevance this case presents to the theorisation of contemporary capitalist urbanisation more broadly. We might imagine, for example, what Dubai's most recent experiment with urbanisation and securitisation might tell us about the gendered, racialised and classed dimensions involved in the politics of migrant construction labour markets elsewhere. This proposition is practical as well as political: normative debates about the 'problem' of what to do with large numbers of migrant builders in rapidly growing cities, or the 'threat' that they are seen to pose, either to the security or the moral fabric of the city, are ones that transect the local and national politics of a diverse array of rapidly growing metropolitan centres in the contemporary moment (see, for example, Wong et al., 2005; Broudehoux, 2007; *The Times*, 2012). Epistemologically, questions about the gendered and embodied politics through which contemporary processes of urbanisation take place, the kinds of local urban politics that emerge in their wake, and the political and social implications for workers employed in urban construction markets reflect how Dubai and the GCC more broadly can be crucial sites for understanding the contemporary political economies of capitalist city-building.

Notes

1. This latter set of South Asian migration networks of course has a much longer history than the past few decades; for example, as Zachariah et al. (2003) point out, connections between the southern Indian state of Kerala and the Gulf region extend back several hundred years. However, there have been a series of major influxes of South and East Asian migrants following the 1970s oil boom, the first Gulf War of 1990 and once again in the wake of high oil revenues at the beginning of the twenty-first century.
2. See also Mohammad and Sidaway's (2012: 607) overview of the dominance of South Asian male migrants in Abu Dhabi's population, who make up an estimated 52 per cent of the city's population.
3. For a rather different take on exploring migrant embodiment, see also Walsh's (2012) discussion of 'embodied' accounts of emotion, social difference and belonging in which the affective moments of migrant life are experienced.
4. The length of workers' visas was shortened to two years in 2011.
5. The federal laws governing foreign workers were recently eased in January 2011 to allow workers who have been employed for two years with an employer to change employers without the sponsor's consent, and to allow workers who

have not been paid by their employer for a period of several months to seek new employment.

6. Interview with the Deputy Chief of Mission at a South East Asian labour-sending country consulate, Abu Dhabi, May 2008.
7. Various interviews with labour welfare officials from a South Asian labour-sending country consulate, Dubai, April 2008.
8. Ibid.
9. Interview with a labour welfare official from a South Asian consular office, Dubai, January 2008.
10. Interview with a Dubai-based construction labour subcontractor, Maruthadi, Kerala, July 2009.
11. Personal communication, a senior architect from a British architecture firm, Dubai, October 2007.
12. Interview with a labour welfare official from a South Asian country consulate, Dubai, 8 April 2008.
13. Interview with the ambassador of a South Asian labour-sending country, Abu Dhabi, 1 May 2008.
14. Interview with the ambassador of a South Asian labour-sending country, Abu Dhabi, 1 May 2008.

Part III

Gulf Migrants:
Broadening Perspectives

7

Bahrain's Migrant Security Apparatus

K. T. Abdulhameed

This chapter examines an aspect of Gulf migration that is understudied in analyses of the region, the phenomenon of migrants recruited to work in the public security apparatus. While this sector of the migrant population is a highly visible feature of several countries in the Gulf, the most significant example is found in Bahrain, where the employment of foreigners in public security forces has its early roots in state structures established under British colonialism. Although there is scant information on the precise number of migrants in Bahrain's military and security services, population data suggest it is more than double the number of Bahraini citizens employed in this sector, reaching up to 20,000 people (figures from 2010).[1] This long-standing practice has become even more controversial following Bahrain's anti-government protests of 2011, in which migrant security forces – mostly from Pakistan, Yemen and Jordan – led the crackdown on citizen protesters. The Bahraini opposition has long accused the government of extending citizenship to some of these migrants, in an attempt to build a loyal gendarme for the regime and alter the sectarian balance of the country through increasing the number of Sunni citizens.

The chapter begins by outlining the historical origins of this type of migration in the Gulf and then turns to a detailed examination of the Bahraini case. It explores the impact of this system on migrant identities, the relationships between citizen populations and these particular migrants, and the ways in which it helps to entrench a system of divide and rule within the country. Part of the analysis in this chapter draws upon in-depth narrative interviews, conducted in 2012, with two Pakistani migrants employed in the Bahraini security apparatus. Interview A is with a 54-year-old male Pakistani who has been granted Bahraini citizenship after working for the Interior Ministry since 1978, Interview B is with a 22-year-old Pakistani male who works for the National Guard and arrived in the country in 2011. These narratives can be seen as a route by which to better understand the situation of migrants, through 'a life history of a person who experiences power from a particular position, in a particular way' (William Roseberry cited in Gardner, 2010: 26).

Origins of Migrant Security Forces in the Gulf

The use of non-citizen migrants as armed forces to defend existing power structures has a long pedigree in the Gulf. According to James Onley, Gulf rulers in the nineteenth century could rely on up to 2,000 *fidawiyah* (armed retainers) acquired through tribal alliances to protect or advance their positions of power (Onley, 2004: 44). In Bahrain, the ruling Al Khalifah tribe was estimated to have 540 armed retainers recruited from neighbouring tribes in 1905 (Onley, 2004: 43). Between 1869 and 1923, the main share of Bahrain's 'ruler expenses', effectively the state budget, was spent on subsidies and 'gifts' given to the nearby Na'im tribe in order to employ these retainers (Onley, 2004: 71). Although the support of armed tribes is not equivalent to a modern security force, the model of rewarding armed groups for their loyalty helped establish a pattern replicated by later regimes. This 'patron–client' system continues to underpin the relationship between Gulf rulers and their security forces.

In addition to neighbouring Arab tribes, Gulf rulers have also enlisted support from non-Arab tribal regions. Dating back to the time of Oman's Al Ya'rubi dynasty (sixteenth and seventeenth century), for example, there is evidence of the presence of 'mercenaries' drawn from nomadic tribes in Baluchistan (now part of Pakistan) (Nicolini, 2007). These Baluch migrants, 'became an institutional part of the Omani governmental forces and major political leaders' at the beginning of the twentieth century (Nicolini, 2007: 84). In 1921 Oman's first modern army unit was established, comprised entirely of Baluch migrants (Peterson, 2004). Bahrain is also now home to a large population of Baluch 'settled migrants', many of whose male descendants continue to serve in and recruit for the Interior Ministry.

Britain encouraged these migratory movements through its effective control of the Gulf state system during the nineteenth century and early twentieth centuries. Britain's primary concern was protection of its lucrative shipping routes to and from India, and the prevention of any encroachment from other powers. Britain's treaties with local tribal leaders in the Gulf gave it ultimate control over the region's military and diplomatic relations, and Gulf ruling families relied on British troops to provide protection from other ruling families – such as in the dispute between Bahrain and Qatar over the Zubara coast – and defence from domestic challenges to their rule. Thus, in addition to reliance on local tribal rulers, Britain would frequently relocate forces to the Gulf from British-controlled India (Macris, 2010: 85). This relationship was to extend into the modern era with the continued training and staffing of the highest echelons of the Gulf's military and security by British advisors.

The discovery of oil reserves in Bahrain, Kuwait and Saudi Arabia in the 1920s and 1930s gave Britain an even greater incentive to maintain its presence in the Gulf, particularly in the context of heightened competition with the US over oil concessions. Despite these geopolitical concerns, however, Britain faced a declining global position in the wake of the Second World War, which was accentuated by its loss of control in the Indian subcontinent in 1949. As Macris notes, 'the British had to address the question of how a superpower "undoes" over a century of paternalistic control of the sheikhdoms on the west side of the Gulf' – without losing access to the profits accessible through their protection (Macris, 2010: 158).

In this changed political context, British strategy shifted towards new mechanisms to ensure continued support of local allies in the Gulf. In the first place, it established a series of its own military bases in the region and took direct control over local military forces. In 1959, Britain established the Headquarters British Forces Arabian Peninsula in Aden, later renamed Headquarters, Middle East Command. From this base, British military personnel were able to counter perceived threats with greater immediacy despite its declining power (Macris, 2010: 124).[2] As the British grappled with the new political context, the ideological frontline of Arab nationalism was extending towards the Gulf. By 1956, Bahrain saw a growing movement for independence from British rule. The convoy of Britain's Foreign Secretary Selwyn Lloyd was attacked by a public procession. Burrows writes that, 'this incident made us realize that we must be prepared to intervene with British forces if required in order to maintain law and order if they were threatened to this extent' (1990: 67). Two years later, the 14 July revolution in Iraq deposed a monarch brought to power by the British, and the country was declared a republic. A weakened British military and its dependent rulers in the Gulf sought ways to create a buffer against the rise of Arab republicanism, and a new agreement for British military support was signed between Britain and Kuwait. In 1961 British troops were deployed to Kuwait with units also stationed in Bahrain, Sharjah and Aden, with additional fighter planes and a supply depot in Bahrain (Macris, 2010: 125).

Despite these efforts, the 1960s sealed the demise of British supremacy in the Gulf, with the eventual disbanding of the Headquarters, Middle East Command in 1967. Nonetheless, British troops continued to play a key role in ensuring the continued dominance of ruling families throughout the Gulf sheikhdoms. In 1966, the Prime Minister of Bahrain stated that his country would like to see, 'the British remain as protectors in the Gulf ... [and] most strongly hopes that the US will be willing to assume some responsibility for Gulf security' (Macris, 2010: 139). Bahrain then went on to develop its own armed forces, 'officered mainly by Jordanians' (Macris, 2010: 169). Following the announcement of Britain's withdrawal from the Gulf in 1968, a Kuwaiti diplomat based in London suggested that 'he was sure a formula could be worked out whereby Kuwait, Abu Dhabi, Qatar, Bahrain and Dubai would undertake to meet the financial cost of a continuing British military presence' (Macris, 2010: 156). Britain offered to continue supplying the Trucial Oman Scouts (Omani troops led by British officers) with officers. At the same time, growing US influence in the region meant that Gulf leaders also looked towards Washington for military support.

Migrant Security Forces in the Era of Independence

With the formal independence of all Gulf States by 1971, British advisors continued to staff and train the highest ranks of the Gulf's military apparatus. Through this control, further reinforced by growing Western arms sales to the Gulf, Britain ensured that the new regimes in the Gulf remained intact and loyal to Western interests. Fred Halliday writes that, 'In the small state of Qatar, for example, enormous power was held until 1972 by two legendary figures; one, an ex-Glasgow policeman named Ronald Cochrane, who had adopted the Muslim name of Mohammad Mahdi, and headed the army, while the other, Ronald Lock, headed the police' (1977: 16). A British colonial police officer involved in violently quelling Kenya's Mau Mau uprising, Ian Henderson, became head of the General Directorate for State Security Investigations in post-independence Bahrain, remaining in his post for 30 years. Dozens of Britons also served in training and advisory roles in the UAE army and police force (Halliday, 1977).

At the same time, however, the composition of the security and military forces underwent a significant shift, with the bulk of new recruits increasingly sought from countries in South Asia. These migrants filled the bottom ranks of the armed forces, officers recruited from other areas of the Arab world served above them, and British (and American) advisors held the top positions. In Bahrain and Oman, mercenaries serving under British 'advisors' were largely recruited from Baluchistan, with higher-ranking and intelligence positions filled by Jordanians. In Oman, 'up to half of the soldiers in the SAF [Sultan's armed forces] are mercenaries from the impoverished plateau of Baluchistan, in Pakistan. All the top personnel, officers and training staff, in the three branches are British ... Jordan has deployed several thousand troops there and also provided experts for the police and intelligence services' (Halliday, 1977: 31–2).[3] In Qatar, the Emiri Guard and parts of the British-established Trucial Oman Scouts merged to form the armed forces. Qatar's police force, up to 6,500 men strong, included 'a large number of expatriates, who seem to be carefully chosen to ensure their loyalty' (Halliday, 1977: 282). The United Arab Emirates also recruited a large number of troops from foreign countries, particularly Jordan, Oman, the Sudan and Pakistan (Cordesman, 1997: 351).

Buttressed by oil profits during the 1970s, these new security and military forces allowed Gulf States to also become benefactors of other regimes and armed forces. Regional cooperation to this effect would 'ensure an integrated and stable repressive system in the whole region' (Halliday, 1977: 30). Perhaps the starkest example of this was the Dhofar rebellion, where opposition forces in Oman not only faced the SAF troops officered by the British, reinforced in large numbers by Jordan, but also garrisons from the UAE and Saudi Arabia, who provided financial aid to Oman as well (Halliday, 1977: 32). Gulf regimes also backed royalist forces battling republican opposition in neighbouring Yemen, with Saudi Arabia, the US and the UK providing weapons, money, refuge and other covert support to battle opposition movements during the country's civil war (Macris, 2010: 131). In this manner, migrant security forces not only helped Gulf regimes ensure the protection of their own non-representative regimes, but they also were instrumental to creating a wider buffer zone against the spread of republican and anti-colonial movements.

In short, the question of migrant-based security forces needs to be seen as instrumental to the development of the wider repressive capacities of the Gulf state. As the practice of recruiting massive volumes of migrant workers allowed rulers to undermine indigenous labour movements, the practice of recruiting foreign forces loyal to the regime has likewise been effective in undermining domestic challenges to Gulf regimes. The example of Bahrain, particularly in the wake of the 2011 uprising, is a pertinent illustration of how central this structure has become to the 'despotic power' of Gulf rulers.

The Case of Bahrain

As noted at the beginning of this chapter, while the number of migrants working in Bahraini security forces is not publically available, there is little doubt that the figure is very high and exceeds the number of citizens working in this sector. The Bahraini security apparatus is made up of a number of institutions, at the top of which sits the Supreme Defence Council. Responsible for Bahrain's defence and security policy, this body is headed by the King and includes the Prime Minister, Crown Prince and heads of other security-related government institutions such as the National Security Agency (NSA), Ministry of Foreign Affairs, Ministry of Defence and Ministry of Interior (MOI).

The Bahraini army (known as the Bahrain Defence Force or BDF) is comprised of the Royal Bahraini Air Force, the Royal Bahraini Army, the Royal Bahraini Naval Force and the Royal Guard. It is very difficult to gauge the size of security institutions due to a lack of publically available data, but the army has been estimated by Dutch news and analysis organisation *Fanack* to be made up of some 8,000 personnel (*Fanack*, 2014). The BDF is part of the inter-Gulf GCC Peninsula Shield Force, a joint military force agreed upon by members of the GCC in 1984, thought to number some 40,000 troops from Gulf countries (Mustafa, 2013). Paramilitary forces, such as the Public Security Force and Special Security Force Command, fall under the Interior Ministry, and are estimated by the same organisation to have 11,000 personnel (*Fanack*, 2014). Separate to both these institutions are the National Guard (three batches of 1,200 personnel) and the NSA (Bassiouni et al., 2011: 65).

The act of migration itself is largely motivated by the pursuit of a better life that is not available in the sending country. While ostensibly migrants employed in security forces occupy a position of power – vested in them by the government and exacted when dealing with citizens – it is also precarious. These workers are dependent, as regular migrants are, on their places of work for wages and employment to make a living – and in the case of migrants in security forces doubly dependent – on the political will of the Bahraini government. Nonetheless, the experience of migrants working in security forces is crucially different from that of migrants working in the private sector. These differences can be seen in modes of recruitment, visa handling and costs, training and benefits offered in employment, and outcomes of the migration process (most significantly, the possibility of naturalisation).

There are a variety of different means by which migrants are recruited to serve in the Bahraini security apparatus. Interviewee A describes that between 1985 and 1998 the number of Pakistani recruits in the SSF (Special Security Forces) rose tenfold, from 500 to 5,000, due to government-to-government coordination. He states:

> [The recruitment methods have changed] because I [spoke to people] in 1988–91 during the Gulf war, directly, to ask them to send Pakistanis, legally, from the Ministry of Interior. Some I recruited through [local] companies – they got release letters because they decided they wanted to work in the Interior Ministry, but the main way was government to government.

According to both interviewees, in 2011 the Bahraini government sent recruiters to a number of Pakistani cities to carry out interviews and medical assessment of potential recruits, encouraging locals to inform their relatives of the recruitment – then arranging and paying for visas for those who were selected. The first interviewee explained that, 'The first question – [interviewers ask is about] education and professional training – I didn't go there [in person, to Pakistan to recruit new personnel] but they will tell me, "tomorrow we are in Karachi so tell [the people you know]"'. According to the second interviewee, a number of members of the National Guard – and also in his estimation a small number of trainee police in his batch – would have paid large sums of money to an unlicensed 'agent' to secure a visa or position in the Bahraini security forces. The interviewee also explained that recruitment by this method occurred mainly when individuals were being brought directly from Pakistan, rather than by a relative in Bahrain.

In 2011, an advertisement created by the Overseas Employment Services (OES) of the Fauji Foundation[4] appeared on the Foundation's own website, in the Pakistani newspaper *Jang*, and on online recruitment agency Paper Job Ads. It stated:

Immediate Need In Bahrain
In Bahrain we need some security staff.
Age: Minimum 20, maximum 25
Height: Minimum 5'10, maximum 6'0
Education: minimum high school graduation, or more
Those people who wish to join us should be at the Fauji Foundation in
Rawalpindi on March 8, 9 and 10 with their passport, ID card, school
certificate – or if you are working proof of employment – and two
passport size photos.

The Pakistani *Express Tribune* newspaper writes that the Bahraini
government recruited members of their National Guard as well as anti-riot
instructors and security guards. There were said to have been 800 vacancies
for which 6,000 to 7,000 applications had been received, with other
officials at the OES claiming there were 200 to 300 vacancies and that an
unspecified number of people had been selected (Lasker, 2011).

Migrants working in security forces are typically housed in distinct areas,
separate from the organically developed towns and cities across the island.
There is thus an important difference in how these migrants are distributed
spatially across the country, compared to other migrants resident in the
country who tend to reside in labour camps and private accommodation.
In the case of migrants employed in public security, the self-contained town
of Safreh serves as a housing project for foreign employees of the security
forces. It is located in the Southern governorate close to the SSF training
base, and has its own consumer outlets specifically for Interior Ministry
employees and their dependents. This compound, which is disconnected
from much of the local population, allows migrants in the security forces
to live as a settled community – and segregates them to a large extent from
the indigenous Bahraini population living in towns and villages where the
security forces are often stationed for duty. By and large, their interaction
with Bahraini citizens occurs at two levels: at their places of employment
(with government employees and officials) and when policing citizens.
Following the Bahraini uprising that began in February 2011, interaction
at the 'street' level has largely been comprised of attacking and dispersing
public protests, and more recently, pitched battles with Bahraini youth.

The interviewees described a strong bond of community among security
personnel based on shared profession, personal contact, nationality and
religion. The subject of Interview A indicated he felt religious affiliation with
the local population, noting, 'the main connection is we are all Muslims'. The

second interviewee indicated that during training, significant emphasis was placed on the idea of equality among security personnel, saying, 'In Safreh even if someone does behave like "you are a Yemeni, you are a Pakistani", then they finish [terminate employment] them straight away. We get taught that "we are all in this together"'. The subject of the interview describes in this sense how members of security personnel displaying discriminatory behaviour based on nationality within the forces are allegedly dismissed from employment, thereby enforcing a sense of community based on profession, regardless of ethnic and linguistic differences.

Neither respondent indicates any sense of discomfort or even recognition of the animosity expressed at their role by a significant portion of the local population, describing Bahrain as a 'peaceful' country with 'friendly people'. The subject in Interview A conveyed a sense of the separation between this particular migrant community and the local citizens, but described the relationship between the two as: 'excellent – most of Pakistanis are working to save Bahrain, in security forces. Who are defending Bahrain right now? The Bahrainis in the forces – they were all sleeping in the barracks.'

Political Naturalisation

Perhaps the most striking feature of this group of migrants is the possibility of political naturalisation – being granted the right to hold a Bahraini passport without meeting the legal requirements – which is virtually impossible for other migrants in the country. Once again, exact statistics on this are not publically available. However, opposition activists and scholars have presented evidence alleging that citizenship has been granted to thousands of migrants (beyond the legal process and conditions of eligibility) as well as a large number of Saudi citizens from the Dowasir tribe (Gengler, 2011). The conferring of citizenship is the ultimate benefit bestowed by the regime, although it can take many years to obtain and requires naturalisation by royal decree once those eligible have met legal requirements and applied for citizenship. Interviewee A mentions the range of work benefits provided by the Bahraini government to members of security forces (for example, housing assistance and healthcare), and notes: 'the best of all this is – and we give thanks for – the passport'. He had applied for the Bahraini passport in 1988 and received it in 2006. Interviewee B (a new recruit) indicated his intention to remain in Bahrain; and to eventually settle his parents in Bahrain. It should be noted, however, that naturalisation is an 'insecure' form of access to the resources of the state, as it is based upon a political decision, rather than a legal process, and therefore can potentially always be revoked by another political decision.

Obtaining citizenship is also a means of moving up the ranks of the security forces, as Interviewee B suggests. He comments that the officer ranks ('those with stars') are held by indigenous Bahrainis, while the positions below are held by naturalised Bahrainis, and the bottom ranks by foreign recruits. In Interview A, the individual describes undergoing training by Pakistani and Baluch recruits who migrated to Bahrain before him. Both interviewees stated that their immediate supervisor and managers were of the same nationality as them (Pakistani). However, outside his 'training batch', the subject in Interview A stated that he worked in an administrative job with indigenous Bahrainis as his superiors in the SSF and the Royal Guard. Within this structure, the government maintains what Bonacich describes as a 'caste system', in which, 'citizens and migrants operate in two separate professional spheres each with its own recruitment rules and wage scales. In this system nationals constitute an "aristocracy of labor" with a clear hierarchical ranking between the two groups' (Louër, 2008a: 37). It should be remembered, however, that the majority of the Bahraini citizen population is not eligible to serve in the security and armed forces because of the exclusion of the Shia population. In this way, the multitude of migrants in the security forces helps maintain a vertical segmentation between sections of the population who would otherwise belong to the same economic class.

The possibility of naturalisation functions very successfully for the Bahraini government, as it helps sustain an active force of 'loyalists' using the carrot of material compensation alongside the stick of insecurity created by potential unemployment, deportation and revoking (or not bestowing) nationality. Within the sphere of contentious politics, it establishes competition between non-local forces and the local population for access to the finite resources of the state, while maintaining the vulnerability and dependency of both. The practice of pitting competition between civilians and non-civilians, as Khalaf (1998) argues, plays the crucial role of creating vertical segmentation wherein traditional class solidarity morphs instead into loyalty based on perceived associations. Migrants in the security forces are able to access certain privileges due to their loyalty to the ruler, while it is very difficult for any sustained opposition to emerge within the ranks of the armed forces.

The recruitment of migrants to work in security forces in Bahrain has both caused and fuelled complaints by opponents of the regime. Competition for limited jobs was exacerbated by the fact that the

> high population of foreign workers increasingly competed with the poor Shiites for job opportunities for both skilled and low skilled labour ... The government was very slow to improve its job training and recruiting efforts. Further, Bahraini Shiites – both of Arab and Persian origin – were not permitted to join the armed forces and were discriminated against for senior positions in the civil service. (Khalaf, 1998)

Conclusion: Bahrain's Uprising: Loyal Gendarmes of the Regime?

In January 2011, with much of the Arab world gripped by the unfolding events of Tunisia and Egypt, 'ideas began to circulate on a number of online forums and social networking platforms, such as Facebook and Twitter, [including] calls for demonstrations to demand political, economic and social reform in Bahrain' (Bassiouni et al, 2011: 65).[5] On 14 February, the tenth anniversary of the promulgation of Bahrain's National Charter and the declaration of the Kingdom's status as a 'constitutional monarchy', scattered unlicensed protests involving thousands of demonstrators took place at various localities. One demonstrator died as a result of a shotgun wound incurred by a member of an MOI police patrol in Daih village. In addition to this, a number of protesters were injured as a result of security forces' attempts to disperse gatherings, and attacks by protesters against police reportedly took place. The funeral of the young man killed took place the following day – and the public procession attracted more than 2,000 mourners, a small number of whom assaulted the police verbally and with metal rods. In an attempt to disperse the gathering of people, which at this point had evolved into a demonstration, MOI personnel are reported to have fired two shotgun rounds after reportedly having exhausted all other crowd dispersal ammunition. Another demonstrator was killed when a shotgun projectile struck him in the back at very close range, fuelling public anger and leading to the eruption of demonstrations at various locations around Bahrain. Protesters eventually gathered at the GCC roundabout (known widely as the Pearl Roundabout), setting up tents and a makeshift sit-in, which the King later authorised in a televised national address.

The Pearl Roundabout fast became the site for civilians to gather and express their discontent as well as discuss the political situation and proposed alternatives, with members of opposition parties making public addresses and an estimated 1,000 or more people setting up tents to stay overnight. Early on 17 February 2011, according to the MOI, four battalions (of over 1,000 security personnel), and onsite units from the NSA, the Ministry of Interior Criminal Investigations Department (CID) and BDF Intelligence department were dispatched to clear the roundabout. During this operation, and the hours that followed, four protesters were killed after being wounded by shotgun pellets fired by MOI personnel at close range. One of the deceased was reportedly part of a group of civilians responsible for assaulting security personnel.

The following day, BDF tanks stationed at the roundabout were faced by a group of approximately 50 demonstrators reportedly chanting anti-government slogans and verbal abuse at military personnel. Military personnel repeatedly issued instructions for the individuals to disperse, and fired warning shots – and MOI security personnel later used tear gas and rubber bullets to disperse the group. In the fracas, one person was fatally wounded and died the following day as the result of being shot in the head, and a number of others were severely injured. These events prompted a political initiative for dialogue between the government and opposition parties, initiated by the Crown Prince. The following day, numbers of protesters returned to the Pearl Roundabout, once again establishing a permanent protest camp there, this time with the Crown Prince's authorisation.

In the days which followed national strikes began, as well as large-scale demonstrations; one including a small number of police. A royal decree pardoned 300 prisoners including twelve political prisoners, who were subsequently released, and activity continued at the Pearl Roundabout while high-level political talks took place in the background. A demonstration was held outside the Criminal Investigation Directorate to demand the release of alleged political prisoners, and a minor cabinet shuffle was ordered by the King. Popular and widespread demonstrations were held by Ministry of Health employees at the Salmaniya Medical Complex, and by students at schools and universities.

During these events in February and March 2011 the question of political naturalisation of security personnel was a key target of popular protest. The number of violent incidents involving foreign members of Bahrain's security apparatus and Bahraini citizens increased dramatically, particularly during the policing and dispersing of demonstrations, at checkpoints and during arrests. Deaths of civilians at the hands of security personnel led to acts of retribution against members of public security forces, as well as the targeting of migrant workers by unknown mobs on a small number of occasions. This characteristic feature of Bahrain's uprising indicates the significance of this form of migration to Bahraini contentious politics, and confirms the manner in which the reliance on migrants in the security forces has effectively established a 'social base' for counter-insurgency and defence of the ruling regime.

The significance of this social base was strongly confirmed at numerous protests. In one demonstration in February 2011, involving thousands outside the MOI headquarters (known as *al-qala'a* – the fortress), participants 'denounced the policy of hiring foreign citizens to serve in the BDF and the local security services'. Other demonstrations were directed at (and staged in the areas surrounding) the embassies of the Republic of Yemen and the Islamic Republic of Pakistan – sending countries of a large proportion of foreign employees staffing Bahrain's security institutions. A smaller, 'counter demonstration' was staged outside the Fateh mosque for the first time on 21 February 2011, expressing discontent with international media coverage of the developments in Bahrain, and pledging allegiance to the royal family. Notable in this demonstration was the presence of expatriate workers, signifying again the success of allegiance to the ruling class over-riding class solidarity. There are no particular indicators as to whether these expatriates were in the employ of the regime or its security forces, but what is significant perhaps is the perception that the protection of expatriates in Bahrain would be provided by the regime and its supporters, a position extolled by the government and its allies.

Further clashes took place in Hamad Town in March 2011, which involved a conflict between Shia student protesters and teenagers from naturalised Sunni families living in the same neighbourhood. The clashes were broken up by units from the MOI Special Security Force Command (riot police), during which injuries were sustained by a number of civilians and MOI employees. Again, at a major public demonstration organised by the seven political opposition societies during March 2011, demonstrators decried what they described as the, 'deliberate policy of political naturalisation, which allowed almost 60,000 foreigners to be granted Bahrain citizenship between 2001 and 2007, has had a disastrous social and economic effect' (Bassiouni, 2011: 110). Another major protest during March 2011 was held at the General Directorate of Nationality, Passports and Residency, 'against the naturalisation policies of the GoB [Government of Bahrain], which they claimed were designed to alter the demographic balance in favour of the Sunni population. Many protesters also denounced the policy of hiring expatriates to work in the security services and described those expatriates as 'mercenaries' (Bassiouni, 2011: 118).

During this time, a number of attacks by unknown individuals against expatriates (particularly those of Asian descent) were reported, as well as attacks on police patrols and officers, and reported incidents of vandalism and the 'marking' of homes belonging to NSA and MOI employees. As a response to information regarding armed vigilante groups in a number of areas, local groups organised themselves to 'protect their lives and property', including a group which stationed itself close to the National Guard facility in Safreh to 'deter against attacks by individuals and vandals' (Bassiouni, 2011: 126).

On 15 March 2011 the King declared Bahrain to be under a State of National Security. As part of this declaration, four organs of the Bahraini security apparatus were responsible for implementing order: the BDF, the MOI, the NSA and the National Guard – all heavily staffed by migrant security personnel. The number of violent clashes spiked, leading to several fatalities among police and civilians – at the site of clashes, and in one case a civilian died after being detained by an MOI unit. In mid-March, in the presence of troops from the GCC Peninsula Shield and overseen by the BDF, over 5,000 personnel were deployed to clear the Pearl Roundabout and protest camp at the Bahrain Financial Harbour. The operation was primarily executed by police from the MOI assisted by National Guard units, with these forces also responsible for crowd control, staffing checkpoints and conducting house arrests. Dispersed from the Pearl Roundabout, which was later demolished, attempts at street demonstrations took place in numerous localities and led to further violent confrontations between MOI units and civilians.[6]

In the aftermath of Bahrain's aborted uprising of 2011, the emergence of social media sites dedicated to the SSFs indicated a strengthening sense of community between ideologically similar, though perhaps socio-economically different, factions of society. Significantly, migrant workers in Bahrain's security forces appear to be extremely active on these sites. The ideological common ground between these migrants and pro-government Bahraini citizens is their support of Bahrain's rulers, as well as a discourse upholding a highly sectarian variant of Sunni Islam. We see an expression of this 'community' on the Facebook site entitled 'The Return of Bahrain & Saudi Arabia Falcons' established in September 2011 and self-described as 'A page concerned with raising the banner of monotheism, publishing the facts and exposing Shia infidels and traitors, as well as the support of the SSF and Army'. Another popular Facebook site entitled 'Fight Against Bahrain Terrorists' established in January 2012 is described as being run by a 'Human Rights Activist', who writes that their 'previous page were [sic] reportedly Abuse by Bahrain Shias, as of today 19-01-2012 page were deleted by Facebook Management. Kindly help us to promote the truth about Bahrain.'[7]

As well as updating followers on security issues in Bahrain, both pages make reference to Islam (for example, through posting quotes from the Quran). On the 'Fight Against Bahrain Terrorists' page, anti-government protesters are generally described as 'terrorists', or on occasion as 'thugs'. Commenters use the terms 'Shia', 'Iranian dogs' to describe protesters, and invoke Islam in phrases such as 'Muslim spirit', 'Muslim brothers', and 'Ahl-e-Sunna' (followers of Sunni Islam).[8] 'The Return of Bahrain Falcons' page repeatedly refers to anti-government protesters as 'Shia Criminal Monkeys', 'Shia criminal terrorists' and 'Iranian traitors', while describing security forces as 'Riffai Heroes' (Riffa is a Sunni-dominated area of Bahrain), and including posts referring to 'Sunni' and 'Ahl-e-Sunna' (followers of Sunni Islam).[9] The majority of text on both pages is in English, with a large number of comments written in Urdu using Latin script – which may suggest that the majority of its visitors are not Arabic speaking, and perhaps not Bahraini.[10] However, both pages invoke nationalism expressed as loyalty to Bahrain and its ruling family, as well as opposition to 'Shia' and 'Iranian' infiltrators.

Finally, it is interesting to note a more recent restiveness among the migrant security population. As expressed on community web portals, March 2014 saw at least two public demonstrations[11] by migrant security personnel and supporters in response to the killing of MOI policemen in a bomb explosion.[12] Posts on the community portal also criticise the Bahraini government for 'sleeping' in the face of a perceived growing threat from a restive population, and for failing to adequately protect the security forces who have allegedly sacrificed their lives in order to defend the status quo.

Both these online and offline developments confirm the salience of Bahrain's migrant-based security forces to any understanding of the events of the last few years. Building upon a centuries-long historical pedigree, the Bahraini government has managed to employ this system of divide and rule to preserve allegiance and obedience from a group that it essentially exploits, in order to protect itself from dissenting citizens. The regime's success in this process lies in enabling the fragile coexistence of several competing elements of society, while managing their levels of disquiet through engendering a fear of each other greater than their discontent with the existing state of affairs. In this sense, scholarly analysis of Bahrain's migrant population needs to place much more emphasis on unpacking the specificity of different employment sectors – incorporating the differential experience of migrant security personnel into our understanding of the country's political and social characteristics.

Notes

1. Figures for employment by nationality issued by the Bahraini Labour Market Authority (LMRA) calculate that 48,111 Bahrainis and 7,912 non-Bahrainis were employed in the public sector in the fourth quarter of 2010. 'Estimated Total Employment by Citizenship and Sector: 2002–2013', http://blmi.lmra.bh/2013/06/data/lmr/Table_A.pdf (accessed August 2014). On the other hand, information issued by the Central Informatics Organisation (CIO) national census of 2010 calculates that 54,975 Bahrainis and 28,082 non-Bahrainis were employed in 'public administration and defense'. 'Working Population (15 Years+) by Major Economic Activity, Nationality and Sex: 2010 Census', www.cio.gov.bh/cio_ara/English/Publications/Census/LabourForce/4.13.pdf (accessed August 2014). Based on this simple calculation, there appear to be approximately 20,000 non-Bahraini public sector employees unaccounted for, leading to speculation that it may well reflect the size of the community of migrants working in public security forces.
2. Britain's Political Resident in the Persian Gulf, based in Bahrain during the 1950s, recorded in his memoirs, 'We therefore had to form the small force mentioned above and, unbelievable as it sounds today when the Trucial States are enormously rich, we actually had a fund for economic and development aid.' And that it was 'agreed that in addition to the normal naval and RAF presence it would probably be adequate for one company of infantry to be held in Sharjah and Muharraq' (Burrows, 1990: 33).
3. Baluchistan is now a province of Pakistan. Prior to the formation of Pakistan, British colonialism in the subcontinent and its control of the Gulf allowed for a recruitment office to be established in Bombay to hire migrant workers for Bahrain as early as 1936 (Addleton, 1992). Geographical 'ownership' over Baluch land and trends of migration among Baluch nomadic tribes also contributed to large-scale Baluch migration to Oman. In addition to this, the inhospitable terrain of Baluchistan itself, as well as the historical and cultural legacy of Baluch mercenaries in Oman, led large numbers of Baluch tribes to enter Oman seeking employment in the armed forces. In 1921 Oman's first modern army unit was established, comprised entirely of Baluch migrants (Nicolini, 2007: 184).

4. The Fauji Foundation is a conglomerate in Pakistan worth over US$600 million on the Karachi Stock Exchange, with investment in a range of sectors including food, energy, agricultural and financial services. It was established as a charity in 1954 to provide employment and welfare benefits to Pakistani ex-military personnel and their dependents, and is run by ex-officers from Pakistan's armed forces (although it is classified as a non-governmental entity).

5. The discussion of the Bahraini uprising in this section is based upon Bassiouni et al., 2011.

6. Detailed testimony issued in the Bahrain Independent Commission for Investigation (BICI) report of November 2011 holds that security forces were held responsible for at least 21 civilian deaths through beatings, shotgun projectiles and excessive use of tear gas, as well as another five civilian deaths as a result of torture in custody. Repeated allegations also include the deliberate maltreatment of women and children, property damage and theft, verbal abuse and the use of religious and sectarian insults during house arrests, and the torture and maltreatment of detainees in police custody. The same report accounts for at least three police deaths at the hands of civilians, and the killing of two expatriate workers by civilians.

7. 'Facebook: Fight Against Bahrain Terrorists', www.facebook.com/pages/Fight-Against-Bahrain-Terrorists/358954004130447 (last viewed 2 April 2014).

8. Ibid.

9. 'Facebook: The Return of Bahrain & Saudi Arabia Falcons', www.facebook.com/pages/The-Return-of-Bahrain-Saudi-Arabia-Falcons (last viewed 2 April 2014).

10. For an example of non-Bahraini members of the army, see 'Facebook: Bahrain Army', www.facebook.com/BahrainArmy (last viewed 1 April 2014).

11. 'Facebook: Fight Against Bahrain Terrorists', www.facebook.com/pages/Fight-Against-Bahrain-Terrorists/358954004130447 (last viewed 2 April 2014).

12. These attacks involving the use of explosives to target security personnel emerged in early 2014. They include an attack in which three policemen (two from Pakistan and one from the UAE as part of a GCC force operating in Bahrain) were killed by a remotely detonated device while dispersing a gathering of protesters in Daih.

8

Expat/Expert Camps: Redefining 'Labour' Within Gulf Migration

Neha Vora

This chapter is about labour camps in Qatar, distinct compounds removed from the city centre designed to either house or employ temporary migrant workers who have been recruited to the country to fill particular jobs that citizens are either unqualified or unwilling to do. Labour camps, as much of the literature on migration to the Gulf Arab States has explored, segregate populations of foreigners by class, race, gender and nationality (Buckley, 2012b; Gardner, 2010; Hanieh, 2011; Kanna, 2012; Vora, 2013). They allow for the containment of the foreign and the policing of perceived security threats by reducing mobility and increasing surveillance of different groups of non-citizens (Gardner, 2010; Kanna, 2012). They are, therefore, spatial expressions of what Longva (1997; 2005) has called an 'ethnocratic' society, where access to resources, political power, belonging and urban space are tied directly to ethnicity, race and national identity. This spatial segregation and containment is also part of the production of labourers as biopolitical subjects: instead of through direct coercion by the state, migrant regulation and the *kafala* system seep into a multitude of everyday processes, geographies and technologies that inform the very bodily practices of migrants in the Gulf States (Rose, 2001).

However, the labour camps I discuss here are not – as many readers familiar with the Gulf context might expect – full of construction workers from South Asia imported to rapidly build the infrastructure that Qatar's petro-wealth demands. Rather, these camps are occupied primarily by white professionals from North America and Europe – 'expats' who have come to the country on temporary renewable visas in order to build Qatar's new 'knowledge economy', along with other economic diversification initiatives the country has undertaken in the last decade.

Recent efforts to diversify away from petroleum-based wealth in the Gulf States are not only the result of the finiteness of natural resources but also of a sense of threatened national identity and ethno-racial purity due to a large proportion of non-citizens. Qatar's knowledge economy in particular is designed to train citizens to replace foreigner workers; the state's hope is that an indigenous knowledge economy will in turn produce more skilled Qatari citizens for the workforce, thereby also reducing the country's heavy reliance on foreign workers, who currently constitute over 85 per cent of the population. This practice, called 'Qatarisation', is official state policy and is actively promoted in multiple ways – companies are offered incentives to incorporate more Qataris, and Qataris receive preferential treatment in many educational and hiring processes.

The keystone of this push to grow an indigenous knowledge economy is the Education City project, overseen by the Qatar Foundation, a non-profit organisation funded by the Qatari government.[1] Situated on the outskirts of Doha, Qatar's capital, Education City houses, among other offerings, branch campuses of six American universities: Northwestern, Georgetown, Cornell, Virginia Commonwealth, Carnegie Mellon and Texas A&M (Harman, 2007; Krieger, 2008). Bringing top universities to Qatar from the United States and elsewhere will purportedly provide the modern skills that Qataris need to achieve the state's vision of national development. Qatar's American universities, therefore, are meant primarily to be an investment in a type of knowledge economy that fosters nativist national futures and enables Qatarisation while also modernising the country. Ironically, economic diversification projects like Education City are also opening new markets for foreign workers, particularly Westerners, who are considered to embody the expertise required to achieve global competitiveness and modernity. In addition, American branch campuses are providing higher education options for the children of middle- and upper-class foreign residents, who previously would have had to leave the country to attend university. In fact, only a handful of Qataris occupy positions on the faculty and in higher administration of Education City institutions, and non-Qataris comprise more than 50 per cent of the student body at most schools.

Because the Qatar Foundation has designed Education City to provide primarily American-style education, recruited primarily Americans to fill key positions, and looked to the United States as a model for the growth of its indigenous knowledge economy, the project has heightened local concerns about too much Western influence, which might result in the loss of Arabic language, Muslim values and traditional Qatari social relations. Education City has also raised questions among Qataris about who is benefitting more from its universities: citizens or migrants? The tension between a desire for modern, Western-influenced national development and the need to preserve vanishing national tradition and ethno-racial purity in the face of foreign bodies and cultures is encapsulated in the Education City project, reflected in the technologies that state and other institutions employ to manage foreign residency, and experienced in a myriad of ways by the expatriates I introduce in this chapter.

Many North Americans have moved to Qatar over the last decade on short-term contracts to work as faculty and administrators in Education City and other sites of knowledge economy.[2] I myself have taught at Texas A&M Qatar (TAMUQ) in Education City for three terms, and have conducted over six months of research among faculty, administrators and students there (Vora, 2014; 2015). These upper-middle-class professionals, like myself and many of the people I met and worked with during my time at TAMUQ, entered quickly into Qatar's expatriate population – an international mix of relatively educated and skilled workers (in contrast to those who would be considered 'migrant labourers') who were brought to the country as experts in their fields, and who found their social status and wealth greatly improved by the decision to live and work in the Gulf. Furthermore, most of these expatriates spent their days shuttling between various compounds – those of the companies where they worked, the shopping malls and hotels where they spent their leisure time, and the gated housing communities and high-rise buildings where they lived. Their nationalities in many ways defined their mobility and opportunities in the country, as did their Western professional accreditations, their English-language skills and – to a large extent – their whiteness.[3]

I argue here that while these expats have access to a lifestyle that seems lavish and far removed from the existences of supposedly 'unskilled' labourers, they are also contained in particular parts of the city through biopolitical technologies, geographies of exclusion and neoliberal forms of governance. They are interpellated as temporary workers, as (white) raced and (upper-middle) classed foreigners, and as groups of residents who belong in certain parts of the city and not in others. They in turn, through their own discourses and everyday practices, reify Qatar's ethnocratic social structure, its ethno-racial hierarchy of labour migration and what Kanna has called 'a neocolonial hierarchy which privileges Europeans and North Americans' (2014: 612).

As I explore in this chapter, professional expatriates are in fact labourers too. And so-called migrant labourers, instead of being unskilled and uneducated, rely on forms of expertise and knowledge in order to become transnational and increase their social and economic capital (see also Kanna, 2012). In this chapter I am interested in two interrelated questions. First, how do desirable and undesirable forms of foreignness get coded on to differently raced, classed and national bodies in the Gulf? In particular, what is the role of whiteness in these processes, and how does whiteness get linked to national and economic development projects? Second, how are markers of 'expertise' deployed in both Qatari state and expatriate discourses to establish the role of Western professionals in economic development, to distinguish between expatriates and migrant labourers, and to manage the day-to-day functioning of migrant governance in the country?

I want to draw connections between the stark social hierarchies in the Gulf and the built environments of compound living and working, pushing back against and providing a counterpoint to the primary focus on working-class labour camps in Gulf migration literature through a focus on the phenomenon of what I call the 'expat/expert camp', and particularly the biopolitical aspects of expatriate life within this type of camp. Biopolitics as a framework allows us to explore how power operates through technologies of regulation and knowledge accumulation in order to manage the minutiae of everyday life, and how subjects themselves become self-regulatory in relation to these technologies. This model of power is one that moves away from ideas of repressive states and capitalism – and away from rational actors within market fundamentalism – towards a more diffuse way of thinking about how institutions of power and inequality, geographies and spaces, and subjects are co-constituted. By providing a different picture of what constitutes labour migration and migrant governance in Qatar and the Gulf States, I suggest new ways of thinking about race (particularly whiteness), belonging, and work in the Gulf that go beyond economically reductive accounts of the migrant as *homo economicus*, Gulf States as modern-day slave economies and the stark citizen/non-citizen dichotomy through which foreign resident life in the region is generally understood.

Shifting the Paradigm of Gulf Labour Migration

The last several years have seen a sharp rise in academic publications, humanitarian reports and media articles from around the world that spotlight the mass labour exploitation, structural violence and slave-like conditions under which many migrants to the Gulf supposedly live and work.[4] Most of these accounts produce a normative migrant labourer who is raced, classed and gendered in a particular way – a young rural man left behind by South Asia's economic development, who, with little to no skill or education, has come to the Gulf for a temporary stay in order to make money to remit back to struggling family members at home.[5] Without economic or social capital, this migrant labourer is easily exploited: he might find himself receiving less pay than promised upon recruitment, have his passport withheld from him, be expected to work long hot hours in the Gulf sun, or live in cramped unsanitary conditions in walled labour camps at the edge of the city.

There are numerous studies that focus on labour exploitation, push and pull factors, remittances and other market-based migration experiences for supposedly unskilled low-wage workers, particularly those in construction or domestic work (see, for example, Al-Awad and Elhiraika, 2003; Gardezi, 1997; Kapiszewski, 2001; Khalaf and Kobaisi, 1999; Nambiar, 1995). While many of these accounts attempt to ameliorate worker conditions by shining a light on human rights abuses and illegal labour practices, this scholarship too often reduces migrant workers solely to their labour, thereby eliding (however unintentionally) their acts of politicisation, such as strikes, and their affective belonging and sociality with Gulf residents, both migrant and citizen (see Buckley, 2012b and Kanna, 2011b; 2012 for more on this elision). While exploitation and violence are indeed endemic to daily migration patterns in the Gulf, this picture is incomplete, and it serves to perpetuate ideas about Gulf countries as exceptional under globalisation (as if migrants are not exploited elsewhere), to reproduce Orientalist ideas about Gulf nationals and governments (which are supposedly more repressive and violent than elsewhere) and to ignore the diversity of people who come to the Gulf to work from around the world, and their positive and negative experiences of migration (Ahmad, 2011; Buckley, 2012b; Vora, 2013).

As Ahmad (2011) has astutely explored in her work on Kuwait, the primary lens for understanding migration in the Gulf – that of rational actor economics, or *homo economicus* – is incomplete in that it fails to account for longer, more intimate connections between migrants, their home countries and the Gulf; as well as for the large role that migrants play in the 'social reproduction' of the population, a role that is not only circumscribed by racial, national and religious factors, but is also deeply gendered as well. In my own work, I have considered how middle-class Indians in particular experience and produce diasporic belonging in Dubai in ways that exceed the neoliberal economic narratives of accumulation and voluntary migration that they themselves participate in recuperating (Vora, 2008; 2013).[6] These excesses of belonging, traced by many accounts of foreign residents in the Gulf that investigate diasporic communities, politicisation and/or affect, challenge what I have previously referred to as a 'triptych' of residency in the Gulf States, where groups are seen to be either (exploited) 'migrant labourers', (consuming) expatriates or (unproductive) locals (Vora, 2013).

Within this formulation, expatriates get treated in the literature most often as consuming individuals regulated by and productive of Dubai's neoliberal market technologies, while migrant labourers are reduced to labour. In fact, Gulf States are represented as ethnocratic societies through descriptions of certain spaces and the populations that occupy them: labour camps and construction sites are where migrant labourers are exploited, and shopping malls and hotels are sites of consumption and leisure for expats and locals, who are supposedly not impacted by the structural violence of the *kafala* system of labour migration governance in the Gulf. In contrast, I suggest an anthropological approach to foreign residents' lived experience that asks how labour comes to be constructed as the primary defining feature for some migrants and not for others. This requires attention to the complex ways in which race, class, gender and nationality infuse Gulf social structures, geographies and forms of governance – allowing us to see how all foreign residents (and citizens as well, although this is outside of the scope of this chapter) are biopolitical subjects who in turn reproduce various ideas about belonging, exclusion, work and expertise in the Gulf States.

There is very little ethnographic scholarship on Europeans and North Americans in the Gulf, and in this scholarship these 'expats' are rarely considered as labouring subjects; there are however two ethnographic accounts that come from a Marxian framework to address the experiences of expatriates as workers in the Gulf. Ali's (2010) work, for instance, on expats in Dubai, claims that expats take up a 'Faustian bargain' by migrating to the Gulf, one in which they trade democratic liberal rights for increased wealth – thus the sub-title of his book, *Gilded Cage*. Expatriates, he argues, knowingly take up this bargain even though there are many potential negative impacts on them, such as jail time, no right to work grievances, and living under autocratic rule. Thus, they exist within the same exploitative system as migrant labourers, although they are less duped and less exploited by that system due to their economic and cultural capital. In a similar vein, Gardner (2008) also puts expatriates and labourers into the same analytic framework, arguing that professional and elite Indians in Bahrain constitute part of a 'transnational proletariat' that is subject to similar forms of structural violence, racism and exploitation as their less educated and lower-paid compatriots.

These accounts address the work experiences of expatriates in the Gulf, and in so doing move towards challenging the male South Asian construction worker as archetypical Gulf migrant. However, these works also reproduce similar problematics of market fundamentalism and *homo economicus*, thus eliding more complex attachments and motivations for migration and residency in the Gulf, in particular the politics and history of race, gender, class, nationality, imperialism and postcoloniality. In most other accounts that reference expatriates, particularly those coming from urban studies and geography, expatriates emerge as a spectre of sorts, an archetypical consuming person of business or leisure whose cosmopolitan global elite status makes Gulf cities and their emerging built environments their playgrounds (see Davis, 2006; Elsheshtawy, 2008; Kanna, 2011a). The focus in much of this work is on the technologies of hailing this normative white subject – the ways in which Gulf cities are built and marketed for the people they imagine will occupy its spaces.[7]

Actual field research that pays attention to the complexities of expatriate desires, community building, and modes of both leisure and work are scarce. One notable exception here is the work of Katie Walsh (2006; 2007), who conducted field research among British expatriates in Dubai in order to understand their everyday forms of belonging and placemaking. Walsh explores in her work how British expatriates, while enjoying national and racial privileges they might not at home, are also subject to financial insecurities, long work hours and a wide range of concerns that might be categorised under the rubric of labour. Walsh's work highlights the need for more sustained attention to the role of race and particularly of whiteness in Gulf daily life.

While it is commonplace to code certain multinational and multiethnic spaces in the Gulf as 'Indian' or 'Arab', while also acknowledging that this naming does not encapsulate the diversity of peoples that inhabit these spaces, there seems to be a reluctance on the part of many scholars to address the whiteness of certain spaces in the Gulf – spaces they themselves often occupy – when the on-the-ground experiences of most Gulf field researchers is that of stark racial segregation, boundary policing, and a sense of where one belongs and doesn't belong in Gulf cities based on skin colour, nationality, gender and class status.

How whiteness operates in conjunction with other markers to produce exclusionary spaces and communities in the Gulf has a longer history that goes back to British imperial ties to the region, and also to more recent American influence there. Kanna (2014) and Coles and Walsh (2010) have explored how imperial forms of racial boundary policing impact the experiences of British and by extension other white expats in the Gulf today, and Vitalis (2007) has traced how American Jim Crow policies produced labour stratification in American oil industries, a stratification that may be responsible for the ethno-racial structuring of contemporary Gulf development projects as well, such as what we see in construction.

Expatriates, then, are inculcated into a system of race in the Gulf that is not at all disconnected from the one they experience at home. And, their lives at home, at work, and at play are deeply affected by an ethno-racial segregation that permeates through the built environments and daily life of Gulf residency. They in turn reproduce certain ideas about whiteness, about racial and cultural difference, and forms of colonial nostalgia in the Gulf, even as they are impacted by new forms of governance and biopolitical technologies that circumscribe their mobility and mark them as outsiders (and sources of corruption) to the nation, as I explore in greater detail below.

The exclusionary spaces that expatriates occupy in Gulf cities, then, are as much to keep others out as to keep expatriates in (Kanna, 2014). Understanding this duality of built environment in the Gulf is crucial to understanding how whiteness operates not only as a marker of leisure, but also as a particular form of labour – one that is expert, non-indigenous, necessary for development, thought of as transposable from one context to another and in need of containment in zones and spaces designated as Western or 'expatriate'.[8]

Daily Life in the Camps

In my first days in Education City in 2010, I met Margaret, a mid-level human resources staff member at one of the American universities in Doha's

Education City, and we immediately became friends. One afternoon, after lunch at a café in the Landmark Mall, she invited me back to her apartment in a newly constructed gated community near the mall. Margaret lived alone in a three-bedroom villa in a gated compound about a ten-minute drive from her work – housing provided for her by her employer. Her living room was cluttered with furniture she had collected in her over five years in Qatar, ranging from modern pieces to antique styles reminiscent of Indian or Persian designs.[9] She had recently purchased a baby grand piano and started taking lessons, so the furniture in the room has been pushed into the corners in order to accommodate this large new arrival. In the hallway leading to the living room were piles of goods that Margaret stocked up on during her recent weekend errands: cases of diet cola, water bottles, beer and wine, and snack foods. She apologised for the mess, telling me how, between work, her boyfriend (who lives in another villa in a neighbouring compound), her music lessons and several charity organisations she is involved in, she hadn't had time to clean up around the house lately.

I understood the feeling quite well. Having arrived in Doha just ten days earlier in order to teach summer session at Texas A&M Qatar (known locally and on the home campus in College Station, Texas as TAMUQ), I had hit the ground running – between finishing my syllabi, learning my way around the city, getting medical tests and my driver's license and dealing with the jet lag of being halfway around the world, my hotel apartment in Doha's swank West Bay neighbourhood, also provided by TAMUQ, looked like a tornado had come through. I hadn't had time to pick up any of my clothes, and had taken to dumping my papers, water bottles, scarves and other daily items on the dining table every day when I got home from work. The cleaning crew of the hotel cleaned around my mess, not wanting to disturb what may be my own form of organised chaos.

Margaret's Doha life took place, like mine, in three or four key sites. Work in Education City, where she arrived every morning at eight and left by four; upscale shopping malls and hotels, where she ate her meals and socialised with friends; and villas in her own and other gated compounds, where she went for her philanthropic work and hobbies, or to visit her boyfriend. In these spaces, she encountered a multinational group of people, including many Americans, Canadians and Europeans who, like her, had come to Doha on renewable three-year contracts to work in administrative or managerial positions. From time to time she also interacted with some upper-middle-class Arabs and South Asians, and the occasional Qatari. In Education City, for example, the majority of Margaret's co-workers were American or

Canadian. Her interactions with Qataris, non-Gulf Arabs, and South Asians were mostly limited to students and service staff. Her circle of 'best' friends, including her boyfriend, were also mostly American, although through her philanthropic work she was acquainted with a handful of Qatari women who occasionally invited her to their home for a *majlis* (social gathering).

Margaret's main mode of transportation was her Honda Civic, which she was renting with a car allowance from her employer, or it was the occasional cab if she went out drinking on the weekends. I too had a company car for my short summer stay, which I used to shuttle back and forth between Education City and my West Bay hotel, and I also took cabs for weekend outings to the many hotels that served alcohol and had night clubs, many of which were located a short drive from my hotel. Margaret and I, along with our colleagues and friends, spent a great deal of time driving between the sites where we lived, worked and played. The areas we inhabited, unlike more congested downtown areas, were not pedestrian friendly, and car culture, despite increasing traffic congestion, reigned in Qatar among its expatriate population.

Like other foreign residents in Doha, Margaret had myriad reasons for living and working in the Gulf, but the primary one she relayed to me was economic. She was earning about 30–50 per cent more than she would for a similar university position in the United States, and without having to pay taxes, housing and transportation costs, or even for her yearly trips back to North Carolina to visit her aging parents. She spent quite a bit on vacations, drinking and restaurants, plus her large recent expenditure for the piano, bought on the cheap from a fellow American expat who was packing up and moving back to the States. Despite her spending, she was still saving over US$10,000 a year in her bank account back in the States, and she had paid off college loans and had no credit card debt.

However, she complained that she had not received a raise in over two years. In fact, Margaret was not at all satisfied with her work life. Although she was making more and saving more than she could in the US, she did not feel adequately challenged or appreciated in her position. Not only was there the constant feeling that less qualified people were being recruited directly from the US for jobs above hers while she stayed at the same pay and position, she was deeply bored with the repetitive administrative tasks that she was asked to do every day – tasks that did not make her daily work life, despite her title, her Master's degree in education and her being recruited for her 'experience' (though paltry) in American academia, much different from that of a secretary.

In fact, many middle-level expatriates in Education City were not embedded in careers but rather in repetitive labour that was packaged as a form of expertise they brought to Doha that the Qatar Foundation would not be able to find indigenously. Faculty, for example, spend much more time teaching than engaged in research and intellectual pursuits in Education City; many are recruited directly into branch campuses after not being able to procure positions within the 'home' spaces of American academia.[10] Others were mid-level administrators who had risen to high-level management positions during their recruitment to Qatar, or after spending a couple of years there, and they were not necessarily qualified for the position they were currently filling were we to compare their credentials to similarly situated assistant deans and heads of staff in the United States. But most Western expatriates in Education City, and in Doha overall, are young people like Margaret who have not figured out yet what their area of expertise is, and rather have taken jobs in Doha based on salary promises, the ability to save and remit money,[11] the inability to find equivalent jobs in their home countries, the journey of finding themselves or the desire to travel and live abroad before they settle down later in life.

Since 2008, the global economic recession has made it harder to procure and maintain employment in Europe and North America for young people with college degrees, and made the Gulf region even more appealing to Westerners. Thus, Margaret and those like her are embedded in the same economic systems that drive 'migrant labourers' to Gulf countries. Once in these countries, like their South Asian and Arab counterparts, they also establish forms of belonging, affective ties and community formations that 'exceed the economic' narratives through which they expressed their reasons for coming to the Gulf and deciding to stay (Vora, 2013).

Margaret's father had worked in Saudi Arabia and other parts of the Gulf, so Margaret had experience living in the region during her childhood. She fondly remembered American compound life in the Gulf as a space of intimate friendships and deep bonds with other families. In addition, she articulated a preference for the lifestyle and culture of Doha over the US. People were friendlier, she claimed, and more family oriented; they were also, unlike Americans in the US, less shallow and less materialistic, and were also more cosmopolitan in their outlook. She felt at home in Doha more than she had anywhere else in the world in many years. However, when she referred to what people are like in Doha, Margaret mostly meant other expats like herself; she rarely noticed or mentioned lower-wage foreign residents at all, nor did she express many positive views on Qataris.

In fact, Western expats live, play and to a degree also work almost entirely segregated from both Qatari citizens and non-Western diaspora groups, including low-income 'labourers'.

Margaret's cosmopolitan life in an international city like Doha was therefore preferable to the US precisely because of the ways in which she was able to participate in and benefit from practices of cultural and racial segregation, preferring to be with what Kanna (2014) calls 'like-minded' individuals without explicitly having to acknowledge the discriminatory structures that privilege whiteness in the Gulf. The sense of whiteness being in peril at home due to multiculturalism, immigration and post 9/11 Islamophobia ironically intensifies the sense of comfort that many Western expatriates feel in their exclusive communities in the Gulf.[12]

Many of Margaret's friends and colleagues – some of whom I counted among my friends and colleagues as well – shared this perception that Doha was a better place to live at the current moment in their lives than the US or Europe, especially given the economic, social and political problems that they felt permeated their home countries. These were all Westerners, mostly white and mostly American, who worked as faculty or staff in Doha's Education City. Their jobs were linked, then, to the rise in Qatar's knowledge economy, which was underpinned by a desire to bring 'international' standard education to the country. This translated to American branch campuses of top universities, along with English-language education, gender-integrated classrooms and programmes that offered globally marketable degrees like engineering and business (Miller-Idriss and Hanauer, 2011).

The faculty and staff of Education City, particularly as one moves up the ladder of income and education, are primarily recruited from North American and European countries, and most earn, like Margaret, more than they would for comparable jobs in their home countries. In addition, because their cosmopolitan ethos, language skills, and for many their whiteness, translated to a 'value-add' within Qatar's job market, these semi-skilled to skilled professionals were coded as experts in education, often in ways they would not be at home (see also Henry, 2013). Thus, having only a bachelors degree can lead to a high-level position in Qatar when that position would require many further years of training or expertise in the home campuses of Education City schools. These expatriates, on top of receiving higher salaries than their Arab or South Asian counterparts, also often have their housing, cars, children's schooling and travel back to their home countries subsidised by their employers. And they have access to top services and consumer products from around the world that are brought into the country for their consumer desires and national tastes.

Given their quality of life, it might seem that these are privileged members of elite classes who simply follow the money and profit from Qatar's exclusionary and hierarchical social and economic practices. However, I argue that these expatriates are also in many ways labouring individuals who face restrictions on speech, permanent residency, mobility, fair employment practices and a range of other challenges that make them not altogether distinct from other groups of foreign residents in the country. In addition, while many have commented on (sometimes negatively) the afterhours lives of Western expats in the Gulf, particularly in regards to excessive drinking, heterosexual sex practices and nightclub life, little attention has been paid to how all foreign residents in the Gulf, including so-called migrant labourers, produce vibrant spaces of socialisation and intimacy that counterbalance the work regimes that define much of their Gulf existence.

How do we understand the narratives of Margaret and her friends through a lens of labour while also expanding our understandings of labour to avoid economically reductive modes of analysing foreign resident life in the Gulf? What do white Western experiences in Doha tell us about the nature of daily life in the Gulf States, and how do the perspectives of this demographic of mobile cosmopolitan 'experts' with disposable income both add to as well as complicate our current understandings of Gulf residency and migration, as well as the rubrics of race, class, nationality and gender in Gulf cities?

Margaret and those like her (including myself as an educator and researcher who benefitted from my Western expertise while in the Gulf, though white privilege was not available to me) were both enabled by our social and geopolitical locations as well as circumscribed by them. Our experiences of Doha's cosmopolitanism were inextricably tied to practices of racial and cultural segregation, practices co-constituted with the built environments of the city, which allow urban professional expatriates segregated existences from the rest of the city's residents while in many ways also working to contain them. In effect, then, sites of white/Western privilege and expat consumption and production also are camps that cordon off and contain this population in relation to other groups of residents, a population that, though interpellated and represented in Gulf state and commercial discourses as cosmopolitan, expert and consuming, is also in the Gulf primarily to perform a particular kind of labour, one that relies less on skill and experience and more on embodied dispositions and performances that can be coded as both 'Western' and as necessary for the project of building a modern 'global city'.

Education City as Expert Camp

Located on the outskirts of Doha, Education City is a sprawling campus containing multimillion-dollar architectural marvels that house top-name American universities, a new student centre, residence halls, administrative offices for the Qatar Foundation, a recreation facility and other buildings that serve the faculty, staff and students who work and study there. The lawns throughout are manicured and watered daily, and there are open gathering spaces for commencements and other activities. With its many roadways, parking lots, and clear demarcation through fences and guarded gates, it truly feels like a distinct space set apart from the rest of Doha – a city within a city (see also Kane, 2011).

In order to enter or exit Education City, one must have an ID badge that specifies their faculty, staff or student status, or be invited as a visitor. These ID badges also scan to open doors around campus, thus designating access based on job status as well. To visit Education City or even any of the university buildings it houses, you need to leave your ID – drivers license or passport – with a guard, and then come back to collect it as you leave. Like expat compounds around the Gulf, Education City appears more impenetrable than it actually is, with buses coming through at all times, with certain gates being unmanned from time to time or with guards who arbitrarily let some people in without the right credentials. However, this is a distinct compound, and one that is marked as Western, and to some extent, white, despite the variety of people one encounters when inside.

Education City is the hallmark of Qatar's investment in knowledge economy, designed specifically to bring American education of the highest international standards to Qatar in order to train its population in the skills required to be globally competitive and to eventually replace foreign professionals with locals, an official state policy called Qatarisation. In addition, the spectacle of Education City and the globally recognised brands of the universities it houses, puts Qatar on the map as a global city that is striving to top world records in several categories through its over-the-top development schemes.[13]

It means a lot for the Qatar Foundation to create an indigenous platform for higher education in Qatar, through an amalgam of the best available global options. Incorporating foreign aesthetics, models and programmes is not new in the Gulf States, who actively try to balance a desire to be cosmopolitan and internationally recognisable with their insecurities about population imbalance and a traditional culture supposedly at risk of vanishing. This has meant bringing in architects, urban planners, engineers, bankers and other professionals from around the world in order to build the rapidly growing economies and geographies of Gulf cities. In the case of Education City, however, global and cosmopolitan translates directly to Western – and particularly American – forms of curriculum, pedagogy, school spirit and educational mission. Students are expected to take SATs and TOEFL exams in order to qualify for entry, and admissions materials, curricula and student affairs all emphasise success based in meritocracy, global citizenship and the ability to compete for jobs within a global economy. As one administrator at Texas A&M told me, the Qatar Foundation is very clear in its privileging of American and Western forms of education as superior and desirable:

> you see, our students want a Western education because they think in engineering its better, you know what I mean?[14] They want what a main campus student would get. At g-town [Georgetown] they want what a main campus student at g-town gets, ok, its, it could be some other world, it could be there were all the French universities, you know what I mean? They would want what that person gets. Maybe 25–30 years from now everything here is high quality Chinese education, whatever.

The planning and operation of the branch campuses, which are beholden to and seen as extensions of the home campus, also require the production of distinctly American spaces. Most schools have to conform to the standard operating procedures of their home campuses. In the case of Texas A&M, these are set by the Texas legislature and include a requirement that students take some aspect of Texas history in order to graduate. However, campuses also have had to change some of their policies in order to accommodate Qatari needs. For example, the start of the school year needed to be pushed back in 2011 due to the Eid holiday. And certain aspects of home campus education – like Georgetown's required 'Problem of God' course and art history classes at Virginia Commonwealth that feature nudes – have encountered resistance from conservative Muslim students and their parents. Thus, the Americanness of branch campuses permeates through Education City, even though it takes different forms in different spaces and articulates with Qatari norms and expectations (see also Vora, 2015).

But why does an American model of education also include a preference for faculty and staff from the United States and other Western countries? It is telling here that there is only one Qatari full-time faculty member across all of the branch campuses. Certain markers of expertise are coded on to certain bodies, and this coding is deeply connected to race and nationality. The expertise imagined to be necessary for Qatar's knowledge economy and for Education City in particular is a form of expertise that is specifically non-indigenous but also potentially assimilable into the Qatari context. It therefore calls into being a sense of a transposable commodity that is embodied by the white Western/American expatriate subject – one who is transnationally competent and cosmopolitan, can easily move between cultural/national contexts and yet maintains a *habitus* that comes out of Western and white histories, knowledges and privilege. These tracers of cosmopolitan habitus have, however, been obscured over time and within the context of postcoloniality and globalisation, and are now conceived of as universal or 'global' in scope, both at home and in the Gulf. Qatar Foundation's mission (as of 2013 when this chapter was first drafted), for example, does not make any claims to Western or American educational forms, but rather to ideas of global eliteness and excellence:

> Qatar Foundation's [QF's] mission is to prepare the people of Qatar and the region to meet the challenges of an ever-changing world, and to make Qatar a leader in innovative education and research. To achieve that mission, QF supports a network of centers and partnerships with elite institutions, all committed to the principle that a nation's greatest natural resource is its people. Education City, Qatar Foundation's flagship project is envisioned as a Center of Excellence in education and research that will help transform Qatar into a knowledge-based society.[15]

However, as I have outlined above, this global excellence is interpreted directly as an American one. The international standards, state-of-the-art offerings, and forms of global citizenship that Qatar Foundation is interested in producing through a Qatari knowledge economy effectively recuperates a white Western form of expertise and cosmopolitanism as 'global', and Qatari and other knowledges, pedagogies and norms as inherently parochial and in need of globalising through the importation of expertise. However, while white Western migrants to Qatar are clearly structurally privileged and able to market upon their embodied expert subjectivities, these migrants are not free from the regimes of migrant governance that operate within the Gulf, and in fact they are regulated and produced, both individually and as populations, as biopolitical labouring subjects who are contained within specific compounds and camps around Doha, like Education City.

The Biopolitics of Expert Camps

As I outlined above, most literature on Gulf labour migration relies heavily either on *homo economicus* explanations or on top-down models of structural violence/exploitation in order to understand migrant choices and experiences. Instead, I suggest here that it is more productive to consider how power circulates among and operates upon Gulf residents through biopolitical technologies (see also Kanna, 2011b; 2012 for a similar argument). This framework allows us to avoid naturalising distinctions between citizens and non-citizens, between different national groups and between so-called migrant labourers and so-called expats in order to understand how subjects are produced and produce themselves within multiple, overlapping and often contradictory vocabularies and logics of belonging and exclusion – ones that include all aspects of daily life in the Gulf, not only those we deem 'labour'. My own journey to work in Doha reveals the minute ways in which I was produced as an expert and a labourer simultaneously.

The process of relocating from the United States to work in Education City is rather complicated, although the steps are to some degree standardised. As a Texas A&M employee, my sponsor company was the Qatar Foundation, and they provided me with my visa to work and reside in Qatar. My employer, on the other hand, was TAMUQ, with whom I had a contract to be a Visiting Assistant Professor in the Liberal Arts department, to be held concurrently with my TAMU tenure-track position, as a short-term joint appointment.

However, I was a unique case – most faculty and staff were hired directly to TAMUQ and did not hold joint appointments. Very few faculty had experience teaching on the main campus at all; more often, staff would relocate semi-permanently from Texas to Doha. Texas A&M at the time had an office on the main campus in College Station – Qatar Support Office – to help with relocation and other issues that employees from the main campus to the branch campus might have, as well as to assist with administration.[16] For faculty and staff relocating to Doha from the US, salaries were set according to equivalent positions in Texas; however, they also came with a 'TAMUQ incentive package' that included a 30 per cent salary bump, housing and other benefits. Other universities in Education City, particularly private ones, did not have to adhere to limitations imposed by state legislatures, and were able to set salaries and curricula more independently than TAMUQ, though most had similar salary structures.

In addition to listing my salary and work expectations, my contract stipulated that:

> As a condition of employment, you shall abide by all Texas A&M University System Policies and Regulations and all University Rules. You also are expected to abide by the applicable laws and regulations of the State of Qatar and to respect the cultural, religious and social customs of Qatar. Your failure to abide by such applicable laws, regulations and customs may be considered a material breach of this offer letter, subject to termination by the University at its sole discretion.

My incentives package document, attached to my contract, explained that I would be provided with housing and either transportation or a transportation allowance during my time in Doha. It also stipulated that, since I was a temporary employee, my earnings would be taxable in the US; for permanent relocators, salary is only taxable over $80,000; thus, Margaret and many of her peers were not paying taxes at all. I was also given specific instructions on what would be expected from me upon arrival in Qatar, including immigration procedures, how to get a driver's license and medical insurance coverage information. My immigration procedures read as follows:

Qatar Immigration:

- Because you will enter Qatar on an 'official visiting visa,' initially you must complete routine immigration actions similar to those of a person permanently relocating to Qatar. Failure to complete this process in a timely fashion could jeopardize your ability to stay in the country.
- Within your first two weeks in Qatar you will receive a medical examination, including a blood test and chest X-ray.

- Part of the Qatar government background check will require your fingerprints.
- You can exit and re-enter Qatar during the period of your visiting visa, however, each exit/entry requires a single exit/entry permit approved and issued by the Qatar Foundation. The Texas A&M University at Qatar Immigration Coordinator needs at least a one-week notice to obtain necessary approval of your exit/entry request.

Once this contract was finalised and signed by all my bosses in Texas and in Doha (department heads, deans, etc.), I submitted a PDF file of my passport to the Qatar Support Office (QSO), who booked me a business class round trip flight on Qatar Airways to Houston.[17] After a long but luxurious 15-hour flight, full of French champagne and Bollywood movies, I landed in Doha International Airport around 10 p.m., where I passed through immigration rapidly with the visit visa that QSO had procured for me. I was met by a young Qatari man holding up a Qatar Foundation placard with my name on it – Sami worked for Human Resources at TAMUQ and was often tasked with picking up new arrivals at the airport in his Range Rover. Sami provided me with my TAMUQ cell phone, informing me that I could make one 15-minute international call to my family in the US, but that other calls must be limited to local ones. He drove me to my hotel apartment, a large tower called Somerset in Doha's swanky West Bay neighbourhood, next to the newly built Kempinski Hotel and across the street from the trendy and popular W, where I would end up spending much of my leisure time while in Doha. At the hotel, I was greeted cordially by the Filipino manager, who handed me an envelope with the keys to my rental car in it – a small Mitsubishi with a name I had not heard of before – and escorted me and my baggage up to my apartment.

The apartment exceeded expectations: it had two large bedrooms and a living room, all with floor-to-ceiling views of the Arabian Gulf, and a large kitchen, dining table and two bathrooms. The hotel had provided some instant coffee and instant noodles for the newly arrived weary traveller, and the kitchen was fully stocked with any utensils I would need to cook or serve food. I also had access to the hotel gym and pool, and a daily lavish breakfast spread (omelette station!) available to me as part of my package that TAMUQ was covering.

For the first two years I stayed at Somerset, TAMUQ even paid for my water cooler service and my in-hotel laundry and dry cleaning. I was living the good life, clearly, in comparison with my College Station existence, where I was the lowest-paid faculty member in my department and struggling to make mortgage payments, as well as in comparison to the majority of non-Western expats in Doha. With the Doha summer salary, all of which (after taxes) was going into my bank account because I had almost no out-of-pocket living expenses, I was able to pay off credit card balances, loans and other debts I had accumulated over the course of grad school and my subsequent move to Texas. I also reserved some of that cash for dining out and drinking with friends in Doha's hotels, shopping for luxury brand items in the city's malls and weekend side trips to Dubai, Oman and India.

However, this good life was not a do-as-you-please existence, but one that, as I was reminded in a plethora of large and small ways on a daily basis, was restricted and channelled by and through various biopolitical technologies and regulatory regimes, even as these forms of governance allowed room for better-positioned expatriates to manoeuvre around them in ways that 'migrant labourers' could not.

First, let me refer back to the two examples from my contract that I provided above. The immigration process was long and complicated before I got to Doha, and once I was there it required days of waiting in lines and interacting with different bureaucratic offices around the city. I was instructed by the Liberal Arts administrator to wait at a bus stop in Education City the morning after my arrival in Doha in order to get medical tests. I joined several other Qatar Foundation employees on a small bus that took us to a hospital even further out of town than Education City. Chatting with those closest to me, I met two faculty members from Georgetown who had just arrived for three-year contracts, an events coordinator for the new multimillion-dollar horse racing stadium that QF had just finished building, a human resources employee relocating from my main campus, as well as a postdoctoral student who was starting a one-year position at Weill Cornell Medical School.

When our bus arrived at the facility, we were met by a young Qatari man, an employee of Qatar Foundation who spoke to the guards at the hospital, who allowed us to bypass the long lines of construction workers and low-level office employees waiting outside and go straight into medical testing. Testing required a blood extraction and an x-ray, plus a short interview. The process involved shuttling from office to office, and took about two hours. Upon leaving, some of the people who had been in line when we went in were still waiting.

The next day, Sami, who had picked me up from the airport, took the new TAMUQ arrivals to get temporary driver's licenses, and again his Qatari nationality and Qatar Foundation employee status allowed us to move to the front of the line. Here we were given a vision test and then issued temporary month-long driver's licenses, which, once our medical tests were completed and we were issued with residency cards, we would exchange for permanent licenses.

In order for HR to apply for our residency, we also had to turn over our passports. Once I received my passport back, after a couple weeks, along with my residency card, I was able to exchange money and buy a new phone – both activities that required official residency status. I could not, however, leave the country unless I had an exit permit from QF, a process that required again turning over your passport and waiting for several days, hoping that the exit permit would come through in time for your trip. However, as an American citizen this was not as fixed or necessary as it would have been for someone with a Global South passport. I could enter Doha on a visit visa, so while it would compromise my residency status if I left the country without an exit permit (which chances were I would be able to do), I could re-enter again as a tourist after paying around US$40, although not without consequences from my employer.

In addition to these bureaucratic hurdles, which both circumscribed my mobility but also highlighted my privilege vis-à-vis other migrants, the labour I performed while in the Gulf required a certain embodied subjectivity and the ability to manage and work within the uniqueness of TAMUQ's student body in ways that were new to me, having never taught outside the United States. I was constantly aware of my charge to 'abide by the applicable laws and regulations of the State of Qatar and to respect the cultural, religious and social customs of Qatar', and so I chose my clothing very carefully to make sure it was not too tight, short or revealing; I regularly came to campus with a shawl to drape over my shoulders; and I consciously performed as a Western anthropologist in front of my classroom, emphasising my American accent and asserting my positionality as someone who was not Indian 'from India' in order to maintain authority. In this way, although I am not white, I carried a symbolic whiteness that established my expertise as an American professor within Education City.

The classroom experience also meant managing gendered, classed and ethno-national interactions between myself and my students, and between different students themselves. I found myself unable to get the women to speak up as much as the men in class, despite my efforts, and I had several students who were unwilling to discuss topics like gay rights or feminism – these were considered 'Western' phenomena that did not translate to the

Qatari/Arab context. In addition, I practiced self-censorship and constantly worried about projects I was assigning, if I was pushing students too far outside their comfort zone and whether I was successful as a teacher in the TAMUQ context. These are not unusual concerns, and they were ones that I had in College Station as well, although they manifested around different topics and interactions. Both spaces required me to self-regulate as well as to produce my identity in relation to my students and the normative college 'culture'.

At Texas A&M's main campus, for example, I was constantly aware of how, as a woman of colour, my students often took my lectures about race or gender as personal opinion rather than as fact, as they would if the information was relayed by a white male professor. At TAMUQ, however, students accepted my expertise more readily, but I had an added level of insecurity in that my stay in Doha was contingent upon not violating cultural standards or offending any high-level Qataris.

For most of the faculty in Education City, who did not hold tenure-track positions in the US like I did, the lack of true tenure and security, mingled with concerns about restricted speech and academic freedom, led to greater insecurities about their careers and longevity in the Gulf. In many ways, they were in limbo, not yet having launched a full-blown career, having to learn to work in new ways and not sure where they would be in a few years time. Thus, myself and those like me existed both as experts and as labour within Education City, and our expertise was both marked upon our bodies and performed by us as embodied habitus within a shared vocabulary of ethno-racial migration in the Gulf, a vocabulary that was encoded on to the geographies of the city as well, both allowing for more elite cosmopolitan forms of mobility, leisure and consumption, while containing expatriate 'foreign matter' into specific spaces and modes of belonging (Gardner, 2010).

As biopolitical subjects, 'migrant labourers' are both regulated by and participate in the *kafala* system, forms of belonging and exclusion, and ethno-racial urban geographies. They are thus not subalterns who cannot speak but rather engaged actors who challenge as well as reproduce the systems into which they are inculcated. For example, Kanna (2012) and Buckley (2012b) have both explored migrant labour activism and daily life within compounds through the lens of biopolitics, highlighting how these workers are not disconnected from larger institutions and politics, and are also able to articulate complex positionalities, affects and claims upon the city despite conditions of exploitation and lack of resources. In the same vein, we can think of expats like myself and Margaret not as having entered into a Faustian bargain or as primarily consumers, but rather as foreign residents who are inculcated into and reproduce regimes of both consumption and production, labour and expertise.

Just a quick look at the processes and technologies of migration and residency for American and other expatriates in Education City reveals the biopolitics of daily life for expatriate professionals, a daily life that is intimately linked to both race and nationality, though not overdetermined by either. By thinking of labour as something that all residents do – like leisure, like politics, like belonging – we open up new ways to think about daily life in the Gulf for differently situated actors, none of whom are reducible to 'labour'. Rather than being outside of and unimportant to the Gulf nation-state, then, foreign residents of all stripes are political subjects who are interconnected with and partaking in the production of citizens as well as non-citizens, and the constantly emergent and blurry boundary between these categories that have until now been treated as rigid and self-explanatory in much of the literature.

Conclusion: Labour Camp as Expert Camp

Recently, an Indian friend handed me an issue of *Little India* magazine, a publication aimed at diasporic audiences in the US, from October 2012. He had been saving it, he told me, since my work was on Indians in Dubai. The cover features four Indian-looking men in blue coveralls against the background of a half-constructed building (see Figure 8.1). Three of the men are gazing directly at the camera, smiling. One is turned away from the camera, at the edge of the frame, and we cannot see his face. The headline below this picture proclaims 'The New Indentured Laborers'.

Inside, the article referenced on the cover begins with the case of two recent suicides by Indian men in Dubai, and the author explains that suicide rates in the UAE are seven times greater among expatriates than citizens, with three out of four of these suicides being by Indians. The article continues to explain, through anecdotes, the forms of exploitation and discrimination Indians face in the Gulf, even the more affluent ones. Several photos accompany this article, the first an expanded version of the cover photo, which now shows that there are three more men in the frame, all also looking at the camera. They appear to have been captured in the midst of chatting or socialising, perhaps while waiting for a bus or on a

Figure 8.1   Little India cover, October 2012

lunch break. Other images include men at the Dubai Creek offloading goods from a dhow, fishermen working with a large net and more men in coveralls walking with a wheelbarrow. They are, we are supposed to infer based on the accompanying text, exploited, working under slave-like conditions, and trapped in the Gulf. However, this inference requires several elisions on the part of the reader, ones that have become so naturalised that we do not even know we are making them.

First, what do we make of the variety of expressions on the faces of the men in the photo? And what about their social and affective lives, which are displayed here even as they are depicted in their work clothes at a work site? Would a similar scene of middle-class expatriates socialising, smiling at the camera and standing in their office elicit a similar headline? We need to reduce these men to their labour – and also to a labour that they are supposedly alienated from – in order to read them as indentured and exploited.[18] Also, the variety of jobs and locations pictured in the accompanying article belie the idea that Indian 'migrant labourers' are confined to camps on the city's edges – in fact, working-class Indians permeate all areas of the city, not just labour camps. The suicide rates, while shocking, are also reflective to some degree of the demographics of the UAE: expatriates do outnumber citizens many times over, and of the expatriate population, most are South Asian.

Creating a narrative of labour exploitation therefore requires choosing some anecdotes over others, in effect removing potential positive experiences, forms of belonging, politicisations and affective ties in the Gulf for Indian working-class foreign residents. This is not to argue for a celebratory picture of construction worker life in the Gulf, but rather for an account that is more complete and complex, and thus more humanising. It is also a call to look at transnational labour migrants not solely as trapped or duped, but as knowledgeable people with certain skills and networks that allow them to become transnational in the first place.

In this chapter, I have focused on redefining 'labour' within Gulf migration, primarily through a focus on the biopolitical and geographic ways in which migrant subjects are constituted. This redefinition allows us to understand how all Gulf residents labour, not only those who look like the men in Figure 8.1; it also avoids making certain populations reducible to an economic activity or mode of production, while others are afforded richer inner lives and forms of belonging and sociality.

I have explored how foreign residents are produced through understandings of a difference between labour and expertise, in which expertise is inflected with race, nationality, class and an embodied Western cosmopolitan *habitus*. In addition, I have argued for a better academic framework for approaching migration in the Gulf that considers governance, regulation and self-regulation not as repressive modes of exploitation, but rather as productive of various subject positions and racialisations.

In concluding, I want to suggest a complementary argument to the one I have just outlined: while in many ways expats are important to consider as labour in the Gulf, so-called migrant labourers are also experts in their own right. The transnational networks of expertise that so-called 'unskilled' labourers tap into in their migration and residency practices push against the ways in which they have been interpellated both in academic and activist literature, as well as by Gulf state discourses. In order to migrate into low-wage positions in the Gulf, people need contacts with recruiters and others who supply visas and help with job applications; they need to be able to borrow and pool money from a range of familial and community resources; they need to have investigated migration procedures, either formally or through word-of-mouth; they need to make sure the family members they are taking care of back home are able to support themselves; and a host of other knowledges and networks required to migrate in the first place.

As Spivak (1996) has so aptly put it, those who can become diasporic are not among the most subaltern of the subaltern. Once in the Gulf, low-wage foreign residents rely on networks to learn geographies, languages, laws and residency processes. They also develop social and affective ties to others, not only from the same nationality, and these ties impact their sense of identity and belonging. In addition, many become politicised as a result of the treatment they experience at the hands of employers, the state and other residents (see Kanna, 2012; Buckley, 2012b; Vora, 2008; 2013).

Shifting our understanding of labour reveals how expertise and labour are embodied in different ways by all Gulf residents; it also challenges us as scholars of the Gulf to look more closely at our own interpellation as experts and expats, and how we reproduce certain understandings about race, nationality and class through our own practices and existences in the Gulf – ones that include within them forms of labour, racialisation and geographic segregation that are not at all disconnected from the daily lived experiences of so-called 'migrant labourers'.

Notes

1. Qatar Foundation, www.qf.com.qa (accessed August 2014).
2. There are no data readily available on the number of Americans or Westerners in Doha. The Qatar Statistics Agency (QSA) does not break down the non-Qatari population by nationality, and numbers from the American embassy do not distinguish between active military located in Qatar and civilian expatriates. The population I am discussing here would fall somewhere within the 7 per cent reported recently by the *Guardian* as 'other' in Qatar's population, and the 20 per cent reported by the QSA who have higher degrees. However, within Education City, in many upscale housing compounds and in the bars and restaurants at fine hotels, white/Western expatriates are ubiquitous.

3. Kanna (2011; 2014) has written about how whiteness symbolises wealth and modernity in Dubai, and is used to promote the emirate as a 'global city'. There are several accounts of whiteness being linked to modernity in developing and postcolonial states. Henry (2013), for example, has recently explored how 'foreign' (i.e. white American) teachers are recruited to Chinese schools as symbols of modern education and imagined national futures.

4. A series of articles published recently in the UK *Guardian* newspaper, for example, highlights Qatar's 'modern day slavery' through descriptions of harsh working and living conditions among Nepali construction workers: www.theguardian.com/global-development/series/modern-day-slavery-in-focus (accessed August 2014).

5. See also Buckley (2012b) for a critique of this 'archetype' of migration in the Gulf.

6. For more on foreign residents' belonging in the Gulf, see Gardner (2010), Johnson (1998), Leonard (2002) and Nagy 2008.

7. My work is also complicit in this type of investigation, for, through my investigation of built environments and state discourses that target 'expats', I rely more on an imagined normative object of these enterprises, instead of on a more complex ethnographic engagement with different individuals who fall into the category of expatriate, and who might both challenge and reify the ways in which they are interpellated by Gulf spaces and institutions (Vora, 2013).

8. See Mitchell (2002) for more on this kind of expertise.

9. For more on expatriate home-making, see Salih (2002) and Walsh (2006).

10. This is not the case for all faculty: some, who have research interests in the region, who speak Arabic and/or are Muslim or grew up in the Gulf or Middle East, actively seek out positions in Gulf universities. I have heard varying accounts from non-Western faculty and staff about their experiences in Education City. Some feel they are not receiving the pay and benefits packages that Westerners receive, while others feel at home and well-treated. This is an area of ethnographic research that I have not yet explored in depth.

11. Here, I am counting Margaret's student loan payments from college, money she sends occasionally to her sisters and parents, and gifts she purchases for friends and family in the US as remittances. This is another epistemic category that relies on certain assumptions and elisions to think about who 'remits' and what counts as remittance, but one that I do not have space to explore further in the context of this chapter.

12. Kanna (2014) recounts similar experiences among white expatriates in Dubai. On one occasion, a white Belgian man even tells him that he would not move back to Belgium because of the rise in immigrants there.

13. In this way, Qatar is much like Dubai, and has garnered similar international attention in recent years.

14. Texas A&M offers only engineering degrees, so that is why this administrator is referencing engineering.

15. Accessed at www.qf.com.qa/discover-qf/qatar-foundation-mission in January 2013. This mission statement has since changed and the link is no longer active. In fact, the entire Qatar Foundation website now reflects more of a

focus on Qatar, its people, and its heritage (www.qf.com.qa). This is perhaps due to criticism from Qataris about Education City's contributions to rapid Westernisation in the country.

16. That office has since been moved to the branch campus, due to budget concerns, according to several of my TAMU colleagues in the US and Doha. It was unclear to me whether QSO was being funded by the Qatar Foundation while it was in the US, or whether its operating budget came out of the generous 'consulting fee' that Qatar Foundation pays the main campus in order to have its brand come to Doha and offer a Texas A&M education to Doha residents.

17. Business-class travel is standard for higher administration and faculty – the only times I have had an opportunity to travel this way have been as a Visiting Assistant Professor at TAMUQ.

18. I made a similar argument in a short interview on *Jadaliyya*: New 'Texts Out Now: Neha Vora, Impossible Citizens: Dubai's Indian Diaspora', www.jadaliyya. com/pages/index/12601/new-texts-out-now_neha-vora-impossible-citizens_du (accessed August 2014).

9

In and Out Moves of the Bahraini Opposition: How Years of Political Exile Led to the Opening of an International Front During the 2011 Crisis in Bahrain

Claire Beaugrand

Introduction

Migration studies in the Gulf have typically concentrated on the phenomenon of massive labour migration in the oil-rich region, the rationale behind migratory policies, as well as the expatriates' experiences. Conversely, the Gulf countries are characterised by insignificant levels of emigration of nationals to other regions, although intra-Gulf mobility – for family and economic as much as political reasons – has always been quite important.[1] The assumed link between politics and migration is one of isolation between the two: foreigners are requested not to engage in political activism (unless, as exiles, they are welcomed to do so to serve the host state's interests or image, like the Palestinian leadership in 1960s Kuwait or the Arab leaders in Qatar). The case of Bahrain invites the researcher to revisit the link between migration and domestic politics in a way rarely seen in the region: if various studies have shown the import of political or religious ideologies through migrants or returning students (Chalcraft, 2010; Louër, 2008b), Bahrain provides the case of a country where decades of political exile of opposition activists widened the framework of the domestic political fight once they returned. While analysts tend to focus on the peculiar sectarian composition of Bahraini society, this chapter argues that the opposition's various experiences of exile – until the new King called for the amnesty of its members in 2001 – also account for the confrontation pattern of the political situation in Bahrain. More specifically, through building upon the literature on diaspora and conflict, the chapter examines the impact on Bahrain of this internationalisation of the political conflict since the 2011 crisis.

Bahrainis abroad do not exactly fit *sensu stricto* the definition of a diaspora even when the term is extended to newer experience of dispersal (Van Hear, 1998). Denys Cuche (2001: 20) characterises diaspora as 'a certain type of social formation, stemming from large migratory movements, identifiable through original features that make it clearly distinguishable from any other form of ethnic regrouping that international migration can create' – these features being 'a permanent state of dispersion', 'a certain rooting in host societies' and 'a common feeling of identity, which is ethnic in character, that proceeds from a self-representation of the disseminated community as an entity sharing a common history and culture'.[2] Bahrainis lack many of these characteristics: emigration, which cannot be described as massive, has been based on political activities; the dispersion of the opponents has rarely been 'permanent'; and rooting in host countries has been rather weak as the majority of the exiles' children returned to the island in 2001. Furthermore, Bahrainis do not even claim to be a diaspora, the main word used as a self-reference being 'political exiles' (*manfiûn*).

Yet a couple of features nevertheless make this branch of literature and its research on the role of diaspora in conflict relevant. The 2011 crisis and the brutal repression that characterised the National Safety period (March–June 2011) has stalled the movement of exiles' reintegration, reactivated links with foreign countries through the emergence of a new generation of activists born and raised in the West, and seen a new wave of exiles who encompass a wide variety of socio-economic backgrounds. Parameters analysed in diasporic communities to explain the attitudes of faraway communities towards conflict at home (Shain, 2002: 128–33) seem increasingly relevant to Bahrainis in exile.

First, Bahrainis in exile have gradually built and maintained their own vision of Bahraininess, more and more distinct from that of the state: this vision, articulating citizenship and migration, widely shared by the opposition inside the country, seems exacerbated by the experience of emigration, and sees opponents or critical individuals being stripped of their rights and gradually pushed outside – even through denaturalisation – while newcomers are welcomed, provided they join the ranks of loyalists that are uncritical of the regime. Second, Bahrainis in exile are organising themselves through a range of different political interest groups, seeking through available legal channels to influence the policies of their host countries. This chapter provides historical depths to this diasporic activism in the host states, which continues to have a perceptible impact on the Bahraini regime's interstate relations.

In the first part, this chapter will look at the British-inherited history of political exile in Bahrain, distinguishing between two traditions of exile:[3] the banished socialist/Marxist revolutionaries of the 1960–1970s who found shelter mostly in Ba'athist Syria, and the leaders of the Shiite Islamist opposition, who, spreading unrest after the Iranian revolution, made their way through the asylum-seeking process in Canada, the United Kingdom, Denmark and other Scandinavian countries (while others were deported to Iran). Against this background, the chapter investigates the way in which political agendas, transnational strategies and mobilisation means designed in the specific context of exile were to be reimported into the native country and adapted there, as the practice of open criticism in the West considerably renewed the terms of the political debates and raised the level of expectations in Bahrain. Lastly, the chapter looks at the mobilisation of international support by opposition forces in the domestic political fight (including the strategies of preventive self-imposed exile) and argues, based on qualitative interviews carried out from 2008 until 2013, that the history of political exile of the Bahraini opposition contributed to the frontal pattern of conflict and the opening of a new international front when the 2011 crisis erupted.

Decades of Opposition Exile

Alone among the Gulf countries, Bahrain has an established track record in deportation that was inherited from British rule over the island.[4] In 1938, the leaders of the movement protesting against the high rate of Indian employment in public administration and the discrepancy in salaries were banished to Bombay (Khuri, 1980: 197–8). Likewise, the episode of the nationalist liberal movement between 1953 and 1956, referred to as *al-haya'a* (the committee), ended with the imprisonment and exile of the three main leaders to Saint Helena, as related in the memoirs of Abd-al Rahman Al Bakir, *From Bahrain to Exile – Saint Helena*, published four years after he was released in 1965 (Joyce, 2000). Other militants left Bahrain to settle in Kuwait or Saudi Arabia. From this time on, two different waves of exile took place: the Marxist and Arab nationalist movements of the 1960–1970s, when Bahrain was still under British protection, and the Shiite Islamist currents of the 1980–1990s.[5]

Waves and Structures of Exile: Marxist and Arab Nationalist Opposition

When asked about the political affiliation that caused them to flee Bahrain, the interviewees from a leftist background referred to the major distinction between the members of the Popular Front for the Liberation of Bahrain (*jabhat sha'abiyya li-tahrir al Bahrayn*) (PFLB) and the National Liberation Front-Bahrain (*jabhat al tahrir al watani al bahrâniyya*) (NLFB). Lawson described the two leftist movements as follows (1989: 85):

> Leftist political organizations have been active in Bahrain since the early 1960s [...]. Between 1968 and 1974, local activists associated with the Arab Nationalist Movement merged with cadres in Oman, Qatar, and the Trucial States to form the Popular Front for the Liberation of Oman and the Arab Gulf (PFLOAG).[6] This organization split in 1974, with the Bahraini section reconstituting itself as the Popular Front in Bahrain (PFB). Support for the PFLOAG/PFB has come primarily from disaffected professionals and intellectuals. The other significant clandestine organizations in the country, the National Liberation Front-Bahrain (NLFB) and the local branch of the Ba'th party, differed from the PFLOAG/PFB less in terms of principles [...] than with regard to more practical matters. The NLFB evidenced pronounced communist, even pro-Soviet, leanings during most of the 1970s and drew its primary support from the more radical trade unionists.

Apart from the fact that the Liberation Front slightly predated the PFB and as such played a role in the March 1965 uprising, leading the way into exile, there is little difference in the who and where of the exiled activists. The informants who belonged to these movements were either students, involved in the activities of the unauthorised parties' students union, or members of the labour movement, when they fled Bahrain for the last time. All of the dozen leftists interviewed left the island between 1965 and 1975, whether they feared repression, or they simply went abroad to complete their studies or attend conferences but were not allowed back in again. This was the case of Abdul Rahman al Nu'aimi (1944–2011), who would later become the head of the PFLB: a graduate in mechanical engineering from the American University of Beirut, at that time a hotbed of Arab nationalism, he left Bahrain following a crackdown on workers' movements at the power station in which he was working in 1968.

The first runaways exited via the pre-independent Qatar, or transited through the pre-Saddam Ba'athist Iraq. All without exception settled for some time in Beirut and Syria, as the official policy of the Arab Republic of Syria has been to automatically grant residency to any Arab citizen – all the more so in the case of nationalists and Gulf dissidents. A difference though, appears in their respective trajectories: the members of the Liberation Front benefitted from training or higher education in Moscow, while the militants of the Popular Front shared in the Dhofari revolutionary experiment, in the revolution's schools or martyr's hospitals. They were later offered shelter and passports by the People's Democratic Republic of Yemen. Layla Fakhro (1945–2006) – often seen as the person who inspired the fictional character *Warda*, the eponymous heroin of the novel by Sonallah Ibrahim – embodied this trajectory as she participated in the Dhofari rebellion, through the establishment of schools in 'liberated areas' before retreating to South Yemen. Although each wandering path is unique, the party's transnational network played an essential role in the settlement and employment of its exiles cadres. As a result, the exile's locations of the Bahraini cadres of the leftist movements were limited mostly to Damascus and Aden up until the end of the Cold War. Like Abdul Rahman al Nu'aimi, who headed the PFLB from Damascus where he spent 33 years, the leader of the trade union movement, Mohamed al-Murbati, first elected as trade union representative at Bahrain airport where he was a technician, spent 27 years in Syria.

As the attraction of the socialist project gradually eroded and the trade union movement was being suppressed by the mid-1970s, another form of opposition emerged, coming from the Shiite segment of the population in the context of the Islamist revival that affected the whole region. Just like the leftist movements recruited mainly among educated urbanites, most of them stemming from notable Sunnite families with close links to the traditional ruling circle – the Shiite movements first affected urban Shiites of Persian origin, the *'ajam*, before reaching the Shiite Arab villages or *Baharna* villages.

Waves and Structures of Exile: Shiite Islamist Movements

The politicisation of Shiites followed two lines: that of the Shiraziyyin, theorised in Kerbala, and that of the *Dawa* sympathisers, formed in Najaf (Louër, 2008b). The Shiraziyyin, led by the Iraqi *hujjat-Allah* Hadi al-Mudarissi, opted for a radical and confrontational strategy with the regime, later showing great enthusiasm for, and organising mass mobilisation in support of, the Iranian revolution. In 1979, Hadi al-Mudarissi, who had been deported from Bahrain, founded the Islamic Front for the Liberation of Bahrain (*jabha islamiyya li-tahrir al Bahrayn*) (IFLB) in Tehran, advocating violence as a legitimate means to achieve political change; it established ties with the office of the Islamic Republic designed to export the revolution, under Ayatollah Hussein Ali Muntazeri (Alhasan, 2011).

After the Bahraini government announced that it had foiled a coup d'état supported by a foreign power on 13 December 1981 and attributed it to the IFLB, the IFLB leadership went into exile in Tehran, Damascus or in scattered numbers towards the countries they considered most friendly to asylum seekers: Sweden, Canada and Denmark. Among them, Sheikh Mahfuz, the future head of the reborn Shirazi trend in 2001, spent most of the 1990s calling for the overthrow of the Khalifa from Syria, while young activists like Abdulhadi al-Khawaja, who later founded the Bahrain Centre for Human Rights in 2002, went to Denmark.[7] During the 1980s, the Bahraini authorities continued to deport young men from the island of Muharraq, suspected of sympathy towards the Shiraziyyin, to Iran. If they were accepted in Iran, they were not necessarily welcomed there, especially after Ayatollah Muntazeri, who was Khomeini's heir apparent and head of the liberation movements, fell into disgrace in the eyes of the Supreme Guide. Some of them stayed in legal limbo and recalled being refugees with no access to employment.[8]

The other part of Shiite Islamist exiles originated in the Bahraini branch of *al-Dawa*, founded in 1972; they left Bahrain more gradually in the 1980s. Contrary to the Shiraziyyin, who did not recoil from armed opposition, the *al-Dawa* remained committed to the doctrine of progressive action through legal channels, having provided most of the MPs forming what came to be known as the 'Religious Bloc', including the cleric Sheikh Eissa Qassem, in the short-lived parliament of 1973–1975. However, in the early 1980s a few members headed by Saeed al-Shehabi and Mansur al-Jamri, son of a Shiite religious figures in Bahrain, Sheikh Abdul Amir al-Jamri (1937–2006), refused this line and founded an opposition movement in exile, the London-based Islamic Bahrain Freedom Movement (*Harakat Ahrar al-Bahrayn al-Islamiyya*), known in English as the Bahrain Freedom Movement, which subtly erases its Islamic character.

Finally, close to this tendency but distinct from it as they left Bahrain with no intention to establish political movements abroad, the leaders of spontaneous youth movements that between 1994 and 1998 protested against corruption and deteriorating economic conditions in their rural communities, referred to as 'villages', joined the ranks of political exiles. In January 1995, when Sheikh Ali Salman, the future chairman of the main opposition political society, was deported, the *Ahrar* of London convinced him and his acolytes during a transit in Dubai to go to the British capital, where they had started advocacy activities.

Political Strategies and Activism in Exile

Apart from Saeed al-Shehabi and a few individuals around him who pursued the *Ahrar* movement, all the Bahraini exiles went back home after the general amnesty of 2001, decreed by the Emir Hamad bin Eissa al-Khalifa, two years after his coming to power. The new rule allowed a revival of Bahraini political life to take place, with the resurgence of opposition movements (named political societies as parties are officially forbidden) and the election of a new parliament, both put on hold in 1975 with the dissolution of the first parliament.

When asked about the motives that drove their decision to return, all the former exiles noted that the question made no sense to them, as staying in their country of asylum was an option they could not seriously consider. In the words of Ahmed al-Ubdaydli, brother-in-law of Layla Fakhro, who left his academic position in Cambridge to come back: 'The question of the return should not be asked in terms of it being worthwhile or not: you *have* to go back to your country. Nobody wants to stay abroad.'[9] Some of the leftists even tried an early return at the beginning of the 1990s, hoping to benefit from the détente that resulted globally from the end of the Cold War and regionally from the liberation of Kuwait. But the majority of those who tried their luck were put in custody at the airport and deported to a third destination, the United Arab Emirates, where they would be permitted to start anew if they gave up their political activities. As a matter of fact, in the 2000s, Bahraini activists who lived in the UAE outnumbered those in Syria, as these newcomers joined the activists who had left Bahrain in the 1970s and 1980s for work and safety reasons. Among the 'deportees' were Hasan Madan, exiled for 26 years and later the Secretary-General of the Progressive Democratic Forum, heir to the NLFB, as well as the trade-unionist Hamid Awachi, exile companion of Mohamed Murbati in Damascus who, according to the complaint both made to the International Labour Organization (ILO) 'attempted to return to Bahrain in April 1993, when he was arrested and held for a week before being expelled from the country'.[10]

These trajectories also need to be analysed through the prism of material and economic conditions, which influenced the nature of their return: the trade unionists, who were economically dependent on international solidarity, have had less leeway to arrange the conditions of their return and even, possibly, bargain with the Bahraini authorities. On the other side, those with secure jobs in exile, for instance in academia, have negotiated for themselves better conditions for their return, and usually adopted more pragmatic positions towards the regime.

This will to return by any means, is what essentially differentiates the exile from any other kind of migrant or diaspora, as defined by Hamid Naficy (1999: 3): 'Exile is inexorably tied to homeland and the possibility of return. However the frustrating elusiveness of return makes it magically potent.' This position affects both the relationships that exiles maintain with their home and establish within their host countries: exile is a form of emigration that is *not* accompanied by the objective of or efforts towards assimilation in the host country; in the case of Bahraini *political* exiles, it was mostly geared towards the political fight. The other side of the exile's experience is the potentiality that it offers in terms of formation, creation and knowledge transfer (Renaudet, 2011).

The Bahraini political exiles took their political struggles with them abroad. They transplanted the Bahraini political space into wider national or international political arenas, and by doing so adopted new techniques and discourses of political struggle. From the 1990s, the national and international intersected in the Western-inspired articulation of notions such as democracy and the defence of human rights. This posture coincided with the end of the Cold War and culminated, for the opponents in London, with the Labour Party's idea of 'ethical Foreign Policy'. Two centres of Bahraini exiles emerged as particularly active in awareness raising and lobbying politicians and international organisations: first, the Bahraini Freedom Movement (BFM) in London; and second, the leftist activists in Damascus around Abdul Rahman al Nu'aimi from the Popular Front, or around the exiled Bahrain trade union movement.

In London, the BFM activists released press statements, organised demonstrations and created a very active website, 'Voice of Bahrain' in both Arabic and English, where they posted and still post regular reports on the human rights abuses carried out by the Bahraini government. According to Saeed al-Shehabi,[11] they established 'working relationships' with all the prominent human rights organisations, particularly Amnesty International, and presented their case to the UNHCR, creating strong pressure on the Bahraini government. They also approached British MPs, the most prominent of whom being Lord Eric Avebury, who published his correspondence with the Foreign Office on the human rights situation in Bahrain in 1996 under the title *Bahrain: A Brickwall*. High profile MP George Galloway also defended the cause of Abdul Amir al-Jamri when he was arrested and imprisoned between 1996 and 1999.[12]

The leftists also adopted the articulated and consensual language of human rights, whether they were trade unionists in contact with the ILO or militants who attended left-wing political meetings and toured Europe and the US to gain support for their cause. Mohamed al-Murbati recreated the structure of workers' movements in exile, parallel to the government-established structures inside the country (e.g. the Joint Labour-Management Consultative Committees that elected a General Committee for Bahraini Workers – GCBW): on 15 February 1978, he announced the establishment of the Bahrain Workers' Union following an agreement among Bahrain's trade unions that was concluded under the supervision of the International Confederation of Arab Trade Unions (ICATU), the Kuwait Workers' Union and the Yemen Workers' Union. The Bahrain Workers' Union's organisational programme was announced and registered with ICATU on 11 April 1984; it was affiliated with the ICATU and the Communist-leaning World Federation of Trade Unions (WFTU) in April 1989.

This period created bridges between members of the opposition who came from various ideological backgrounds. The leftists abandoned revolutionary actions and proclaimed their faith in reformism and liberal democracy – conscious that the time of national liberation movements leading to the regime's overthrow was over;[13] so did an important segment of the Shiite Islamists, playing down the idea of implementing Islamic Law to instead emphasise democratic aspirations. All the segments of the opposition united around a rallying cry made of four major claims: the restoration of the 1973 Constitution, the election of a parliament, the lifting of the 1975 state security law and the release of political detainees and return of exiles.

In spite of this united front abroad, the exiles of different segments did not maintain the same kind of links with their home country nor the same mobilisation capacities inside Bahrain during the 1990s. In the words of Laurence Louër:

> Contrary to many exiled movements, including the Islamic Front for the Liberation of Bahrain, the Islamic Bahrain Freedom Movement succeeded in staying legitimate in the eyes of the opponents who remained at home and to coordinate with them. The task was especially difficult because charismatic leaders were among the insiders. The fact that the IBFM [Islamic Bahrain Freedom Movement] enjoyed a family link to the insiders probably facilitated the maintenance of the political tie. (2008b: 203)

This success in the 'difficult task' was due partly to the fact that the very popular clerical figure Sheikh al-Jamri, who was an iconic figure of the 1994–1998 *intifada* was the father of Mansur al-Jamri, founder of the IBFM (*Harakat Ahrar al-Bahrayn al-Islamiyya*). Moreover, the choice made by the leader of the youth uprising, Sheikh Ali Salman, to join London when he was forced out of Bahrain in 1995, illustrates these relations between the inside/outside movements, although not all the exiles joined the IBFM. Yet, the legitimacy of the IBFM would be seriously affected when part of the leadership connected with the popular oppositional figures of the interior came back home, and when the very popular oppositional figures of the interior, like Sheikh Eissa Qassem, distanced themselves from it. Saeed al-Shehabi, cut off from former comrades and having failed to impose his views during the initial process of the Shiite opposition re-foundation, remained isolated in London, advocating, within the IBFM, a line deemed too radical if not adventurist by the rest of the Shiite opposition at the time.

The Return and Reintegration Process

While a few individuals chose to work with the government, notably the IBFM member Dr Majid al-Alawi, who became Bahraini Minister of Labour until the 2011 crisis, the majority of the interviewed former exiles who wished to return to politics, journalism or militancy in trade unions joined the opposition ranks. Their unchanged political commitment is illustrated by the fact that many of them mentioned declined the offer to sign a letter of apology to be allowed back into the country before 2001.[14]

The composition of the opposition 'political societies', that were made legal in 2002, reflects the different opposition movements that emerged since the independence of Bahrain: the Progressive Democratic Forum (*al minbar al demuqrati al taqaddumi*), the National Democratic Action (*al 'Amal al demuqrati al watani*, nicknamed *Wa'ad* – or 'promise' in English) and the Islamic Action (*al 'Amal al Islami* or *Amal* – hope) represent respectively the legacy of the Liberation Front-Bahrain, the Popular Front and the IFLB. A fourth opposition group, al-Wefaq National Islamic society (the Concord) provided a political umbrella for a wide spectrum of Shiite currents convinced of the virtue of reformism.

When invited to reflect on the results of their ostracisation, interviewees made similar remarks, best formulated by Murtadha Badr, a former activist of IFLB, elected in 2002 at the head of Manama municipal council. The exiles, as opposed to the detainees, have 'learnt abroad the importance of the media and public relations; they brought the problems of Bahrain to the world's attention'.[15] In other words, by constituting a wide-reaching network, including international lobbying groups, they placed their struggle at a transnational level. Badr talks about the shift of the political fight from a violent ground on to a peaceful political field. 'We changed and we also obliged the government to change its strategy from violence to politics. Now the government does recognise the political societies, i.e. the reality on the ground.' Acknowledging this reality is also the lesson that many leftists drew from their different experiences abroad, with several confessing that they felt they had returned to a deeply religious society which their foreign ideological beliefs prevented them from fully understanding at the time they left.

The reintegration process was nevertheless full of disappointment. The years of violence and exile have created a profound mutual mistrust. In spite of the 2001 gesture of general amnesty, a symbolic conflict of memory and legitimacy has been going on since the coming to power of the Emir Hamad.

The exiled political leaders came back having built their political legitimacy on the united and uncompromising call for the restoration of the 1973 Constitution. This is the basis on which they had their followers endorse the National Charter by referendum, with a sweeping 98.41 per cent vote in favour of reforms. Yet, the unilateral declaration of the 2002 Constitution that diluted the powers of the elected parliament, by creating an upper chamber, clearly showed the top-down character of the reform process. The opposition consider the 2002 Constitution as a 'gratuitous constitution' (*dustur minha*), not a 'contractual one' (*dustur ta'aqqudi*).[16] It is this discrepancy between the opposition programme and the 2002 Constitution that led to the boycott of the following general elections by three of the four opposition movements, and is also expressed in the recurrent discourse about the 'incompleteness' of the reforms and their lack of legitimate foundations. While often overlooked in the largely sectarian analysis of the deadlock of the post-2001 political system in Bahrain, the form of mutual denial of legitimacy played a significant role in understanding the confrontational politics in Bahrain during the 2000s. For the opposition, the general amnesty and call to return was an acknowledgment of its existence as political opposition; whereas it became soon clear that it was, for the regime, no different from any act of royal benevolence or *makruma* that would not affect its rule.

The strategy of participation adopted by three of the four opposition political societies, first in 2002 by the Democratic Forum and most importantly in 2006 conjointly by al-Wefaq and Wa'ad, did not bridge this gap of trust, nor did it bring a proper reconciliation mechanism for reforming the structure of the Bahraini political system. Its main consequence was to divide further the Shiite opposition: those who denied legitimacy to the Al-Khalifa and judged them definitely unable to reform themselves reverted to tactics of gathering support outside of the country, along with a confrontational approach with the regime on the ground. This is the line advocated by the Movement for Democracy and Liberties, or *al-Haq*, an offshoot composed of disaffected members of the formal opposition societies that opted against participation in the 2006 elections and advocated civil disobedience and street protests in the peripheral dis-enfranchised villages – and later the Islamic Loyalty Current (*al tayyar al wafa' al islami*) headed by Abdul Wahab Hussain.

The leaders of these so-called 'unregistered' societies, advocating a more radical and uncompromising line, were not among the political exiles, whether Hassan Mushaima, Abdul Jalil al-Singace from *al-Haq* or Abdul Wahab Hussain from *Al-Wafa'*. Yet, being a minority within the opposition, they resorted to a strategy of awareness raising *outside of Bahrain*: in August 2006, for instance, Hassan Mushaima and Abdul Jalil al-Singace, who had participated in the 1994–1998 *intifada*, toured the UK and the US to report about the human rights situation in Bahrain (conditions of detention, unfair trials and allegations of torture) as well as to present to the UN Secretariat a petition asking for the establishment of a new Constitution drafted by an elected body. It is worth noting that this non-participatory approach, on the ground, presented commonalities with the uncompromising line of the London-based Bahrain Freedom Movement that had been commanding little audience in Bahrain since the massive return of the exiles in 2001. Both movements joined forces to call for the boycott of the parliamentary elections in 2010, diverting most of the campaign's attention to the repression of their street actions.

In these years there emerged a particular vision of the nation: first developed by the BFM on its website and newsletter, and built in decades-long exile, it portrays the 'homeland' as a country of oppression, torture and detention, and more interestingly, a land under 'the *colonial* rule of the Al-Khalifa' (*isti'amar*) imposed on the indigenous population for two centuries and recently enforced by '*mercenaries*' (*murtazaqa*) – a theme deep-rooted among the *Baharna*, the island's indigenous Shiite population, that reflects among them the widespread feeling of discrimination.

This vision of endogeneity takes place against a double background of migration policies. The most visible one was the phenomenon of political naturalisation that Saleh Bandar brought out in the open in September 2006, in what has become famous as 'the Bandargate'. Bandar revealed a secret plan conceived by some members of the royal family to overrun the Shiite majority by 'Sunnising' the electorate, an objective reached through the naturalisation of foreigners and especially members of security forces from Jordan, Yemen and Pakistan – with which the country has a famous history of military cooperation. According to one opponent who lived during the 1990s riots as a child, animosity towards the police was largely prevalent in this period when children used to call their playing 'hide and seek' *mutadhahirîn/shaghab* (short for *shurta mukafat al shaghab* – anti-riot police) literally demonstrators/police. Second, contrary to most of the GCC countries, tensions between Bahrainis and foreigners have also appeared at the bottom end of the labour market (Louër, 2008a). Yet the moderate opposition worked to diffuse them: while the Crown Prince built his legitimacy on a programme of reforms geared towards an economic revamp that would include a labour reform to make the foreign workforce more expensive and thus less attractive to employers, the opposition 'party' al-Wefaq supported this initiative in parliament and mobilised its forces in the trade unions to defend the rights of foreign workers,[17] thus contributing to the latter's salary rise and cost-levelling with nationals.

The International Front of the 2011 Crisis

When the crisis erupted in February 2011, it soon appeared, with the first victims among demonstrators and even more with the entry of GCC forces into Bahrain, that the security option would ensure the regime's victory in the domestic political fight. Confronted with the violent crackdown under the National Safety Law from March until June 2011, the reformist opposition[18] to the regime mobilised fairly rapidly three different kinds of international resources and networks, corresponding to transnational strategies set up during exile periods: trade union networks, transnational human rights activism and political lobbying and advocacy.

In these three domains, the main narrative has evolved and the rhetoric advocating violent fight or rebellion was overshadowed by a strategy of peaceful and law-abiding protest, in tune with new modes of contentious actions. Yet, the government has been denying the sincerity of this evolution from proclaimed revolutionary or religious-based goals towards Western-style rhetoric of rights. It still considers the opposition as sectarian-motivated, Iran-inspired and animated by a desire for regime change, which clearly delegitimises its political claims in the eyes of its Sunni constituencies as well as in the other GCC countries. It struggles to convince the West and the opinion of its own public, receptive to the opposition's narrative but deaf to its radical past. Conversely, its own repressive line, justified by the idiosyncrasies of 'Iranian perfidious intentions', appears largely as violating the standards of liberal democracy.

Labour Unions

During the 2000 decade under King Hamad, Bahraini trade unionism was revived and restructured under a new 2002 labour law. As a measure implementing a 2002 decision that planned to transform the GCBW into an independent federation, the General Federation of Bahraini Trade Unions (GFBTU) was created in January 2004. This was done in the presence of international and Western-based sister organisations, giving the GFBTU a less radical or Marxist-oriented tinge than the former exiled trade union. Soon it was controlled by the main opposition groups. During the 2011 crisis, the two complaints launched by the GFBTU resulted in very potent pressures on the Bahraini government, following mass dismissals of workers who allegedly missed work to attend the protest.[19]

First, in June 2011, the GFBTU delegates to the International Labour Conference lodged a complaint with the ILO regarding the non-observance by Bahrain of the Discrimination Convention of 1958.[20] Despite lingering questions – backdated wages, employers' contributions to the Social Insurance Organization during the dismissal period, allowances and promotion – the reinstatement of dismissed workers was, according to the GFBTU, one area were the government showed a particularly cooperative attitude.[21] The ILO sent a mission to the Kingdom in March 2102, which resulted in the signature of a tripartite agreement between the Labour Minister, the president of the GFBTU and the vice-president of the Bahraini Chamber of Commerce and Industry (BCCI). The GFBTU attributed to the ILO mission of inquiry the significant increase in the number of reinstated workers and acknowledged its role in preventing reinstated workers from being asked to sign a letter in which they would promise not to engage in political activities, reply to a general strike call or claim backdated salaries.[22]

Second, and maybe more importantly since the US is Bahrain's largest trading partner, the American Federation of Labour and Congress of Industrial Organizations (AFL-CIO), linked through sister organisations to the GFBTU, filed a complaint with the US Department of Labor in April 2011. It alleged that the Government of Bahrain had violated the Labor Chapter of the US–Bahrain 2006 Free Trade Agreement (FTA). As a result, the US Department of Labor issued a report on 20 December 2012 in which it concluded that 'the Government of Bahrain appears to have acted inconsistently with its commitments under Article 15.1 of the FTA', and recommended to engage in 'consultation with the Government of Bahrain'.[23] Although the termination of the FTA was avoided, the threat remains present and the government of Bahrain hired legal help to get advice on the file.[24] It pushed the Bahraini regime to increasingly focus on the region, depend on neighbouring GCC states for help and hope for a rapprochement with the Saudis.

While trade unionism had become a potent aspect of the opposition's leverage outside the country, it was weakened on the domestic scene for being too politicised. Above all a matter of nationals, the GFBTU was considered a fiefdom of the opposition, an assumption illustrated by the call for a general strike on 20 February 2011. To counter this influence, and further extending politics into trade unionism, the government amended the 2002 law to introduce the notion of pluralism within trade unions, which led to the creation of the pro-government Bahrain Labour Union Free Federation on 18 July 2012.

Human Rights Activism and Political Lobbying

Human rights activism is undoubtedly the domain where the fight between the government and opposition has been the most acrimonious, first because it appeals to the public opinion of the main Western allies of the monarchy, and second because those who excel at campaigning for human rights are deemed the most uncompromising among the opposition. Their exile experience has indeed been so influential that al-Wefaq, typically characterised as having a mass following at home, has sought to design a transnational strategy to catch up with the visibility of radical opposition in the West since the beginning of the 2011 crisis. Moreover, the fact that some former exiles had taken the nationality of their host countries complicated the situation by giving them additional ways of protection and leverage for mobilisation abroad: for instance, in what became known as the 'trial of the 13' political opponents, two of those sentenced to life were nationals of European countries, namely Sweden (al Miqdad) and Denmark (Abdulhadi al-Khawaja), that sent diplomatic representatives to the trial sessions. When Abdulhadi al-Khawaja started a hunger strike in 2012, his case was raised and debated in the Danish parliament.

The passing of sectarian political activism to human rights-focused activism is best illustrated by the career of Abdulhadi al-Khawaja. To human rights defenders in the West, Abdulhadi al-Khawaja is the smiling icon of the peaceful fight against oppression, symbolised by his three-month hunger strike in 2012; in the eyes of the government of Bahrain, he remains a fierce sectarian political opponent seeking its fall. Abdulhadi al-Khawaja spent more than 20 years in exile.[25] A student in London in 1979, he joined the *Shirazi* IFLB before settling in Damascus, where he founded the Committee to Defend Political Prisoners in Bahrain (CDPPB) in 1983 aimed at denouncing arbitrary detentions, torture, unfair trial (including that of the 73 involved in the alleged coup), nationality stripping and forced deportation. In 1989, he left for Denmark, where he was granted asylum and then nationality in 1992, and where he established the Bahrain Human Rights Organisation in Copenhagen. Affiliated with the Geneva-based World Organisation Against Torture (OMCT) it actively denounced arbitrary arrests permitted under the 1974 State Security Law. At his return from exile in 2001, benefitting from the general amnesty decreed by the new Emir Hamad, he founded the Bahrain Centre for Human Rights (BCHR).

As seen above, the 1990s was the decade of BFM rapprochement with human rights NGOs, the UN and British parliamentarians and of the reframing of the political fight into a democratic rhetoric (Louër, 2008b: 203). Abdulhadi al-Khawaja acquired all the experience and professional track record of a human rights defender, so that when he returned to Bahrain he became a pivotal figure in the international human rights network in the region: in 2003, he was part of the fact-finding mission to Iraq for Amnesty International, who entrusted him with the task of developing its programme in the Middle East. Throughout the 2000s, his reputation became more and more established and his work acknowledged.[26]

It is not clear when and why the BCHR adopted a clear line of zero accommodation with the autocratic regime, yet on the spectrum of Bahraini politics it is widely regarded as uncompromising. Katja Niethammer (2006: 20) describes the radicalisation of the BCHR in the following terms:

> To fish for the more radical (or less patient) fringes of the Shiite movement is, therefore, an obvious choice. [...] Observably the more confrontational approach taken by the BCHR is more attractive to the youth than the elders. The BCHR and its allies address two main audiences and hence employ two different strategies: Pro-democracy rhetoric is directed mainly to US and UK audiences. The Bahraini audience on the other hand is addressed in sectarian terms.

The crisis, and its Egypt-styled mass mobilisation, blurred the lines between the radical and reformist lines of the opposition's minority and majority: in the face of brutal repression the pragmatists of the majority al-Wefaq emphasised the denouncing of human rights abuses; conversely the Western NGOs and activists largely circulated the people's desire for radical change. Their presence also prevented the situation from further deteriorating as the government placed restrictions on media coverage since the passing of the National Safety Law. As a result, the political fight was transferred on to the field of human rights defence, with high-visibility measures like the King-endorsed initiative of calling for an independent commission of inquiry, the creation of multiple Bahraini human rights organisations stemming from the newly politically aware Sunnis that would break the monopoly of the BCHR,[27] and the establishment, dictated by a will to respect 'pluralism', of a second, more government-leaning, trade union federation, the Bahrain Labour Union Free Federation (BLUFF).

Yet, in this battle waged at the level of transnational activist organisations, the radical exiled opposition started with a clear advantage because it used its experience of physically staying in a Western country to credibly appropriate its signifiers: in her 'letter from a Bahraini prison' published on 24 March 2013 on the *Jadaliyya* website, Zeyneb Al-Khawaja, the daughter of Abdulhadi born in Syria and raised in Denmark, masterfully evokes the figure of Martin Luther King Jr, immediately casting her battle into the framework of the civil rights movement, so powerfully evocative in the US:

> I replied: 'I am glad you weren't with Rosa Parks on that bus, to tell the woman who sparked the civil rights movement, 'that it was all for nothing but a chair.' When the doctor started asking about the African American movement, I offered my Martin Luther King book.[28]

Experiences such as these indicate that perhaps the experience of exile had eventually turned against those who imposed it in the first place. Bahrain Watch, a digital platform designed to monitor government actions, is another example of a new type of technique in tune with notions of professionalism and efficacy. Based on careful research, and liaising with domestic organised groups, the online organisation managed to persuade a South Korean company to cancel its shipment of teargas to Bahrain in 2013.

Moreover, while the pragmatic al-Wefaq has mainly focused on the domestic situation in the decade following the 2001, it started, pushed by its radical competition, to make its way through the maze of US and European Union advocacy channels, confronting the government narrative with an increasingly radical response. While some al-Wefaq members settled in Beirut, two MPs who had resigned from al-Wefaq left during the National Safety Law in a preventive move of self-imposed exile and eventually took up advocacy: Matar Matar, beaten in custody, fled to Washington, DC[29] while Ali-Alaswad moved to the British capital. The long-tested practice of nationality stripping added the Fairuz brothers, both former MPs, to the London community of exiles in November 2012. As a matter of fact, threats to revoke citizenship, or rumours thereof, have been commonly used to try and intimidate opposition forces, starting with the al-Wefaq mentor, Eissa Qassem.

While the former leftists were still connected with European Communist parties, al-Wefaq attempted to gather support from influential political figures in national parliamentary institutions and the European Parliament, as well as senior civil servants and decision makers. While they are not received openly, all foreign stakeholders in the Bahraini conflict make sure they are in close touch with them.

Finally, this strategic move to seek support among the regime's core allies and security providers, the US, the UK, France and Germany, brought to the fore the contradiction that exists in both the government and the opposition camp regarding their relations with the dominant powers. On both sides, the conflict is cast in anti-imperialist terms via a sectarian twist: among the hardliners of the royal family, the links between the opposition and the Western powers is seen as a Western conspiracy against them, and necessitates a strengthening of the Gulf institutions to ensure its own security. Among the radical opposition seeking a regime change, the Khalifa ruling family is dependent upon Saudi Arabia's Al-Saud dynasty, which is backed militarily by the US.

Conclusion

The story of the way that Bahraini authorities dealt with their opposition is one of hoisting themselves with their own petard: having forcibly exiled their opposition and particularly the most radical Shiites, who eventually found their way into Western countries, the latter came back with the same political fight but formulated in a manner emphasising the discourse of rights, which found sympathy among Western public opinion. While the denial of entry (through the refusal to renew passports and any kind of national affiliation to Bahrain) may have worked as a way to keep the opposition at a distance, the exiles' ability to obtain Western nationality increased their ability to leverage diplomatic pressure on the Bahraini government.

When the 2011 crisis erupted and repression unfolded, the activists who had maintained transnational links could activate important networks that enabled them to push forwards. Though being completely overlooked in the debate and analyses of the political crisis in Bahrain, the legacy of the opposition's ostracisation helps us to understand, along with the sectarian divide, the internationalisation of the conflict.

Notes

1. Bahraini workers did come to work in Saudi oilfields in the 1950s and early 1960s (in Aramco and for the Trans-Arabian Pipeline). Others made their way to the UAE in the early 1960s to work as teachers, in the oilfields or in

government administration, where they were joined by scores of activists in the 1970s and 1980s who sought work and safety.

2. Author's translation.

3. The material of the first part is drawn from a paper entitled 'The Return of the Bahraini Exiles (2001–2006): The Impact of the Ostracization Experience on the Opposition's Restructuring', presented on 5 July 2008 at the BRISMES Annual Conference, University of Leeds. The author wishes to thank all who commented on it.

4. The list of the political deportations by the British political advisor includes, in addition to that of the *dawasir* tribe after an attack on the locality of A'ali in 1920, that of al-Zayani and bin Lahej in 1923, Khalaf al-Asfoor in 1928 and Sa'ad al Shamlan in 1938.

    According to Marc Owen Jones (2013), the British also punished exiled members of the royal family, but these latter were better equipped to escape the punishment: when Khalid bin Ali Al Khalifa and his sons Ali and Salman were found guilty of instigating and carrying out two attacks on the village of Sitra in 1923, Khalid bin Ali 'was fined and his property confiscated. [...] his sons Ali and Salman were exiled to India. However, before they could be deported, Ali and Salman escaped to mainland Arabia. They then returned to Bahrain and carried out a revenge attack on the village of Sitra, shooting nine people. There were thirty-four witnesses to the shooting, and Sheikh Hamad reluctantly sentenced the perpetrators to exile, on pain of death if they returned. Despite the apparent finality of this sentencing, Ali bin Khalid returned to Bahrain about six months later without British permission.'

5. By comparison, Kuwait, endowed with a Constitution in 1962, neutralised its Arab nationalist opposition by rigging the 1967 elections and later supporting loyalist candidates among Islamist and tribal ranks. Oman defeated the Dhofar rebellion militarily, as it had done with the Jabal Akhdar rebellion supporting the Imamate a decade earlier.

6. The nebulous movement was first known as the Popular Front for the Liberation of the Occupied Arabian Gulf, whose stated aim was to fight British imperialism and overthrow its local 'stooges'. Originally it united regional forces to support the Dhofar rebellion in the western part of Oman (hence the renaming Popular Front for the Liberation of Oman and the Arab Gulf), but as the Dhofar rebellion failed it was divided between the Bahraini and Omani branches in 1974. Al-Nu'aimi became the Secretary-General of the Popular Front for the Liberation of Bahrain (Beaugrand, 2011).

7. During a trial held behind closed doors in May 1982, 73 defendants were found guilty of planning to overthrow the regime by force and sentenced to minimum jail terms of 15 years; many others, particularly students, suspected of supporting the dissidence were also arrested. Interview with the lawyer Abdullah al-Shamlawi, Manama, 10 July 2012.

8. Interview with a *bidun*, Muharraq, January 2007.

9. Interview with the author, Bahrain, Eissa Town, March 2008.

10. Case No 1949 (Bahrain) – Complaint date: 7 September 1997. The Bahrain Workers' Union and the World Federation of Trade Unions (WFTU). Accessible on ILO website at: www.ilo.org/dyn/normlex/en/f?p=1000:

50001:0::NO::P50001_COMPLAINT_FILE_ID:2896505 (accessed August 2014).

Since its creation, Bahraini trade unions resorted six times to the ILO complaints procedure, three being filed by the exiled Bahrain Workers' Union (one before 1965 by the Arab Workers of Bahrain, one by the ICATU and the latest one by the General Federation of Bahraini Trade Unions, created in 2002): www.ilo.org/dyn/normlex/en/f?p=1000:20060:0:FIND:NO:20060:P20060_COUNTRY_ID,P20060_COMPLAINT_STATU_ID:103396,1495812 (accessed August 2014).

11. Interview, London, May 2008.

12. Phil Davison, Obituary, 'Sheikh Abdul Amir al-Jamri: Leader of Bahrain's Shia Majority, Jailed for His Civil Rights Campaigning', *Guardian*, 20 December 2006.

13. In a January 2008 interview, one of them deplored that they had been on the losing side of history (*al khassirun*).

14. According to various informants who tried to return to Bahrain *before* the royal amnesty of 2001, admission to the country would depend on their agreeing to sign a statement of apology and pledge not to get involved again in opposition politics.

15. Interview, Manama, March 2008.

16. Interview with a founding member of *Wa'ad*, Manama, June 2012.

17. Many rights activists will defend the record of Nabil Rajab, the head of the Bahrain Human Rights Centre, attacked for his alleged selective (and Shiite-biased) understanding of human rights, by stressing his involvement in defending foreign workers' human rights. Interview with a Bahraini activist, 3 March 2014.

18. *Islahi*, as opposed to *isqati*. This distinction, which is a structural one among the Bahraini opposition, also reflects the divergence of slogans between 'the people want the reform of the regime' and 'the people want the fall of the regime' (*al sha'ab yurid islah/isqat al nitham*).

19. According to the King-appointed Bahrain Independent Commission of Inquiry (BICI), 4,507 employees were dismissed among which 2,462 were private sector employees and 1,945 working in the public sector. BICI Report: 397, www.bici.org.bh/BICIreportEN.pdf (accessed August 2014).

20. See the Report of the Officers of the Governing Body, ILO, 313th Session, Geneva, 27 March 2012, www.ilo.org/wcmsp5/groups/public/---ed_norm/---relconf/documents/meetingdocument/wcms_176474.pdf (accessed August 2014).

21. Interview with Karim Radhi, the Assistant Secretary-General, GFBTU, Manama, 27 March 2012.

22. The file was closed with the ILO in March 2014.

23. www.dol.gov/ilab/reports/pdf/20121220Bahrain.pdf (p. ii).

24. Farah Halime, 'Bahrain Hires US Lawyers to Fight Complaints Over Sacked Workers', *The National,* 27 June 2011.

25. See the Bahrain Centre for Human Rights website, www.bahrainrights.org/en/node/1438 (accessed August 2014).

26. In 2004, al-Khawaja was granted the membership of the Advisory Board of the Damascus Center for Human Rights Studies. Since 2007, he has been a member of the International Advisory Network of the Business and Human Rights Resource Centre, headed by former Irish President Mary Robinson, former UN High Commissioner for Human Rights. From 2008 to 2011, al-Khawaja was the Middle East and North Africa Protection Coordinator with Front Line Defenders. His human rights campaigning activities were rewarded at the International Conference of Human Rights Defenders in Dublin and the Arab Program for Human Rights Defenders made him its 'Regional Activist' in 2005. See www.bahrainhrd.org/abdulhadi.html for more information (accessed August 2014).

27. These include Manama Centre for Human Rights, launched in March 2012; Bahrain Civil Network for Human Rights; the Gulf European Centre for Human Rights; Forum of Civil Society Institutions in Arabian Gulf States; Bahrain Human Rights Monitor; Society of Bahraini Human Rights Activists. The members of the National Institution for Human Rights created by a royal decree of November 2009 were appointed in 2013.

28. 'Zainab Al-Khawaja: Letter From A Bahraini Prison', *Jadaliyya*, www.jadaliyya. com/pages/index/10808/zainab-al-khawaja_letter-from-a-bahraini-prison- (accessed August 2014). Zeyneb Al-Khawja wrote the letter to explain the reasons why she went on hunger strike.

29. Matar Matar attended the Tom Lantos Human Rights Commission Hearing on 'Implementation of the Bahrain Independent Commission of Inquiry Report' on 1 August 2012, http://tlhrc.house.gov/docs/transcripts/2012_08_01_ Bahrain/JPM%20Opening%20Remarks.pdf

Part IV

Conclusion

10

Migrant Rights in the Gulf: Charting the Way Forward

Adam Hanieh

Following the December 2010 confirmation of Qatar as the host country for the 2022 World Cup, an unprecedented number of new construction projects were announced in preparation for the tournament. Estimated costs of these projects ran to US$100 billion over just five years (*Reuters*, 2010), and included the construction and renovation of twelve stadiums, new highways and road systems, a causeway linking Bahrain and Qatar, a high-speed rail network and 55,000 hotel rooms (FIFA, nd: 10–37). These projects were part of a much larger national development plan, for which the government projected to spend over US$200 billion on construction projects alone by 2022 (Deloitte, 2013). This vast expansion of the country's infrastructure would depend upon hundreds of thousands of migrant workers joining the labour force – with estimates of the necessary number of new workers ranging from 500,000 to one million (Kelso, 2011).

These expectations of a massive population boom were quickly confirmed, with the number of residents growing at a staggering 10.5 per cent between August 2012 and August 2013, an average of 20 new people each hour, largely due to the influx of migrant workers into the country (QSAPSA, nd). At the same time, reports began to appear of rampant abuse throughout the country's construction sites, despite promises by the Qatari government that it would comply with international labour standards in the recruitment and employment of these workers. Human Rights Watch claimed that the government's pledges around labour standards were 'unclear' and failed 'to include the specific, concrete, and public commitments that Human Rights Watch has sought to ensure respect for the rights of workers and an avoidance of the abusive conditions so many have faced in Qatar' (HRW, 2012: 36). Amnesty International wrote that 'abuses against migrant workers in the construction sector in Qatar are grim' (Amnesty International, 2013: 6) and that if steps to address these are 'not taken as a matter of urgency, the construction for the World Cup is likely to entail considerable human suffering' (2013: 11). The Building and Wood Workers International, following a visit to Qatar in October 2013, decried 'the climate of fear' in the country and argued that the principles embodied in the 'Workers' Charter' – a document written by the Qatar 2022 Supreme Committee, the body in charge of the FIFA preparations – were 'not well defined, do not refer to internationally recognized standards, and do not include workers' rights or trade union rights' (BWI, 2013).

These concerns culminated in a powerful series of investigative articles published by the *Guardian* Newspaper in early 2014, which claimed that more than 400 Nepalese migrant workers had died in the Qatari construction sector since the World Cup bid was won (Doward, 2014). An additional 700 Indian migrant workers had died over the same time period – equivalent to 20 workers a month (Parry, 2014). The death rate was described by one Human Rights Watch analyst as 'horrendous' and providing 'an indication of an unfolding tragedy in Qatar' (BBC, 2014). The intimate connection between exploitation of migrant workers and the expansion of the country's infrastructure base was explicitly confirmed by the IMF, which acknowledged that the conditions of work had made 'global headlines' and that any change in the availability or cost of this labour 'would hinder growth, since the success of Qatar's current development model depends importantly on the ability to rapidly hire expatriate workers' (IMF, 2014).

As the death toll on Qatar's construction sites reached these alarming levels, migrant workers in the rest of the Gulf also saw a sharp deterioration in their living and working conditions. In Saudi Arabia, for example, over 250,000 migrants were deported from the country between November 2013 and January 2014, equivalent to nearly 3 per cent of the country's migrant workforce (*Guardian*, 2014). Clashes in the wake of the deportations left at least three people dead, with tens of thousands of migrants placed in detention camps described by Human Rights Watch as 'makeshift centers without adequate food, shelter, or medical attention' (HRW, 2013). Media and human rights organisations also noted rising levels of abuse against migrant workers in other parts of the GCC, reflected in statistics around psychological trauma and worker suicides. During the first quarter of 2012, Indian workers in Oman were killing themselves at the rate of one every six days (*The Times of India*, 2012). In Bahrain, media reports in early

September 2013 indicated that a migrant worker had committed suicide every four days since the beginning of the year (Khalaf, 2013). A study by the Community Medicine Department of the United Arab Emirates University found that at least one-quarter of migrant workers were clinically depressed and that 2.5 per cent had attempted to take their own lives (Al-Maskari et al., 2011). In January 2014, a Nepalese women's organisation reported that over 80 per cent of their clients who had returned from the Gulf had mental disorders and that 60 per cent required serious psychological assistance (Subedi, 2014).

These worsening trends have sharply posed the question of what can be done to improve living and working standards for migrants in the Gulf. As Mohammed Dito emphasised in Chapter 4, a foundational aspect to migrant exclusion is the *kafala* system – a complex set of bureaucratic pathways that acts to bind workers to particular employers, permits no job mobility and frequently sees workers taking on large personal debts in order to obtain employment. Moreover, labour rights are tightly circumscribed, and none of the GCC states (with the exception of Kuwait) have ratified two key ILO conventions governing the right to freely form and join worker organisations, to organise and to collective bargaining (Conventions No. 87 and 98). Migrant workers are banned from forming unions, and participation in political activities in all GCC states remains heavily restricted.[1] Because residency is tied to a work contract, any protests can be met with termination of employment and immediate deportation. Domestic workers, in particular, face enormous barriers to any collective action – unlike other workers, they are not covered under GCC labour laws, and their widespread isolation in private houses means that it is much more difficult to connect with their compatriots.

Given this lack of basic legal protections, international NGOs and labour organisations have typically placed their advocacy efforts on encouraging governments in the region to pass legislation aimed at improving work conditions for migrants. A key focus of these efforts has been the reform of the *kafala* system – notably ending the practice of charging fees for workers recruited through agencies, providing clear and understandable contractual rights, allowing workers to change jobs without employer consent, prohibiting the confiscation of passports, eliminating exit visa requirements and improving workplace inspections around health and safety. Along these lines, campaigns in labour-sending countries – particularly those waged by international labour bodies – have targeted the largely unregulated industry of labour recruitment agencies that subcontract to the Gulf. In

December 2013, for example, the ILO and the EU launched a €2.4 million project, entitled Promoting Effective Governance of Labour Migration from South Asia, which aimed at reducing abuses by recruitment agencies and providing more reliable information to prospective workers from India, Nepal and Pakistan about working conditions in the Gulf (ILO, 2013b).

Efforts such as these have been useful in raising international awareness about the conditions of migrant workers in the Gulf. The growing campaign around Qatar's treatment of migrant workers indicates that these campaigns do have a real impact, helping to draw together public support and placing pressure on both sending and receiving countries to address the abuses associated with migrant work in the Gulf. At the same time, however, it is important not to overlook the various struggles and actions of Gulf migrant workers themselves. As John Chalcraft has argued, much of the literature on the Gulf has ignored this agency, preferring instead an approach that makes 'the profoundly unequal and consequential control over *persons*, their livelihoods and social and political relations, appear merely as the neutral and technocratic management of *things* ... They have done little to illuminate, except as primary sources, the political role played by migrants in the changing fate of monarchies in the Gulf' (Chalcraft, 2010: 2). The dominant approach tends to discount – or in many cases simply ignore – the fact that migrant workers in the Gulf continue to organise, protest and engage in a variety of different strategies of resistance, despite the very substantial barriers to such actions described throughout this book.

There are increasing signs that such struggles are gaining traction. Throughout 2013, there were several examples of migrant labour disputes in the GCC, belying the claim that migrant workers can be simply reduced to a dormant and passive body of labour. These included a strike by Nepalese workers in Sitra, Bahrain, following a death by suicide of a 22-year-old worker on 23 August (Migrant Rights, 2013), a strike of up to 10,000 South Asian workers in Oman in March, in protest of poor safety conditions and the death of an Indian worker on the job (Al-Akhbar, 2013a), and a demonstration in October by over 1,300 Ethiopian nurses in Kuwait, who were challenging non-payment of salaries and racial discrimination in wage levels (Migrant Rights, 2014).

Perhaps the most significant protest action – in terms of size, breadth and strategic location – was a four-day strike in May 2013 of thousands of workers employed by Arabtec, a major UAE construction company with close links to the Emirati ruling family and part of the consortium that built Dubai's Burj Khalifa, the world's tallest building. The striking workers were demanding that their US$95 dollar monthly food allowance be paid as part of their wages rather than provided in-kind through the company (construction workers in the UAE typically earn a monthly salary of no more than US$245, and often much less) (Al-Akhbar, 2013b). The strike was particularly noteworthy because it involved workers from different building sites spread across Dubai and Abu Dhabi, and thus illustrated a coordinated campaign of workers – a rarity in the Gulf where protests tend to be confined to specific worksites.

The response of both the company and UAE authorities to the strike was predictable, with a police spokesperson commenting to a local newspaper that UAE law 'does not allow [workers] to have a leader or make a strike' and an Arabtec representative claiming that 'unwarranted stoppage has been instigated by a minority group who will be held accountable for their actions' (Kannan, 2013). The reality behind these threats was soon made clear, with 43 workers given deportation orders and forced to return home as a result of their involvement in the strike. The removal of these perceived 'trouble makers' in the wake of the strike was a powerful reminder of the social control enabled by the transient nature of labour in the Gulf. Precisely because of the connection between a fixed work contract and residency rights, codified in the *kafala* system, and the lack of any labour rights or practicable route to citizenship, the strike illustrated once again the vastly unequal power relations between employers and migrant workforces in the Gulf.[2]

Nonetheless, despite these deportations and the repression associated with the strike, the workers' action appeared to have a significant impact, with the company agreeing in September 2013 to raise wages by up to 20 per cent for its 36,000-strong UAE workforce (*Construction Week Online*, 2013). The strike confirmed that labour mobilisations could have an effect on employer practices in the Gulf, particularly if these actions are coordinated over multiple workplaces. As Rima Kalush, an Arab migrant rights activist, noted in regards to the strike:

> Both governments and employers (a distinction difficult to make in some cases) feel empowered to subject migrant workers to low wages and poor conditions because they are easily replaceable. But this 'advantage' has occasionally been overcome when a large number of migrant workers strike on large-scale project; delays in construction or the provision of

services cannot always be tolerated, and in some cases strikes end with some concessions to migrants' demands. Strikes are really the only form of collective bargaining migrants have at their disposal as they are not allowed to unionize. (Chen, 2013)

Transnational Organising and International Solidarity

The question of 'what can be done' also needs to take into consideration the fact that the Gulf's working classes are highly mobile subjects spread over numerous borders. This fluid and transient existence means that class formations in the Gulf need to be viewed outside of a methodologically nationalist frame – implicating millions of past, present and future workers across neighbouring countries. This transnational nature of class points to the potential impact that cross-border labour organising may have on challenging the highly unequal power relations in the Gulf. While these transnational actions remain weak and underdeveloped, there are some indications that regional and international organisations are beginning to place more emphasis on linking migrant work forces in the Gulf.

In South Asia, for example, several NGOS have launched campaigns to pressure their governments to take a more proactive stance towards their citizens in the Gulf. These NGOs include the Nepalese Pravasi Nepali Coordination Committee (PNCC), which has played an important role in documenting and campaigning around recent Nepalese worker deaths in Qatar, and Lawyers for Human Rights International (LFHRI), an organisation based in India that has supported Indian migrants imprisoned and tortured in the UAE. In the Philippines, Migrante International, an alliance of Filipino migrant workers, has played a key part in advocacy for the conditions of Filipino migrants across the world. Migrante now has an office in the UAE, from where they provide legal advice, shelter, counselling and other services for victims of employer abuse, particularly domestic workers.

One of the key thrusts of Migrante's campaigning work is its emphasis on challenging the structural causes of underdevelopment in the Philippines that drives migration in the first place, and forces migrants into the vulnerable and highly exploitable situations such as those found in the Gulf. As the organisation noted in a statement released on the occasion of the 2013 UN High Level Dialogue on Migration and Development, 'Filipinos are pushed into migration due to unemployment, declining wages and increasing costs of basic services from privatisation and public-private partnerships (PPPs) … The lack of development of the [Philippine] economy, resulting in high unemployment and low wages, means that Filipinos are trapped in cycles of migration generation after generation with no long term solution' (Ellao, 2013). Migrante's approach highlights the importance of addressing the root causes of migration within any cross-border campaign to improve the conditions of workers in the Gulf; an orientation which US immigrant rights activist David Bacon has called 'the right to stay home' (2013).

Running against the grain of international lobbying efforts that view foreign embassies and source-country governments as allies of migrant workers, Migrante places a sharp emphasis on the complicity of the Philippines government in the mistreatment of migrant workers in the Gulf. Migrant work is an important source of government revenue (from the fees charged to overseas workers) and also helps to divert domestic attention from the poor living standards in the Philippines itself (Ellao, 2013). As a result, Migrante believes that the government has sought agreements with many countries in order to 'facilitate the sending of more OFWs [overseas foreign workers] as cheap labour' and shows little interest in standing up for improved working conditions that may imperil these labour flows (Ellao, 2013). This critical standpoint is also borne out in the case of the Indian government, which recently accused Indian women workers in Saudi Arabia of 'nefarious attempts' to organise a strike that would 'spoil the goodwill that exists for Indians in Saudi Arabia' (*The Economic Times*, 2014).

Much like labour, capital accumulation in the Gulf is also highly transnational, meaning that international solidarity that confronts corporate complicity can present a potentially powerful tool in tackling the exploitation of migrants. A recent example of this is the innovative campaign launched by prominent artists in solidarity with workers at Abu Dhabi's Saadiyat Island (Island of Happiness), a massive development project projected to cost US$27 billion that involves the construction of museums, hotels, resorts, golf courses and housing for more than 125,000 residents. The artists' campaign targets global art institutions collaborating with projects on the Island, including the Guggenheim Abu Dhabi, Louvre Abu Dhabi and the Sheikh Zayed National Museum (built in collaboration with the British Museum). As part of their actions, the artists have staged demonstrations at the Guggenheim New York and launched Gulf Labor: 52 Weeks in October 2013, a campaign that features a specially created piece of art, or text of a related action or event, by a different contributor each week for the coming year.[3] The campaign has prompted the Guggenheim to respond publically to the allegations of poor worker conditions, and led the Abu Dhabi Tourism Development and Investment Company (TDIC) – the state-run master developer for all of Saadiyat's major construction projects – to publish a new Employment Practices Policy that promised to prohibit employers from withholding wages and passports, outlaw the collection of recruitment fees and other relocation costs and improve the housing conditions for workers. TDIC also committed to hiring the accounting firm PricewaterhouseCoopers to conduct annual compliance audits of working conditions on Saadiyat.[4]

One of the problems, however, faced by all of these campaigns – from Qatar's World Cup to the Guggenheim in Abu Dhabi – is the weakness of regional Arab labour and social movements. As this book has noted, the structuring of migrant labour in the Gulf is not solely a question that affects migrant workers and the ordinary citizens of these states, but one that impacts the entire region. Despite this fact, there have been very few Arab voices raised against workers' conditions in the Gulf. Cross-regional solidarity – based around the *kafala* system, the right to organise, labour conditions and, ultimately, extension of the rights of citizenship – could help dramatically transform the situation faced by workers in the Gulf. Migrant workers need to be seen as allies and an integral part of the Arab world – not disposable bodies that can be sent home when no longer needed.

Conclusion

Campaigns such as these help to illuminate a key conclusion of this book – the necessity of placing migrant labour at the core of any understanding of the political structures of the Gulf States. The heavily racialised treatment of migrant workers, and the abuses associated with this, are not simply the outcome of poor legislative oversight or unscrupulous labour recruitment agencies. Rather, as Abdulhadi Khalaf (Chapter 2) and Omar AlShehabi (Chapter 5) have pointed out, the exploitation of migrant workers lies at the heart of how ruling classes in the Gulf are able to reproduce themselves and the corresponding hierarchies of Gulf society – it is essential to understanding 'what Gulf ruling families do when they rule'. The temporary and precarious conditions of migrant work not only underpins the Disneyland of fantastic mega-projects that dot the skyline of all Gulf cities, but also acts to divide and stratify Gulf citizenry in particular ways. It is for this reason that the exploitation of migrant work is structurally foundational to how Gulf rulers maintain and extend their power over society.

In examining this structural imperative of transient labour to the Gulf's political physiognomy, this book has emphasised that conceptions of migration to the Gulf need to incorporate not just the low-waged (largely male) workers on the region's construction sites, but other, often rather less-discussed, types of movement – from the high-skilled Western professionals in the 'expat' camps discussed by Neha Vora (Chapter 8), to the 'migrant mercenaries' analysed by K. T. Abdulhameed (Chapter 7) or the return of political exiles surveyed by Claire Beaugrand (Chapter 9). Each of these migration patterns – by no means an exclusive list – help to reinforce, shape and contest the nature of power structures in the Gulf. Moreover, as Omar AlShehabi has highlighted (Chapter 5), these forms of migration hold important implications for how urban life is experienced in the Gulf. Indeed, in many ways Qatar's preparation for the World Cup strikingly underscores the observations made by AlShehabi. Long after the spectacle has passed, Qatar's city space will have been dramatically reconfigured in a vision of 'rootless urbanism', one in which transient, temporary populations are invited to visit, consume and enjoy – but denied the ability to stay.

Key to understanding these social, political and economic implications of all forms of migration is the way that migrants are both governed and spoken about. This includes, of course, the *kafala* system discussed in some detail by Mohammed Dito (Chapter 4) and explored in virtually all the chapters of this book. But it also means, as Neha Vora (Chapter 8) and Michelle Buckley (Chapter 6) have drawn out, an appreciation of the governance and language surrounding migration that acts to construct particular subjectivities of the migrant's lived experience – including those of gender, race and class. Understanding the interplay of these is essential to both building solidarity with migrants themselves and, crucially, contesting the prevalent discourse about their presence in the Gulf – notably the 'sex', 'safety', and 'security' trifecta highlighted by Buckley.

Against the prevailing view of the Gulf that tends to diminish or downplay questions of labour and migration, the chapters in this book have attempted to point to some new questions and ways of thinking about these issues, linked through a variety of cross-disciplinary perspectives and case studies. There remains a great deal more that needs to be said about the intersection of labour, migration and citizenship in the Gulf – but the position of migrant workers needs to be placed front and central to our understanding of the political and economic dynamics of the region.

Notes

1.   In Bahrain and Kuwait, migrant workers are permitted to join established unions (but not to form their own). In practice, however, there is a great deal of reluctance from these unions to recruit or ally with migrant workers.
2.   Indeed, these deportations mirrored a similar strike in January 2011, also involving Arabtec, in which 70 workers were deported from the UAE.
3.   See the organisation's website at http://gulflabor.org/
4.   Although there appears to have been some improvement in conditions since these commitments, significant problems do remain. Indeed, the most recent PricewaterhouseCoopers compliance report in December 2013 noted that the number of workers who said they had paid recruitment fees to agents increased from 75 per cent in 2012 to 86 per cent in 2013, and the number who had been forced to pay their own relocation costs had increased to 92 per cent from 77 per cent over the same time period. Moreover, concerns have been raised by Gulf Labor that the actions of TDIC appear to be aimed at presenting a facade of compliance with international standards, without challenging underlying patterns.

Biographies

K. T. Abdulhameed is a writer and freelance researcher from Bahrain.

Omar AlShehabi is a Bahraini Assistant Professor in Economics at the Gulf University for Science and Technology, and the director of the Gulf Centre for Development Policies in Kuwait. He is a former lecturer at University College, Oxford, and has previously worked at the World Bank, the IMF and McKinsey and Co. His first manuscript, 'Uprooting', was published in Arabic in 2012.

Claire Beaugrand joined the Institut Français du Proche-Orient (Ifpo) in June 2013 after working as a Senior Gulf Analyst at the International Crisis Group (ICG). She is one of the core researchers of the European Research Council-funded WAFAW project (When Authoritarianism Fails in the Arab World), coordinating the program on 'the role of diasporas, migrants and exiles in the Arab revolutions and transitions period'. Her PhD thesis was written at the London School of Economics and investigated the emergence and persistence of statelessness in Kuwait.

Michelle Buckley is an Assistant Professor of Human Geography at the University of Toronto, Scarborough. She is a former Lecturer at Mansfield College, Oxford, and at the School of Environment and Technology at the University of Brighton. Her research is broadly concerned with uncovering the transnational labour geographies that sustain contemporary urbanisation in the Gulf region and beyond.

Mohammed Dito is a labour market researcher. His main research interests are migration, youth employment and labour market governance. From 1998 to 2005 he was Head of the Employment Service Bureau at the Bahrain Ministry of Labour, and currently acts as a Policy Advisor to the Bahrain Labour Market Regulatory Authority.

Adam Hanieh is a Senior Lecturer in Development Studies at SOAS, University of London. He is author of *Capitalism and Class in the Gulf Arab States* (Palgrave-Macmillan, 2011) and *Lineages of Revolt: Issues of Contemporary Capitalism in the Middle East* (Haymarket Books, 2013).

Abdulhadi Khalaf is Professor Emeritus of Sociology. Until his retirement in 2012, he was Senior Researcher at the Centre for Middle East Studies, Lund University, Sweden. His academic and political involvement in Gulf affairs is reflected in his publications and frequent political commentaries published regularly in Arab periodicals.

Neha Vora is an Assistant Professor of Anthropology at Lafayette College in the United States. Her research interests include migration and diaspora, urban development, citizenship and belonging, and race and gender, particularly within the Gulf Arab States. Her first book, *Impossible Citizens: Dubai's Indian Diaspora*, was published in 2013 by Duke University Press. She is currently working on a project that investigates the impacts of knowledge-economy transformation and branch campus expansion on residents of Doha, Qatar, both citizen and foreign resident. In particular, she is interested in how liberal educational ideologies like egalitarianism, multiculturalism and feminism are implemented and received by differently situated actors within Qatar's American universities.

References

Abdulla, F. (2012) '[Doctors' Society's Elections Today Amidst Controversy Regarding the Voting of Foreigners (Arabic)]', *Al-Wasat* (Bahrain), 13 April 2012. www.alwasatnews.com/2021/news/read/284690/1.html (accessed August 2014).

Abu Dhabi Urban Planning Council (2007) [*Abu Dhabi Urban Structure Framework Plan (Arabic)*], Abu Dhabi: Abu Dhabi Urban Planning Council. http://gsec.abudhabi.ae/Sites/GSEC/Content/AR/PDF/Publications/plan-abu-dhabi-full-version,property=pdf.pdf (accessed August 2014).

Addleton, J. (1992) *Undermining the Centre: The Gulf, Migration and Pakistan* (Pakistan: Oxford University Press).

Ahmad, A. (2011) 'Beyond Labor: Foreign Residents in the Gulf States', *Migrant Labor in the Gulf*. Doha, Center for International and Regional Studies, Georgetown School of Foreign Service Qatar.

Ahmed, A. (2007) 'Bachelors Being Evicted from Villas', *Gulf News*, 9 August. www.gulfnews.com/nation/Society/10145546.html (accessed August 2014).

Al-Akhbar (2013a) 'Thousands of Migrant Workers Strike at Oman Airport', 12 March. http://english.al-akhbar.com/content/thousands-migrant-workers-strike-oman-airport (accessed August 2014).

Al-Akhbar (2013b) 'UAE Government to Deport Striking Workers', 25 May. http://english.al-akhbar.com/node/15900 (accessed August 2014).

Al Alawi, M. (2011) '[The Tsunami of Foreign Labour in the Gulf Labour Market (Arabic)]', *Asharq Al Awsat*, 1 February. http://aawsat.com/leader.asp?section=3&article=606409&issueno=11753 (accessed August 2014).

Al Arabiya (2008) 'Emiratis Have Recorded their Lowest Percentage in the Country Compared to Expatriates', 24 February 2008. www.alarabiya.net/articles/2008/02/24/46070.html (accessed August 2014).

Al-Awad, M. and Elhiraika, A. B. (2003) 'Cultural Effects and Savings: Evidence from Immigrants to the United Arab Emirates', *Journal of Development Studies*, 39(5): 139–52.

Al Bakir, A. (1965) Min al Bahrayn ila al-manfa Sant Hilina (From Bahrain to Exile – Saint Helena) (Beirut: Dar Maktabat al Hayat).

AlGhatta, L. (2013) 'Stop Street Violence', *Gulf Daily News*, 22 July. http://m.gulf-daily-news.com/NewsDetails.aspx?newsid=357659 (accessed August 2014).

Alhasan, H. (2011) 'The Role of Iran in the Failed Coup of 1981: The IFLB in Bahrain', *The Middle East Journal*, Autumn 2011: 603–17.

Al Hussaini, A. (2011) 'Bahrain: The One Dinar Protest', *Global Voices*, 7 March. http://globalvoicesonline.org/2011/03/07/bahrain-the-one-dinar-protest/ (accessed August 2014).

Ali, S. (2010) *Dubai: Gilded Cage* (London and New Haven: Yale University Press).

Al Jandaly, B. (2007) 'Sharjah Ban on Worker Buses in City Criticised', *Gulf News*, 3 May. http://gulfnews.com/news/gulf/uae/employment/sharjah-ban-on-worker-buses-in-city-criticised-1.183397 (accessed August 20014).

Al Kuwari, A. (2004a) '[Fixing the Demographic Imbalance (Arabic)]', *Al Jazeera*. www.aljazeera.net/specialfiles/pages/81f1f6de-12f5-4840-a9b7-33fc8d7c75dc

Al Kuwari, A. (2005) [Towards a better understanding for the reasons of the population imbalance in oil producing parts of the Arabian peninsula (Arabic)] (Kuwait: University of Kuwait, 2005).

Al-Maskari, F. et al. (2011) 'Prevalence of Depression and Suicidal Behaviors among Male Migrant Workers in United Arab Emirates', *Journal of Immigrant and Minority Health*, 13(6): 1027–32.

Al Najar, B. (1983) *Foreign Labour in the Countries of the Arabic Gulf*, (Beirut: Center of Arab Unity).

Al-Naqeeb, K. (2012) *Society and State in the Gulf and Arab Peninsula: A Different Perspective* (London: Routledge).

Al-Qudsi, S. (2006) 'Unemployment Evolution in the GCC Economies: Its Nature and Relationship to Output Gaps', Centre for Market Research & Information (CLMRI), Labour Market Study No.22.

AlRaya (2012) 'Hoax Companies Trading in Visas Charge 60 thousand Riyals from Each Worker', 21 December. www.mohamoon-qa.com/Default.aspx?action=DisplayNews&ID=9960# (accessed August 2014).

Al Seef, A. (2007) Abd Allah Al Tariki: [Rock of Oil and Sands of Politics (Arabic)] (Beirut: Riyadh Al Rayyes).

Al Sharq (2012) 'Unemployed Persons Start Fake Enterprises to Trade in Residency Permits', 11 February. www.alsharq.net.sa/2012/02/11/119450 (accessed August 2014).

AlShehabi, O. (2012) [Uprooting: Mega Real Estate Projects and the Exacerbation of the Demographic Disorder in the GCC (Arabic)] (Beirut: Centre for Arab Unity Studies).

AlShehabi, O. (2013) 'Divide and Rule in Bahrain and the Elusive Pursuit for a United Front: The Experience of the Constitutive Committee and the 1972 Uprising', *Historical Materialism*, 21(1): 94–127.

AlShehabi, O. (2014) 'Radical Transformations and Radical Contestations: Bahrain's Spatial-Demographic Revolution', *Middle East Critique*, 23(1): 29–51.

AlShirawi, A. (2005) *[Labour Papers (Arabic)]* (Beirut: Dar al-Kunuz al-Adabiyya).

Al Slaise, Y. (2011) 'Bahrain: Schools Break Out in Protest', *Global Voices*, 2 March. http://globalvoicesonline.org/2011/03/02/bahrain-schools-break-out-in-protest-videos/ (accessed August 2014).

Al-Wasat (2010a) '[Constituting 2.5% of the Voting Bloc: 8,150 Gulf Nationals and Foreigners Vote in the Municipal Elections (Arabic)]', *Al-Wasat* (Bahrain).

Al-Wasat (2010b) '[Owners of Small Businesses Renew their Sit-in at the Labour Market Authority (Arabic)]', *Al-Wasat* (Bahrain), 4 October. www.alwasatnews.com/2950/news/read/482102/1.html (accessed August 2014).

Al-Wasat (2011) '[Foreign Residents in Bahrain Demand Representation in the Shura, Municipal Councils and the Chamber of Commerce (Arabic)]', *Al-Wasat* (Bahrain), 27 July. www.alwasatnews.com/3244/news/read/574303/1.html (accessed August 2014).

Amar, P. (2009) 'Operation Princess in Rio de Janeiro: Policing "Sex Trafficking," Strengthening Worker Citizenship, and the Urban Geopolitics of Security in Brazil', *Security Dialogue*, 40(4/5): 513–41.

AMEinfo (2008) 'Value of Major Gulf Projects Exceeds $2 Trillion for First Time', 30 March. http://ezine.meed.com/MEED-160710-Top-100-Projects-Supplement/ (accessed August 2014).

Amnesty International (2013) *The Dark Side of Migration: Spotlight on Qatar's Construction Sector Ahead of the World Cup*. http://bit.ly/1lf4pgm (accessed August 2014).

ANIMA (2009) 'Foreign Direct Investment in the Med Countries in 2008: Facing the Crisis', *Anima Investment Network Study*, No. 3, 20 April. www.animaweb.org/uploads/bases/document/Inv_Et3_Med-FDI-Survey-2008_VE_29-5-09_locked.pdf (accessed August 2014).

ANIMA (2011) Investments and Partnerships in MED Region, 2010.

Arnold, F. and Shah, N. M. (1986) *Asian Labor Migration: Pipeline to the Middle East* (Boulder and London: Westview).

Asfar, R. (2009) Unravelling the Vicious Cycle of Recruitment: Labour Migration from Bangladesh to the Gulf States, International Labour Office (Geneva: ILO).

Avebury, E. (1996) Bahrain: A Brickwall; Correspondence between Lord Avebury and the Foreign and Commonwealth Office of the British Government on the Human Rights Situation in Bahrain (London: Parliamentary Human Rights Group).

Awad, I. (2009) *The Global Economic Crisis and Migrant Workers: Impact and Response* (Geneva: International Migration Programme, International Labour Organization).

Ayubi, N. H. (1995) *Over-stating the Arab State: Politics and Society in the Middle East* (London: I. B. Tauris).

Azamn Daily (2013) '[Black Market Trading in Migrants' Permits is Troubling Local Market and Society (Arabic)]', 10 September. http://bit.ly/1phkfbg (accessed August 2014).

Bahrain 2010 Census (2010) *Bahrain 2010 Census*. www.census2010.gov.bh/results_en.php (accessed April 24,2014).

Bahrain CIO (Central Informatics Organisation) (2010) *Population Statistics*. www.cio.gov.bh/cio_ara/English/Publications/Census/Population/1.pdf

Bahrain CIO (Central Informatics Organisation) (2011) *Bahrain National Accounts*. www.cio.gov.bh/cio_ara/English/Publications/National%20Account/2011/NA2011.pdf (accessed August 2014).

Bahrain Economic Development Board (2008) *Bahrain Economic Vision 2030*. www.bahrainedb.com/en/about/Pages/economic%20vision%202030.aspx#.U--DtvmSzB1 (accessed August 2014).

Bahrain Survey and Land Registration Bureau (2012) '[Size of Real Estate Deals Has Exceeded Half a Billion Bahraini Dinars (Arabic)]', *Bahrain Survey and Land Registration Bureau*. www.slrb.gov.bh/News/details.aspx?slrb=3R+LaFXbV3NRdy38VE7clu2LUqi1Ufyo (accessed August 2014).

Bacon, D. (2013) The Right to Stay Home: How US Policy Drives Mexican Migration (Boston: Beacon Press).

Baldwin-Edwards, M. (2011) 'Labour Immigration and Labour Markets in the GCC Countries: National Patterns and Trends', *Kuwait Programme on Development, Governance and Globalisation in the Gulf States, London School of Economics*, No. 15.

Bassiouni, M. C., Rodley, N., Al Awadhi, B., Kirsch, P. and Arsanjani, M. H. (2011) *Report of the Bahrain Independent Commission of Inquiry* (Manama: Bahrain Independent Commission of Inquiry).

Baumol, W., Litan, R. and Schramm J. (2007) *Good Capitalism, Bad Capitalism, and the Economics of Growth and Prosperity* (New Haven: Yale University Press).

BBC (2011) 'Bangladeshis Complain of Bahrain Rally "Coercion"', *BBC News*, 17 March. www.bbc.co.uk/news/world-south-asia-12773696 (accessed August 2014).

BBC (2014) 'Indian Worker Death Rate in Qatar "normal"', *BBC News*, 19 February. www.bbc.co.uk/news/world-middle-east-26260765 (accessed August 2014).

Beauge, G. and Sader, M. (1981) 'The Pattern for Employment, Migration and Labour in the Gulf Countries', *Population Bulletin of ECWA*, No. 21, December: 85–103.

Beaugrand, C. (2011) 'Abd al-Rahman Al-Nu'aimi: Forty Years of Bahraini Opposition', *OpenDemocracy*, 20 September.

Beblawi, H. and Luciani, G. (eds) (1987) The Rentier State: Nation, State and the Integration of the Arab World (London: Croom Helm).

Bhattacharya, P. (1993) 'Rural-Urban Migration in Economic Development', *Journal of Economic Surveys*, 7(3): 243–81.

Biblawi, H. (1987) 'The Rentier State in the Arab World', *Arab Studies Quarterly*, 9(4): 383–98.

Biblawi, H. (1990) 'The Rentier State in the Arab World', in G. Luciani (ed.), *The Arab State* (London, Routledge).

Bilsborrow, R., Oberai, A. and Standing, G. (1984) Migration Surveys in Low-Income Countries: Guidelines for Survey and Questionnaire Design (London: Croom Helm).

Birks, J. and Sinclair, C. (1980) *Arab Manpower: The Crisis of Development* (London: Croom Helm).

BLMN (Bahrain Labour Market Newsletter) (2013) 'New Visas by Size of Establishment'. http://blmi.lmra.bh/2013/03/mi_dashboard.xml (accessed August 2014).

BNA (Bahrain News Agency) (2007) 'Labour Minister Recieves Indian Ambassador', 25 July. www.bna.bh/portal/en/news/415612?date=2011-3-20 (accessed August 2014).

Bowman, D. (2008) 'More than 500 Firms hit for Withholding Wages', *Arabian Business* 26 April. www.arabianbusiness.com/517567-more-than-500-firms-hit-for-withholding-wages (accessed August 2014).

Boyle, P. J., Graham, E. F. and Yeoh, B. (2003) 'Labour Migration and the Family in Asia' *International Journal of Population Geography*, 9: 437–41.

British National Archives (1972) File Number: 1972, FCO 8/1822.

Bromley, S. 1991) *American Hegemony and World Oil* (Cambridge: Polity Press).

Broudehoux, A.-M. (2007) 'Delirious Beijing: Euphoria and Despair in the Olympic Metropolis', in M. Davis and D. B. Monk (eds), *Evil Paradises: Dreamworlds of Neoliberalism*, pp. 87–101 (London: The New Press).

Browne, I. and Misra, J. (2003) 'The Intersection of Gender and Race in the Labor Market', *Annual Review of Sociology*, 29: 487–513.

Brumberg, D. (2001) 'Dissonant Politics in Iran and Indonesia', *Political Science Quarterly*, 116(3): 381–411.

Brush, B. and Sochalski, J. (2007) 'International Nurse Migration: Lessons from the Philippines', *Policy Politics Nursing Practice*, 8(1): 37–46.

Bryman, D. L. and Green, J. D. (1999) 'The Enigma of Political Stability in the Persian Gulf', *The Middle East Review of International Affairs*, 3(3).

Buckley, M. (2011) 'Building the Global Gulf City: Tracing Transnational Geographies of Capital and Labour in Dubai, UAE', unpublished doctoral dissertation (Oxford: School of Geography and the Environment, University of Oxford).

Buckley, M. (2012a) 'From Kerala to Dubai and Back Again: Migrant Construction Workers and the Global Economic Crisis', *Geoforum*, 43(2): 250–59.

Buckley, M. (2012b) 'Locating Neoliberalism in Dubai: Migrant Workers and Class Struggle in the Autocratic City', *Antipode*, 45(2): 256–74.

Buckley, M. (2013) 'Locating Neoliberalism in Dubai: Migrant Workers and Class Struggle in the Autocratic City', *Antipode*, 45(2): 256–74.

Buckley, M. (2014) 'On the Work of Urbanization: Migration, Construction and the Commodity Moment', *Annals of the Association of American Geographers*, 104(2): 338–47.

Buckley, M. and Hanieh, A. (2014) 'Diversification by Urbanization: Tracing the Property-Finance Nexus in Dubai and the Gulf', *International Journal of Urban and Regional Research*, 38(1): 155–75.

Burns, G. (2009) 'Men Take Lead at the Unemployment Line', *Chicago Tribune*, 3 April. http://articles.chicagotribune.com/2009-04-03/news/0904020524_1_job-losses-job-market-unemployment (accessed August 2014).

Burrows, B. (1990) *Footnotes in the Sand: The Gulf in Transition* (Norwich: Michael Russell Publishing).

Bush, R. (1999) *Economic Crisis and the Politics of Reform in Egypt* (Boulder: Westview Press).

BWI (Building and Wood Workers International) (2013) 'BWI Mission Decries Qatar's Lack of Urgency to Stop Abuses', 10 October. www.bwint.org/default.asp?Index=5117&Language=EN (accessed August 2014).

Canterbury, D. C. (2013) *Capital Accumulation and Migration* (Leiden: Brill, 2012).

Castles, S. and Miller, M. J. (2003) *The Age of Migration: International Population Movements in the Modern World* (Basingstoke: Macmillan).

Castles, S. and Miller, M. J. (2009) *The Age of Migration: International Population Movements in the Modern World*, 4th edition, (Basingstoke: Macmillan).

CDSI (Central Department of Statistics & Information, Kingdom of Saudi Arabia) (2010) 'Economic Establishment Census 2010'. http://cdsi.gov.sa/2010-07-31-07-01-16 (accessed August 2014).

Chalcraft, J. (2010) *Monarchy, Migration and Hegemony in the Arabian Peninsula*. Kuwait Programme on Development, Governance and Globalisation in the Gulf States (London: London School of Economics and Political Science).

Chang, D-O. (2009) 'Informalising Labour in Asia's Global Factory', *Journal of Contemporary Asia*, 39(2): 161–79.

Chaudhry, K. (1997) *The Price of Wealth: Economies and Institutions in the Middle East* (Ithaca: Cornell University Press).

Chen, M. (2013) 'Why the Dubai Strike Matters', *Huffington Post*, 4 June. www.huffingtonpost.com/michelle-chen/why-the-dubai-strike-matt_b_3385183.html (accessed August 2014).

Coles, A. and Walsh, K. (2010) 'From "Trucial State" to "Postcolonial" City? The Imaginative Geographies of British Expatriates in Dubai', *Journal of Ethnic and Migration Studies*, 36(8): 1317–33.

Construction Week Online (2013) 'UAE's Arabtec Raises 36,000 Labourer Wages by 20%', 30 September. www.constructionweekonline.com/article-24487-uaes-arabtec-raises-36000-labourer-wages-by-20/#.Ux8WgPTV_YQ (accessed August 2014).

Cordesman, A. H. (1997) *Bahrain, Oman, Qatar, and the UAE* (Boulder: Westview Press).

Cornelius, W. and Tsuda, T. (2004) 'Controlling Immigration: Limits of Government Intervention', in W. A. Corneliues et al. (eds), *Controlling Immigration: A Global Perspective* (Stanford: Stanford University Press).

Cowen, D. and Siciliano, A. (2011) 'Surplus Masculinities and Security', *Antipode*, 43(5): 1516–41.

Cravey, A. (1998) 'Gendering the Latin American State', *Progress in Human Geography*, 22(4): 523–42.

Crystal, J. (1995) *Oil and Politics in the Gulf: Rulers and Merchants in Kuwait and Qatar* (Cambridge: Cambridge University Press).

Cuche, D. (2001) 'Diaspora', *Pluriel-Recherches. Vocabulaire historique et critique des relations interethniques*, Cahier No. 8, Paris, L'Harmattan, pp. 14–23.

Das Augustine, B. (2009) 'Massive Project Spending Planned in Gulf Region', *Gulf News*, 28 September. www.thefreelibrary.com/Massive+project+spending+planned+in+Gulf+region-a0208555764 (accessed August 2014).

Davis, M. (2006) 'Fear and Money in Dubai', *New Left Review*, 41: 1–14.

Davis, M. (2008) 'Sand, Fear and Money in Dubai', in M. Davis and D. B. Monk (eds), *Evil Paradises: Dreamworlds of Neoliberalism* (London: The New Press).

Davis, U. (2000) 'Conception of Citizenship in the Middle East: State, Nation and People', in N. A. Butenschøn, U. Davis, M. Hassassian (eds), *Citizenship and the State in the Middle East: Approaches and Applications* (New York: Syracuse University Press).

De Angelis, M. (2000) 'Trade, the Global Factory and the Struggles for a New Commons', paper presented at the Conference of Socialist Economists, London, 12 July 2000.

De Haan, A. (1999) 'Livelihoods and Poverty: The Role of Migration – a Critical Review of the Migration Literature', *Journal of Development Studies*, 36(2): 1–47.

Deloitte (2013) *Insight into the Qatar Construction Market and Opportunities for Real Estate Developers*. http://www.deloitte.com/view/en_XE/xe/services/financial-advisory/ff9deoddb950f310VgnVCM3000003456f70aRCRD.htm (accessed August 2014).

Disney, N. (1977) 'South Korean Workers in the Middle East', *Middle East Report*, 61: 22–26.

Doward, J. (2014) 'Qatar World Cup: 400 Nepalese Die on Nation's Building Sites Since Bid Won', *Guardian*, 15 February. www.theguardian.com/football/2014/feb/16/qatar-world-cup-400-deaths-nepalese (accessed August 2014).

DTZ (2008) 'Bahrain September 2008', *DTZ Middle East Market Update Series*.

Dubai Airports (2014) 'Fact Sheets, Reports & Statistics', *Dubai Airports*. www. dubaiairport.com/en/media-centre/facts-figures/pages/factsheets-reports-statistics.aspx?id=9 (accessed August 2014).

Dubai Land Department (2007) 'About Real Estate Regulatory Agency', *Dubai Land Department*. www.dubailand.gov.ae/english/about_us/about_rera.aspx (accessed August 2014.)

Dubai Land Department (2012) 'Foreign Investors Pump AED 22 Billion in Dubai Real Estate During H1 2012', *Dubai Land Department*, 14 August. www.dubailand. gov.ae/EngNewsDetail.aspx?newsId=135 (accessed August 2014).

Dubai Statistics Center (2009) *Household Expenditure and Income Survey*. www.dsc. gov.ae/EN/StatisticalProjects/Pages/ProjectReports.aspx?ProjectId=18 (accessed August 2014).

Economic Times (2014) 'India Warns Women Workers in Saudi Against Going on Strike', 23 March. http://articles.economictimes.indiatimes.com/2014-03-23/ news/48491479_1_indian-embassy-indian-workers-saudi-arabia (accessed August 2014).

EDC (2007) 'Construction Opportunities in the Gulf Cooperation Council (GCC)', 23 August. http://bit.ly/1mSuL3b (accessed August 2014).

Ehrenreich, B. and Hochschild, A. (2002) *Global Woman: Nannies, Maids and Sex Workers in the New Economy* (London: Granta).

Ellaboudy, S. (2010) 'The Global Financial Crisis: Economic Impact on GCC Countries and Implications', *International Research Journal of Finance and Economics*, 41: 177–90.

Ellao, J. (2013) 'Filipino Migrants' Rights Advocates Join High Level Talks on Migration', *Bulatlat*. http://bulatlat.com/main/2013/10/07/filipino-migrants-rights-advocates-join-high-level-talks-on-migration/ (accessed August 2014).

Elsheshtawy, Y. (2008) 'Navigating the Spectacle: Landscapes of Consumption in Dubai', *Architectural Theory Review*, 13(2): 164–87.

Elsheshtawy, Y. (2010. *Dubai: Behind an Urban Spectacle* (New York: Routledge).

(ESCWA) Economic and Social Commission for Western Asia (2007) 'International Migration and Development in the Arab World: Challenges and Opportunities', *Population and Development Report*, 3rd edition. www.escwa.un.org/information/ publications/edit/upload/sdd-07-2.pdf (accessed August 2014).

Esim, S. and Smith, M. (2004) *Gender and Migration in Arab States: The Case of Domestic Workers* (Beirut: ILO).

Executive Office of the Council of Ministers for Labour and the Council of Ministers for Social Affairs in the GCC (2008) '[*An Analytical Study of International Conventions for the Protection of All Migrant Workers and Members of their Families (Arabic)*]', Manama.

Fagotto, G. (2013) 'The State-Migration Nexus in the Gulf: In Light of the Arab Uprisings', *IAI Working Papers* 13, Istituto Affari Internazionali.

Fanack (2014) 'Bahraini Defense Force', http://fanack.com/en/countries/bahrain/ administration-politics/bahraini-defence-force/ (accessed August 2014).

Fargues, P. (2011a) 'Immigration without Inclusion: Non-nationals in Gulf State Nation Building', paper presented at the 2011 Gulf Research Meeting, University of Cambridge, 7 July 2011.

Fargues, P. (2011b) 'Immigration without Inclusion: Non-nationals in Nation-Building in the Gulf States', *Asian and Pacific Migration Journal*, 20(3–4): 273–92.

Farrag, M. (1999) 'Emigration Dynamics in Egypt', in R. Appleyard (ed.), *Emigration Dynamics in Developing Countries, Volume 4: The Arab Region*, pp. 44–88 (Geneva: IOM and UNFPA).

Fergany, N. (2001) [*Aspects of Labour Migration and Unemployment in the Arab Region (Arabic)*] (Cairo: Almishkat Centre for Research).

Fernandez, B. (2011) 'Household Help? Ethiopian Women Domestic Workers' Labor Migration to the Gulf Countries', *Asian and Pacific Migration Journal* 20 (3–4): 433–57.

FIFA (nd) '2022 World Cup, Bid Evaluation Report: Qatar'. www.fifa.com/mm/document/tournament/competition/01/33/74/56/b9qate.pdf (accessed August 2014).

Fields, G. (1975) 'Rural–Urban Migration, Urban Unemployment and Underemployment, and Job Search Activity in LDCs', *Journal of Development Economics*, 2(2): 165–88.

Financial Express (2009) 'Travel Trade in Jeopardy as Manpower Export Falls', 2 April: 1.

Foad, H. (2009) 'The Effects of the Gulf War on Migration and Remittances', unpublished paper, Department of Economics, San Diego State University.

Forstenlechner, I. and Rutledge, I. J. (2011) 'The GCC's "Demographic Imbalance": Perceptions, Realities and Policy Options', *Middle East Policy*, 18: 4.

Foucault, M. (1977) *Discipline and Punish: The Birth of the Prison* (New York: Random House).

Freeman, G. (1995) 'Modes of Immigration Politics in Liberal Democratic States', *International Migration Review*, 29(4): 881–902.

Fuccaro, N. (2001) 'Visions of the City: Urban Studies on the Gulf', *Middle East Studies Association Bulletin*, 35(2): 175–87.

Futurebrand (2006) 'Futurebrand's Gulf Real Estate Study', *Futurebrand*.

Futurebrand (2009) 'Futurebrand's Annual Gulf Real Estate Study', *Futurebrand*.

Gardner, A. (2008) 'Strategic Transnationalism: The Indian Diasporic Elite in Contemporary Bahrain', *City and Society*, 20(1): 54–78.

Gardner, A. (2010) *City of Strangers: Gulf Migration and the Indian Community in Bahrain* (Ithaca, Cornell University Press).

Gardezi, H. (1997) 'Asian Workers in the Gulf States of the Middle East', in B. S. Bolaria and R. V. E. Bolaria (eds), *International Labour Migrations* (New York: Oxford University Press).

Gause, G. (2000) 'The Persistence of Monarchies in the Arabia Peninsula: A Comparative Analysis', in J. Kostiner (ed.), *Middle East Monarchies* (Boulder: Lynne Rienner Publishers).

Gengler, J. (2011) 'Facts on the Ground: A Reliable Estimate of Bahrain's Sunni–Shi'i Balance, and Evidence of Demographic Engineering'. http://bahrainipolitics.blogspot.com/2011/04/facts-on-ground-reliable-estimate-of.html (accessed August 2014).

Gerth, H. H. and Wright Mills, C. (1945) *From Max Weber: Essays in Sociology* (New York: Oxford University Press).

Ghaffar, A. (2004) '[Expatriate workers in the states of the Gulf Cooperation Council: Negative Effects on Demography (Arabic)]' (unpublished paper).

Ghobash, M. (1986) *Immigration and Development in the United Arab Emirates* (Cairo: Al Wafa Press).

Gibson, K. and Graham, J. (1986) 'Situating Migrants in Theory: The Case of Filipino Construction Workers', *Capital and Class*, 10(2): 130–49.

Government of Abu Dhabi (2008) *The Abu Dhabi Economic Vision 2030*. https://gsec. abudhabi.ae/Sites/GSEC/Content/EN/PDF/Publications/economic-vision-2030-full-version,property=pdf.pdf (accessed August 2014).

Gowan, P. (1999) *The Global Gamble: Washington's Faustian Bid for World Dominance* (London: Verso).

Grewal, S. (2013) 'Shock at Verdict in Maid Case', *Gulf Daily News*, 8 May. www. gulf-daily-news.com/NewsDetails.aspx?storyid=352834 (accessed August 2014).

Gulf Labour Markets and Migration Project (2014) 'Percentage of Non-nationals in Government Sector, Private Sector and Other Sectors in GCC Countries', *Gulf Migration*. http://bit.ly/1tcqKOl (accessed August 2014).

Guardian (2014) 'Saudi Arabia Says it Has Deported More Than 250,000 Foreign Migrant workers', 22 January. www.theguardian.com/world/2014/jan/22/saudi-arabia-deported-foreign-migrant-workers (accessed August 2014).

Gulf News (2013) 'Global Remittance Flow Grows 10.77% to $514 Billion in 2012: World Bank', 20 April. http://gulfnews.com/business/economy/global-remittance-flow-grows-10-77-to-514-billion-in-2012-world-bank-1.1172693 (accessed August 2014).

Halliday, F. (1977) *Mercenaries* (Nottingham: Russell Press).

Halliday, F. (1984) 'Labor Migration in the Arab World', *Middle East Report*, 123: 3–10.

Hanieh, A. (2010a) 'Khaleeji-Capital: Class-Formation and Regional Integration in the Middle-East Gulf', *Historical Materialism*, 18(2): 35–76.

Hanieh, A. (2010b) 'Temporary Migrant Labour and the Spatial Structuring of Class in the Gulf Cooperation Council', *Spectrum: Journal of Global Studies*, 2(3): 67–89.

Hanieh, A. (2011) *Capitalism and Class in the Gulf Arab States* (New York: Palgrave Macmillan).

Hanieh, A. (2013) *Lineages of Revolt: Issues of Contemporary Capitalism in the Middle East* (Chicago: Haymarket Books).

Hari, J. (2009) 'The Dark Side of Dubai', *The Independent*, 7 April. www.independent. co.uk/opinion/commentators/johann-hari/the-dark-side-of-dubai-1664368.html (accessed August 2014).

Harman, D. (2007) 'American Education Thriving ... in Qatar', *Christian Science Monitor*, 99: 1–11.

Harris, J. and Todaro, M. (1970) 'Migration, Unemployment and Development: A Two Sector Analysis', *American Economic Review*, 60(1): 126–42.

Harroff-Tavel, H. and Nasrim, A. (2013) *Tricked and Trapped: Human Trafficking in the Middle East* (Beirut: International Labour Organization, ILO Regional Office for the Arab States).

Harvey, D. (1985) 'The Geopolitics of Capitalism', in D. Gregor and J. Urry (eds), *Social Relations and Spatial Structures* (London: Macmillan).

Harvey, D. (1999) *The Limits to Capital* (London: Verso).

Heller, M. and Safran, N. (1985) 'The New Middle Class and Regime Stability in Saudi Arabia', *Harvard Middle East Papers*, Modern Series 3, Center for Middle Eastern Studies, Harvard University. Cambridge, MA.

Henry, E. S. (2013) 'Emissaries of the Modern: The Foreign Teacher in Urban China', *City & Society* 25(2): 216–34.

Herb, M. (2009) 'A Nation of Bureaucrats: Political Participation and Economic Diversification in Kuwait and the United Arab Emirates', *International Journal of Middle East Studies*, 41(3): 375–95.

Hertog, S. (2010) 'The Sociology of the Gulf Rentier Systems: Societies of Intermediaries', *Comparative Studies in Society and History*, 52(2): 1–37.

Hertog, S. (2012) 'Redesigning the Distributional Bargain in the GCC', BRISMES Annual Conference, 26–28 March 2012, London School of Economics and Political Science.

Hollifield, J. (2000) 'The Politics of International Migration', in C. Brettell and J. Hollifield (eds), *Migration Theory* (London: Routledge).

HRW (Human Rights Watch) (2012) *Building a Better World Cup: Protecting Migrant Workers in Qatar Ahead of FIFA 2022* www.hrw.org/sites/default/files/reports/qatar0612webwcover_0.pdf (accessed August 2014).

HRW (Human Rights Watch) (2013) 'Saudi Arabia: Labor Crackdown Violence', 1 December. www.hrw.org/news/2013/11/30/saudi-arabia-labor-crackdown-violence (accessed August 2014).

Hvidt, M. (2011) 'Economic and Institutional Reforms in the Arab Gulf Countries', *Middle East Journal* 65 (1): 85–102.

Ibrahim, S. (2002) *Warda* (Paris: Actes sud).

ILO (International Labour Organization) (2005) 'The Employment Relationship: Report V(1)', ILO International Labour Conference, 95th Session, 2006.

ILO (International Labour Organization) (2009a) *The Current Global Economic Crisis: Sectoral Aspects* (Geneva: Governing Body Report, International Labour Organization).

ILO (International Labour Organization) (2009b) 'International Labour Migration and Employment in the Arab Region', Arab Employment Forum.

ILO (International Labour Organization) (2010) 'Decent Work for Domestic Workers', ILO International Labour Conference. www.ilo.org/wcmsp5/groups/public/---ed_norm/---relconf/documents/meetingdocument/wcms_104700.pdf (accessed August 2014).

ILO (International Labour Organization) (2012) 'Rethinking Economic Growth: Towards Productive and Inclusive Arab Societies', ILO Regional Office for the Arab States/UNDP Regional Bureau for Arab States, Geneva.

ILO (International Labour Organization) (2013a) *Domestic Workers Across the World: Global and Regional Statistics and the Extent of Legal Protection* (Geneva: ILO).

ILO (International Labour Organization) (2013b) 'Promoting Effective Governance of Labour Migration from South Asia Project Launching', press release. www.ilo.org/kathmandu/info/public/pr/WCMS_233175/lang--en/index.htm (accessed August 2014).

IMF (International Monetary Fund) (2010) 'Qatar: 2010 IMF Article IV Consultation – Staff Report', *International Monetary Fund*.

IMF (International Monetary Fund) (2014) 'Qatar – 2014 Article IV Consultation Concluding Statement of the IMF Mission', February 19–20. www.imf.org/external/np/ms/2014/030714.htm (accessed August 2014).

India Real Estate Monitor (2012) 'India Tops the First Time Property Buyers List in Dubai', 5 April. http://indiarealestatemonitor.com/property-news/india-tops-the-first-time-property-buyers-list-in-dubai/ (accessed August 2014).

International Labour Office and Arab Employment Forum (2009) *International Labour Migration and Employment in the Arab Region: Origins, Consequences and the Way Forward*, Beirut-Lebanon, 19–21 October 2009.

Iradian, G. (2009) *GCC Regional Overview*, Institute of International Finance. www.iif.com/download.php?id=hYrSHS7htxw= (accessed August 2014).

John, I. (2011) 'Property Visa for 3 Years', *Khaleej Times,* 29 June. www.khaleejtimes.com/DisplayArticle09.asp?xfile=data/theuae/2011/June/theuae_June819.xml&section=theuae (accessed April 24, 2014).

Johnson, M. (1998) 'At Home and Abroad: Inalienable Wealth, Personal Consumption and Formulations of Femininity in the Southern Philippines', in D. Miller (ed.), *Material Cultures: Why Some Things Matter*, pp. 215–38 (London: UCL Press).

Joyce, M. (2000) 'The Bahraini Three On St. Helena, 1956–1961', *Middle East Journal*, 54(4): 613–23.

Kamrava, M. (2012) 'The Political Economy of Rentierism in the Persian Gulf' in M. Kamrava (ed.), *The Political Economy of the Persian Gulf* (New York: Columbia University Press).

Kamrava, M. and Babar, Z. (eds) (2012) *Migrant Labor in the Persian Gulf* (London: Hurst & Co).

Kane, T. (2011) 'Transplanting Education: A Case Study of the Production of "American-style" Doctors in a Non-American Setting', PhD dissertation in social anthropology, The University of Edinburgh.

Kanna, A. (2007) 'Dubai in a Jagged World', *Middle East Report*, 243(37): 22–30.

Kanna, A. (2011a) *Dubai, the City as Corporation* (Minneapolis: University of Minnesota Press).

Kanna, A. (2011b) 'The Arab World's Forgotten Rebellions: Foreign Workers and Biopolitics in the Gulf', *SAMAR: South Asian Magazine for Action and Reflection*, 31 May.

Kanna, A. (2012) 'A Politics of Non-recognition? Biopolitics of Arab Gulf Worker Protests in the Year of Uprisings', *Interface: A Journal For and About Social Movements*, 4(1): 146–64.

Kanna, A. (2014). '"A Group of Like-Minded Lads in Heaven": Everydayness and the Production of Dubai Space', *Journal of Urban Affairs*, 36(2): 605–20.

Kannan, P. (2013) 'Striking Arabtec Workers in UAE "Helped to Return Home"', *The National*, 27 May. www.thenational.ae/news/uae-news/striking-arabtec-workers-in-uae-helped-to-return-home#ixzz2vf4epzpT (accessed August 2014).

Kapiszewski, A. (2001) *Nationals and Expatriates: Population and Labour Dilemmas of the Gulf Cooperation Council States* (Reading: Ithaca Press).

Kapiszewski, A. (2004) 'Arab Labour Migration to the GCC States', in International Organization for Migration and League of Arab States (eds.), *Arab Migration in a Globalized World* (Geneva: International Organization for Migration).

Kapiszewski, A. (2006) 'Arab Versus Asian Migrant Workers in the GCC Countries', paper presented at the United Nations Expert Group Meeting on International Migration and Development in the Arab Region, Population Division, Department of Social and Economic Affairs, United Nations Secretariat, Beirut.

Kathem, N. (2007) [*The Natures of Possessiveness: A Reading into the Diseases of the Bahraini Condition (Arabic)*] (Beirut: The Arab Institute for Research and Publishing).

Kelso, P. (2011) 'Qatar Will Use World Cup As a Catalyst to Improve Conditions for Migrant Workforce', *Telegraph*, 12 January. http://www.telegraph.co.uk/sport/football/international/8253092/Qatar-will-use-World-Cup-as-a-catalyst-to-improve-conditions-for-migrant-workforce.html (accessed August 2014).

Khalaf, A. (1985) 'Labor Movements in Bahrain', *MERIP Report*, 132: 24–9.

Khalaf, A. (1998) 'Contentious Politics in Bahrain: From Ethnic to National and Vice Versa', the Fourth Nordic Conference on Middle Eastern Studies. www.smi.uib.no/pao/khalaf.html (accessed August 2014).

Khalaf, A. (2000) 'Unfinished Business: Contentious Politics and State-Building in Bahrain', Research Reports in Sociology, Lund University.

Khalaf, A. (2003) 'What the Gulf Ruling Families Do When They Rule', Orient.

Khalaf, A. (2005) 'Problems of Succession in the GCC States', Sixth Mediterranean Social and Political Research Meeting, European University Institute.

Khalaf, A. (2006) 'Rules of Succession and Political Participation in the GCC States', in A. Khalaf and G. Luciani (eds), *Constitutional Reform and Political Participation in the Gulf*, Gulf Research Center.

Khalaf, A. (2013) '[The Price of Well-Being in the Gulf Countries] (Arabic)]', *As-safir al-Arabi*, 18 September.

Khalaf, S. and Kobaisi, S. A. (1999) 'Migrants' Strategies of Coping and Patterns of Accommodation in the Oil-Rich Gulf Societies: Evidence from the UAE', *British Journal of Middle Eastern Studies*, 26(2): 271–98.

Khalil, A. (2007) 'UAE Denies Mass Expulsion of Striking Asia Workers'. www.middle-east-online.com/English/?id=22891 (accessed August 2014).

Khan, A. (2010) 'The Living and Working Conditions of Temporary Expatriate Contractual Workers in the GCC Countries: Defining a Policy Agenda', presentation at ILO, Kuwait Economic Society and University of Sharjah Workshop, Kuwait, 5 December.

Khan, A. and Harroff-Tavel, H. (2011) 'Reforming the Kafala: Challenges and Opportunities in Moving Forward', *Asian and Pacific Migration Journal*, 20(3-4): 293.

Khan, M. H. and Sundaram, K. (eds) (2000) *Rents, Rent-Seeking and Economic Development: Theory and Evidence from Asia* (Cambridge: Cambridge University Press).

Khuri, F. (1980) *Tribe and State in Bahrain: The Transition of Social and Political Authority in an Arab State* (Chicago: Chicago University Press).

Kinninmont, J. (2013) 'Citizenship in the Gulf', in A. Echagüe (ed.), *The Gulf States and the Arab Uprisings* (Madrid: FRIDE and the Gulf Research Center).

KNA (Kuwait National Assembly) (2014) 'Trading in Residency Permits in Kuwait'. www.kna.kw/clt/run.asp?id=1328#sthash.FXMzEOTH.dpbs (accessed August 2014).

Koolhaas, R. and Mau, B. (1995) *S, M, L, XL: The Generic City* (New York: The Monacelli Press).

Kotilaine, J. (2009) 'Rebalancing via Deleveraging', *GCC Economic Monthly*, NCB Capital, October.

Krieger, Z. (2008) 'An Academic Building Boom Transforms the Persian Gulf', *The Chronicle of Higher Education*, 54(29): A26.

Krimly, R. (1993) *The Political Economy of Rentier States: A Case Study of Saudi Arabia in the Oil Era, 1950–1990* (Washington, DC: George Washington University).

Krings, T., Bobek, A., Moriarty, E., Salamonska, J. and Wickham J. (2009) 'Migration and Recession: Polish Migrants in Post-Celtic Tiger Ireland', *Sociological Research Online*, 14(2–3).

Kuwait Central Statistics Bureau (2011) *Kuwait National Accounts*. www.csb.gov.kw/Socan_Statistic_EN.aspx?ID=19 (accessed August 2014).

Lackner, H. (1978) *A House Built on Sand: A Political Economy of Saudi Arabia* (Reading: Ithaca Press)

Lasker, R. H. (2011) 'Bahrain National Guard to Recruit Former Soldiers from Pakistan', *Pakistan Defense*, 11 March. www.defence.pk/forums/strategic-geopolitical-issues/97523-bahrain-national-guard-recruit-former-soldiers-pakistan.html#ixzz2GrTVZov3 (accessed August 2014).

Lawson, F. H. (1989) *Bahrain: The Modernization of Autocracy* (Boulder: Westview Press).

Leonard, K. (2002) 'South Asian Women in the Gulf: Families and Futures Reconfigured', in S. Sarker and E. N. De (eds), *Trans-Status Subjects: Gender in the Globalization of South and Southeast Asia*, pp. 213–31 (Durham and London, Duke University Press).

Lewis, W. A. (1954) 'Economic Development with Unlimited Supplies of Labour', *Manchester School of Economic and Social Studies*, 22: 139–91.

LMRA (Bahrain Labour Market Regulatory Authority) (2014) 'Free Visa Traders Are Behind the Growth of the Phenomenon', Media Blog. http://blog.lmra.bh/ar/archives/4232 (accessed August 2014).

Long, D. (1997) *The Kingdom of Saudi Arabia* (Gainesville: University Press of Florida).

Longva, A. (1997) *Walls Built on Sand: Migration, Exclusion, and Society in Kuwait* (Boulder: Westview Press).

Longva, A. (1999) 'Keeping Migrant Workers in Check: The Kafala Syatem in the Gulf', *Middle East Report*, 29(211): 20–2.

Longva, A. N. (2005) 'Neither Autocracy nor Democracy but Ethnocracy: Citizens, Expatriates and the Socio-political System in Kuwait', in P. Dresch and J. Piscatori (eds), *Monarchies and Nations: Globalization and Identity in the Arab States of the Gulf* (London: I. B. Tauris).

Lori, N. (2011) 'National Security and the Management of Migrant Labor: A Case Study of the United Arab Emirates', *Asian and Pacific Migration Journal*, 20(3–4): 315–37.

Losurdo, D. (2011) *Liberalism: A Counter-History*, translated by G. Elliott (London and New York: Verso).

Louër, L. (2008a) 'The Political Impact of Labor: Migration in Bahrain', *City and Society*, 20(1): 32–53.

Louër, L. (2008b) *Transnational Shia Politics: Religious and Political Networks in the Gulf* (New York: Columbia/Hurst).

Luciani, G. (1987) 'Allocation vs. Production States: A Theoretical Framework', in H. Beblawi and G. Luciani (eds), *Nation, State and Integration in the Arab World*, Volume 2 (London, Croom Helm).

Mabee, B. (2013) *The Globalization of Security*. www.palgraveconnect.com/pc/doifinder/10.1057/9780230234123 (accessed August 2014).

Macris, J. R. (2010) *The Politics and Security of the Gulf: Anglo-American Hegemony and the Shaping of a Region* (New York: Routledge).

Mahdavy, H. (1970) 'The Patterns and Problems of Economic Development in Rentier States: The Case of Iran', in M. Cook (ed.), *Studies in the Economic History of the Middle East* (London: Oxford University Press).

Malecki E. and Ewers, M. (2007) 'Labor Migration to World Cities: With a Research Agenda for the Arab Gulf', *Progress in Human Geography*, 31(4): 467–84.

Mann, M. (1986) 'The Autonomous Power of the State: Its Origins, Mechanisms and Results', in J. A. Hall (ed.), *States in History* (New York: Basil Blackwell).

Marfleet, P. (2006) *Refugees in a Global Era* (Basingstoke: Palgrave).

Marshall, T. H. (1965) *Class, Citizenship and Social Development* (New York: Anchor).

Martin, P. (2009) *The Recession and Migration: Alternative Scenarios*. www.age-of-migration.com/uk/financialcrisis/updates/1c.pdf (accessed August 2014).

Marx, K. (1866) 'Letter from Karl Marx To Francois Lafargue in Bordeaux', London, 12 November. https://marxists.anu.edu.au/archive/marx/works/1866/letters/66_11_12.htm (accessed August 2014).

Marzooq, A. (2011) '780 Monthly Naturalized Individuals in Bahrain', *Al-Wasat Newspaper*, 19 March. www.alwasatnews.com/2021/news/read/284690/1.html (accessed August 2014).

Massey, D. (1984) *Spatial Divisions of Labour: Social Structures and the Geography of Production* (London: Macmillan Education).

Massey, D. (1990) 'Social Structure, Household Strategies, and the Cumulative Causation of Migration', *Population Index*, 56(1): 3–26.

Massey, D. (1999) 'International Migration at the Dawn of the Twenty-First Century: The Role of the State', *Population and Development Review*, 25(2): 303–22.

Massey, D., Arango, J., Hugo, G., Kouaouci, A., Pellegrino, A., and Taylor J. E. (1998) *Worlds in Motion: Understanding International Migration at the End of the Millennium* (Oxford: Clarendon Press).

McCall, L. (2005) 'The Complexity of Intersectionality', *Signs: Journal of Women in Culture and Society*, 30(3): 1771–94.

McDowell, L. (2008) 'Thinking Through Work: Complex Inequalities, Constructions of Difference and Transnational Migrants', *Progress in Human Geography*, 32(4): 491–507.

McDowell, L. (2009) *Working Bodies: Interactive Service Employment and Workplace Identities* (Oxford: Wiley-Blackwell).

McDowell, L., Batnitzky, A. and Dyer, S. (2007) 'Division, Segmentation, and Interpellation: The Embodied Labors of Migrant Workers in a Greater London Hotel', *Economic Geography*, 83(1): 1–25.

MEED (2010) 'Supplement: The MEED Projects Top 100', *MEED*. www.meed. com/supplements/2010/the-GCCs-top-100-projects/the-meed-projects-top-100/3007933.article (accessed August 2014).

Migdal, J. S. (1988) *Strong Societies and Weak States: State–Society Relations and State Capabilities in the Third World* (Princeton: Princeton University Press).

Migrant Rights (2013) 'Workers Strike after Compatriot's Suicide', www. migrant-rights.org/2013/09/workers-strike-after-compatriots-suicide/ (accessed August 2014).

Migrant Rights (2014) 'Kuwaiti Migrants Endure Delayed Wages and Government Apathy', 7 February. www.migrant-rights.org/research/kuwaiti-migrants-endure-delayed-wages-government-apathy/ (accessed August 2014).

Miller-Idriss, C. and Hanauer, E. (2011) 'Transnational Higher Education: Offshore Campuses in the Middle East', *Comparative Education*, 47(2): 181–207.

Mitchell, T. (2002) *Rule of Experts: Egypt, Techno-Politics, Modernity* (Berkeley: University of California Press).

Mohammad, R. and Sidaway, J. D. (2012) 'Spectacular Urbanization amidst Variegated Geographies of Globalization: Learning from Abu Dhabi's Trajectory through the Lives of South Asian Men', *International Journal of Urban and Regional Research*, 36(3): 606–27.

MOIA (Ministry of Overseas Indian Affairs) (2012) *Annual Report 2011–2012* (New Delhi: Government of India, Ministry of Overseas Indian Affairs).

Mustafa, A. (2013) 'Saudi Minister: GCC To Set Up Force of 100,000', *Defense News*, 26 December. www.defensenews.com/article/20131226/DEFREG04/312260016/ Saudi-Minister-GCC-Set-Up-Force-100-000 (accessed August 2014).

MWPS (Migrant Workers Protection Society) (2012) 'Satyavathi's Story', 22 October. www.mwpsbahrain.com/cases/case.aml (accessed August 2014).

Naficy, H. (1999) 'Framing Exile: From Homeland to Homepage', in H. Naficy (ed.), *Home, Exile, Homeland: Film, Media, and the Politics of Place* (New York: Routledge).

Nagy, S. (2008) 'The Search for Miss Philippines Bahrain: Possibilities for Representation in Expatriate Communities', *City and Society*, 20(1): 79–104.

Nambiar, A. C. K. (1995) *The Socio-economic Conditions of Gulf Migrants* (New Delhi: Commonwealth Publishers).

National, The (2010) 'Homeowners Take Charge of Services', 12 November. www. thenational.ae/thenationalconversation/editorial/homeowners-take-charge-of-services (accessed August 2014).

Niblock, T. (2007) *The Political Economy of Saudi Arabia* (London: Routledge).

Nicolini, B. (2007) 'The Baluch Role in the Persian Gulf during the Nineteenth and Twentieth Centuries', *Comparative Studies of South Asia, Africa and the Middle East*, 27(2): 384–96.

Niethammer, K. (2006) 'Voices in Parliament, Debates in Majalis, and Banners on Streets: Avenues of Political Participation in Bahrain', *European University Institute Working Paper*.

OECD (2010) *StatExtracts*. http://stats.oecd.org/Index.aspx?datasetcode=SNA_TABLE1 (accessed August 2014).

Ollman, B. (2003) *Dance of the Dialectic: Steps in Marx's Method* (Illinois: University of Illinois Press).

Oman NCSI (National Centre for Statistics and Information) (2012) *Annual Statistical Abstract 2012*. www.ncsi.gov.om/NCSI_website/websites_en.aspx (accessed August 2014).

Ong, A. (2006) *Neoliberalism as Exception: Mutations in Citizenship and Sovereignty* (Durham: Duke University Press).

Ong, A. (2011) 'Hyperbuilding: Spectacle, Speculation and the Hyperspace of Sovereignty', in A. Roy and A. Ong (eds), *Worlding Cities: Asian Experiments in the Art of Being Global* (Oxford: Wiley-Blackwell).

Onley, J. (2004) *The Politics of Protection in the Gulf: The Arab Rulers and the British Resident in the Nineteenth Century* (Exeter: University of Exeter Press).

Ouroussoff, N. (2008) 'City on the Gulf: Koolhaas Lays Out a Grand Urban Experiment in Dubai', *New York Times*, 3 March. www.nytimes.com/2008/03/03/arts/design/03kool.html?_r=1&ref=middleeast (accessed August 2014).

Overbeek, H. (2002) 'Neoliberalism and the Regulation of Global Labor Mobility', *The Annals of the American Academy of Political and Social Science*, 581(1): 74–90.

Owen Jones, M. (2013) 'Bahrain's History of Political Injustice', *Your Middle East*, 29 April. www.yourmiddleeast.com/opinion/marc-owen-jones-bahrains-history-of-political-injustice_14064 (accessed August 2014).

PACI (Public Authority for Civil Information) (2012) *Statistics – Tables 19 and 20*. www.paci.gov.kw/index.php (accessed August 2014).

Pamuk, H. (2011) 'UAE's Emarat Faces Higher Premiums after Fuel Shortage', *Reuters*, 27 April, http://uk.reuters.com/article/2011/04/27/uae-emarat-gasoline-idUKLDE73Q1A020110427 (accessed August 2014).

Panitch, L. and Gindin, S. (2003) 'Global Capitalism and American Empire', in C. Leys and L. Panitch (ed.) *Socialist Register 2004: The New Imperial Challenge* (London: Merlin Press).

Parry, L. (2014) 'More than 500 Indian Migrant Workers Have Died in Qatar in Two Years As Shocking Death Toll is Laid Bare Ahead of 2022 World Cup', *Daily Mail*, 18 February, www.dailymail.co.uk/news/article-2562370/More-500-Indian-migrant-workers-died-Qatar-two-years-shocking-death-toll-laid-bare-ahead-2022-World-Cup.html#ixzz2v5seFDRm (accessed August 2014).

Percot, M. (2006). 'Indian Nurses in the Gulf: Two Generations of Female Migration', *South Asia Research*, 26(1): 41–62.

Perrons, D. (2004) *Globalization and Social Change: People and Places in a Divided World* (London: Routledge).

Peterson, J. E. (2004) 'Oman's Diverse Society: Northern Oman', *Middle East Journal*. www.jepeterson.net/sitebuildercontent/sitebuilderfiles/Oman_Diverse_Society_Northern_Oman.pdf (accessed August 2014).

Pilling, D. (2011) 'Asia: The Rise of the Middle Class', *Financial Times*, 4 January. www.ft.com/intl/cms/s/0/5841236e-183a-11e0-88c9-00144feab49a.html#axzz1S1y8zc1f (accessed August 2014).

Pradella, L. (2014) 'New Developmentalism and the Origins of Methodological Nationalism', *Competition and Change*, 18(2): 180–93.

Pratt, G. (1999) 'From Registered Nurse to Registered Nanny: Discursive Geographies of Filipina Domestic Workers in Vancouver, B.C.', *Economic Geography*, 75(3): 215–36.

Puar, J. (2007) *Terrorist Assemblages: Homonationalism in Queer Times* (North Carolina: Duke University Press).

Purcell, M. (2002) 'Excavating Lefebvre: The Right to the City and its Urban Politics of the Inhabitant', *GeoJournal*, 58: 99–108.

Qatar Statistics Authority (2009) *Labour Force Survey* (Doha: Qatar Statistics Authority).

Qatar Statistics Authority (2010) *Annual Statistical Abstract 2010*. www.qix.gov. qa/portal/page/portal/QIXPOC/Documents/QIX%20Knowledge%20Base/ Publication/General%20Statistics/Annual%20Abstract/Source_QSA/Annual_ Abstract_QSA_AnBu_AE_2010.pdf (accessed August 2014).

QSAPSA (Qatar Statistics Authority Population Structure Archive) (nd) Ministry of Development Planning and Statistics. www.qsa.gov.qa/eng/ (accessed August 2014).

Rahimi, S. (2007) 'UAE Threatens Deportation after Violent Protest', *Arabian Business*, 28 October. www.arabianbusiness.com/uae-threatens-deportation-after-violent-protest-53412.html

Rahman, M. M. (2011) 'Emigration and the Family Economy: Bangladeshi Labor Migration to Saudi Arabia', *Asian and Pacific Migration Journal*, 20(3–4): 389–411.

Renaud, B. (2010) 'Dubai's Real Estate Boom and Bust of 2002–2008: Dynamics and Policy Responses', *Housing Finance International*, 24(4): 6–17.

Renaudet, I. (2011) 'Le détour par la France des médecins espagnols au XIXᵉ siècle: entre exil politique et formation scientifique', *Cahiers de la Méditerranée*, 82: 67–78.

Reuters (2010) 'Factbox: Qatar's Construction Plan for the World Cup', www.reuters. com/article/2010/12/06/us-qatar-construction-idUSTRE6B533D20101206 (accessed August 2014).

Reuters (2011) 'Sectarian clases erupt in Bahrain', 3 March. www.reuters.com/ article/2011/03/03/us-bahrain-clashes-idUSTRE7227N420110303 (accessed August 2014).

Reuters (2012) 'Bahrain Says it Arrested 29 During Protest on Friday', 22 September. www.reuters.com/article/2012/09/22/us-bahrain-protest-idUSBRE88L03X20120922 (accessed August 2014).

Robinson, K. (2000) 'Gender, Islam, and Nationality: Indonesian Domestic Servants in the Middle East', in K. Adams and S. Dickey (eds), *Home and Hegemony: Domestic Service and Identity Politics in South and Southeast Asia* (Ann Arbor: University of Michigan Press).

Rose, N. (2001) 'The Politics of Life Itself', *Theory, Culture & Society*, 18(6): 1–30.

Ross, M. (2001) 'Does Oil Hinder Democracy?' *World Politics*, 53(3): 325–61.

Russell, S. S. (1989) 'Politics and Ideology in Migration Policy Formulation: The Case of Kuwait', *International Migration Review*, 23(1): 24–47.

Sadiki, L. (1997) 'Towards Arab Liberal Governance: From the Democracy of Bread to the Democracy of Vote', *Third World Quarterly*, 18(1): 127–48.

Saif, I. and el-Rayyes, T. (2009) 'Labour Markets Performance and Migration Flows in Jordan', National Background Paper, Robert Schuman European University Institute Florence, Italy.

Salih, R. (2002) 'Shifting Meanings of "Home:: Consumptions and Identity in Moroccan Women's Transnational Practices between Italy and Morocco', in N. Al-Ali and K. Koser (eds), *New Approaches to Migration? Transnational Communities and the Transformation of Home* (London and New York: Routledge).

Sater, J. (2013) 'Citizenship and Migration in the Arab Gulf Monarchies', *Citizenship Studies*, 18(3–4): 292–302.

Saudi Gazette (2013) '"Abolish the Kafala System and End Problems in Labor Market', 21 January. www.saudigazette.com.sa/index.cfm?method=home. regcon&contentid=20130123150276 (accessed August 2014).

Schmid, C. (2012) 'Henri Lefebvre, the Right to the City, and the New Metropolitan Mainstream', in N. Brenner, P. Marcuse and M. Mayer (eds), *Cities For People, Not For Profit: Critical Urban Theory and the Right to the City* (London: Routledge).

Scott, J. (1998) *Seeing Like a State: How Certain Schemes to Improve the Human Condition Have Failed* (New Haven: Yale University Press).

Seccombe, I. and Lawless, R. (1987) 'Work Camps and Company Towns: Settlement Patterns and the Gulf Oil Industry', *Occasional Papers Series*, 36, University of Durham, Centre for Middle Eastern and Islamic Studies.

Sen, A. (2000) 'Social Exclusion: Concept, Application, and Scrutiny', *Social Development Papers* No. 1, Office of Environment and Social Development, Asian Development Bank.

Shah, N. (2004) 'Arab Migration Patterns in the Gulf', in International Organization for Migration and League of Arab States (eds.), *Arab Migration in a Globalized World* (Geneva: International Organization for Migration).

Shah, N. (2008) 'Recent Labor Immigration Policies in the Oil-Rich Gulf: How Effective Are they Likely to Be?', ILO Asian Regional Programme on Governance of Labor Migration, Working Paper No. 3.

Shah, N. (2009) 'The Management of Irregular Migration and its Consequences for Development: GCC', *Working Paper*, 19, Asian Regional Programme on Governance of Labour Migration, Bangkok, ILO.

Shain, Y. (2002) 'The Role of Diasporas in Conflict Perpetuation or Resolution', *SAIS Review*, 22(2): 115–44.

Shamsi, M. (2006) 'Evaluation of Labour Policies in the GCC', United Nations Expert Group Meeting on International Migration and Development in the Arab Region (Beirut: Department of Economic and Social Affairs United Nations Secretariat).

Sherbiny, N. (1981) 'Manpower Planning in the Oil Countries', in N. Sherbiny (ed.), *Research in Human Capital and Development: Volume 1* (JAI Press: London).

Silvey, R. (2004) 'Transnational Domestication: State Power and Indonesian Migrant Women in Saudi Arabia', *Political Geography*, 23(3): 245–64.

Skocpol, T. (1985) 'Bringing the State Back In: Strategies of Analysis in Current Research', in P. Evans, D. Rueschemeyer and T. Skocpol (eds), *Bringing the State Back In* (New York: Cambridge University Press).

Smith, B. (2010) 'Scared By, Of, In, and For Dubai', *Social & Cultural Geography*, 11(3): 263–83.

Soman, R. (2013) 'Illegal Money Transfers Thriving in the GCC', *bqdoha.com*, 2 October. http://bqdoha.com/2013/10/illegal-money-transfers-thriving-in-the-gcc (accessed August 2014).

Soto, R. and Haouas, I. (2012) 'Has the UAE Escaped the Oil Curse?', The Economic Research Forum (ERF), Working Paper 728.

Soto, R. and Vásquez Alvarez, R. (2011) 'The Efficiency Cost of the Kafala in Dubai: A Stochastic Analysis', Pontificia Universidad Catolica de Chile, Documento de Trabajo No. 399.

Spiro, D. (1999) *The Hidden Hand of American Hegemony Petrodollar Recycling and International Markets* (Ithaca: Cornell University Press).

Springborg, R. (2013) 'GCC Countries as "Rentier States" Revisited', *The Middle East Journal*, 67(2): 301–9.

Spivak, G. C. (1996) 'Diasporas Old and New: Women in a Transnational World', *Textual Practice*, 10(2): 245–69.

Standing, G. (ed.) (1985) *Labour Circulation and the Labour Process* (London: Croom Helm).

Stark, O. (1984) 'Rural-to-Urban Migration in LDCs: A Relative Derivation Approach', *Economic Development and Cultural Change*, 32(3): 475–86.

Stark, O. (1991) *The Migration of Labor* (Cambridge, MA: Blackwell Publishers).

Stark, O. and Bloom, D. E. (1985) 'The New Economics of Labor Migration', *American Economic Review*, 75(2): 173–8.

Stark, O. and Taylor, J. E. (1989) 'Relative Deprivation and International Migration', *Demography*, 26: 1–14.

Subedi, A. (2014) 'Ex-Migrant Workers Shudder at Thought of Gulf Predators', *Republica*, 23 January. www.myrepublica.com/portal/index.php?action=news_details&news_id=68425 (accessed August 2014).

SwedWatch (2005) 'Just Another Commodity? A report on the situation of Migrant Workers in Swedish Companies in Saudi Arabia', July.

Takriti, A. (2013) *Monsoon Revolution: Republicans, Sultans, and Empires in Oman, 1965–1976* (Oxford: Oxford University Press).

Tala Island (2007) 'Tala Island Owners Association Agreement'. www.tala-amwaj.com/Downloads/OwnersAssociationAgreement.pdf (accessed August 2014).

Taylor, E. J. (1999) 'The New Economics of Labour Migration and the Role of Remittances in the Migration Process', *International Migration*, 37(1): 63–88.

TEN Real Estate (2011) 'Amwaj Islands', *TEN Real Estate*. http://realestate.theemiratesnetwork.com/developments/bahrain/amwaj_islands.php (accessed August 2014).

Tétreault, M. A. (2000) *Stories of Democracy: Politics and Society in Contemporary Kuwait* (New York: Columbia University Press).

Tibi, B. (1990) 'The Simultaneity of the Unsimultaneous: Old Tribes and Imposed Nation States in the Modern Middle East', in P. Khoury and J. Kostiner (eds), *Tribes and State Formation in the Middle East* (Berkeley: University of California Press).

Times, The (2012) 'Influx of Workers and Prostitutes for Olympics Raises Sexual Health Fears', 17 March. www.thetimes.co.uk/tto/health/article1962770.ece (accessed August 2014).

Times of India, The (2012) 'An Indian Ends Life Every Sixth Day in Oman', 30 April. http://timesofindia.indiatimes.com/nri/middle-east-news/An-Indian-ends-life-every-sixth-day-in-Oman/articleshow/12934364.cms (accessed August 2014).

Trade Arabia (2011) 'Bahrain Minister Warns on Fuel Subsidy', *Trade Arabia*. 21 November 2010.

Turner, B. S. (2006) 'Citizenship, Nationalism and Nation-Building', in G. Delanty and K. Kumar (eds), *The SAGE Handbook of Nations and Nationalism* (London: SAGE).

UAE National Bureau of Statistics (2005) *1985 UAE Population Census Results*. www.uaestatistics.gov.ae/ReportPDF/DSS_CENSUS_Population%20by%20 Emirates%201975–2005.xls (accessed August 2014).

UAE National Bureau of Statistics (2009) *Labour Force Survey* (Abu Dhabi: UAE National Burea of Statistics).

Union View (2008) 'Hidden Faces of the Gulf Miracle', *Union View*, No. 21.

U.S. Energy Information Administration (2014) 'World Crude Oil Price'. www.eia. gov.

Van Hear, N. (1998) *New Diasporas: The Mass Exodus, Dispersal and Regrouping of Migrant Communities* (London: UCL Press).

Van Waas, L. (2010) 'The Situation of Stateless Persons in the Middle East and North Africa,, UNHCR, October 2010. www.unhcr.org/4ce63e079.pdf (accessed August 2014).

Vitalis, R. (2006) *America's Kingdom: Mythmaking on the Saudi Oil Frontier* (Palo Alto: Stanford University Press).

Vitalis, R. (2007) *America's Kingdom: Mythmaking on the Saudi Oil Frontier* (Stanford, Stanford University Press).

Vlieger, A. (2012) 'Domestic Workers in Saudi Arabia and the Emirates: Trafficking Victims?' *International Migration*, 50(6): 180–94.

Vora, N. (2008) 'Producing Diasporas and Globalization: Indian Middle-Class Migrants in Dubai', *Anthropological Quarterly*, 81(2): 377–406.

Vora, N. (2011) 'From Golden Frontier to Global City: Shifting Forms of Belonging, "freedom," and Governance among Indian Businessmen in Dubai', *American Anthropologist*, 113(2): 306–18.

Vora, N. (2013) *Impossible Citizens: Dubai's Indian Diaspora* (North Carolina: Duke University Press).

Vora, N. (2014) 'Between Global Citizenship and Qatarization: Negotiating Qatar's New Knowledge Economy within American Branch Campuses', *Ethnic and Racial Studies*, 37(12), forthcoming.

Vora, N. (2015) 'Is the University Universal? Mobile (Re)Constitutions of American Academia in the Gulf Arab States', *Anthropology & Education Quarterly*, 46(1), forthcoming.

Walsh, K. (2006) '"Dad Says I'm Tied to a Shooting Star!" Grounding (Research On) British Expatriate Belonging', *Area*, 38(3): 268–78.

Walsh, K. (2007) '"It Got Very Debauched, Very Dubai!' Heterosexual Intimacy amongst Single British Expatriates', *Social & Cultural Geography*, 8(4): 507–33.

Walsh, K. (2012) 'Emotion and Migration: British Transnationals in Dubai', *Environment and Planning D: Society and Space*, 30(1): 43–59.

Weber, M. (1978) *Economy and Society: An Outline of Interpretive Sociology* (Berkeley: University of California Press).

Weiner, M. (2006) 'On International Migration and International Relations', in A, Messina and G. Lahav (eds), *The Migration Reader: Exploring Politics and Policies* (Boulder: Lynne Rienner Publishers).

World Bank (2009) *From Privilege to Competition: Unlocking Private-led Growth in the Middle-East and North Africa* (Washington, DC: World Bank).

World Bank (2013) 'Migration and Remittance Flows: Recent Trends and Outlook, 2013–2016', *Migration and Development Brief*, No. 2.

Willoughby, J. (2006) 'Ambivalent Anxieties of the South Asian-Gulf Arab Labour Exchange', in J. W. Fox, N. Mourtada-Sabbah and M. Al-Mutawa (eds), *Globalization and the Gulf* (London: Routledge).

Willoughby, J. (2008) 'Segmented Feminization and the Decline of Neopatriarchy in GCC Countries of the Persian Gulf', *Comparative Studies of South Asia, Africa and the Middle East*, 28(1): 184–99.

Wimmer, A. and Glick Schiller, N. (2002) 'Methodological Nationalism and Beyond: Nation-state Building, Migration and the Social Sciences', *Global Networks*, 2(4): 301–34.

Wong, T., Yeow, M. and Zhu, X. (2005) 'Building a Global City: Negotiating the Massive Influx of Floating Population in Shanghai', *Journal of Housing and the Built Environment*, 20: 21–50.

Wurzel, U. (2009) 'The Political Economy of Authoritarianism in Egypt', in L. Guazzone and D. Pioppi (eds), *The Arab State and Neo-liberal Globalization: The Restructuring of State Power in the Middle East* (Reading: Ithaca Press).

Yeoh, B. and Willis, K. (2004) 'Constructing Masculinities in Transnational Space: Singapore Men on the "Regional Beat"', in P. Jackson, P. Crang and C. Dwyer (eds), *Transnational Spaces* (London: Routledge).

Zachariah, K., Mathew, E. T. and Irudaya Rajan, S. (2003) *Dynamics of Migration in Kerala: Dimensions, Differentials, Consequences* (New Delhi: Orient Longman).

Zollberg, A. R. (2006) 'International Migration in Political Perspective', in A. Messina and G. Lahav (eds), *The Migration Reader: Exploring Politics and Policies* (Boulder: Lynne Rienner Publishers).

Index

Compiled by Sue Carlton

history of opposition exile
199–210
importance of media 208
leftist movements 201–2, 204,
205–6, 208, 215
relationships with human rights
organisations 206
return and reintegration 207–10
Shiite Islamist movements 203–7
strategies and activism 204–7
workers' movements 206
youth movements 204
political naturalisation 127–8,
161–3, 164–5, 210
security apparatus 158
strikes 9, 164, 212, 226
Bahrain Centre for Human Rights
(BCHR) 203, 213, 214
Bahrain Defence Force (BDF) 158, 164,
165, 166
Bahrain Economic Development Board
104
Bahrain Freedom Movement (BFM)
(London) 204, 205, 206, 207,
210, 213
Bahrain Human Rights Organisation
– Copenhagen 213
Bahrain Labour Union Free Federation
(BLUFF) 212, 214
Bahrain Tender Board 90
Bahrain Watch 215
Bahrain Workers' Union 206
Bahraini Doctors' Society 128
Al Bakir, Abd-al Rahman 200–1
Baluch migrants 154, 157, 162
Bandar, Saleh 210
Bangladesh 57, 69, 94, 143
BAPCO oil company 9
Bedouin tribes 11–12, 79
Beirut 202, 215
biopolitics 170, 172, 173, 175, 177, 194
expert/expat camps 186–92
Bonacich, E. 162
Britain, military advisors to Gulf
countries 155, 156–7

British administration
importing workforce 6
and legacy of deportation 200–1
and origins of migrant-based
security forces 153, 154–6
regional influence of 12
Buckley, M. 191
Building and Wood Workers
International 224
bureaucracy 13, 22, 116, 189–90
Burrows, B. 155

capital accumulation 8, 13–14, 25, 34,
66, 143, 229
capitalism 3, 10, 14, 23, 26, 173
global 70–1
as spatialised 66, 68, 73
Chalcraft, J. 226
Chaudhry, K. 43
citizens
alienation 27–8, 31, 124
issuing permits 79
low participation in productive
process 26, 28
privileges 15–16, 27, 50, 99
in rentier state 45
unemployment 25, 29, 73
citizenship 3, 4, 30, 48–50, 138
citizen and non-citizen relationship
3, 27–8, 49–50, 51–2, 99, 111, 173
documents 5
granted to migrants in security
services 153–4, 161–3
Jinsiyya and *Muwatana* distinction
50
redefinition of 49
as tool for social control 48–50
and welfare system 4, 15–16
see also political naturalisation
class formation
as spatial structure 66–8, 71–2, 73
'spatial fix' concept 68–70
Cochrane, Ronald (Mohammad
Mahdi) 156
Coles, A. 177

migrant workers *continued*
 control of 16–17, 22–3, 24, 145–6
  see also migration management
 criminalisation of 95–6
 debt bondage 86, 89
 in domestic services *see* domestic
  services sector
 and exclusion 81, 97–8, 99–100,
  138, 225
 fragmented institutional framework
  89, 96
 international solidarity 228–30
 irregular/illegal 26, 48, 88, 94, 95–6
 lack of integration 6, 99
 lack of mobility 83
 long-term migrants 98–9
 psychological illness 224–5
 rights 29–30, 73–4, 99, 223–4
  restricted 16, 27–8, 30, 37, 57, 67,
   72, 79, 225, 227
 second generation migrants 67, 98
 in security forces *see* migrant-based
  security forces
 suicide 48, 192, 194, 224–5, 226
 temporary status 30, 64, 72, 98, 102,
  172
 as users of urban space 101–2, 111
  see also expatriates, real estate
   ownership; rootless urbanism
 working and living conditions 9, 48,
  86–9, 223–4, 225–6
  artists campaign 229–30
  construction sector 113, 135, 144
 see also expatriates
migrant-based security forces 153–69
 history of 6, 154–8
 in independence era 156–8
 migrants' experiences 158–9, 160–1
 origins of 153, 154–6
 political naturalisation 161–3, 164–5
 recruitment methods 159–60
 segregation 160
 and social-media sites 166–7
Migrante International (Philippines)
 228–9

migration
 control and management 40–1, 48
 implications for power structures in
  Gulf 61–2
 politics of 39–56
 as positive sum game 58, 59
 as process of class formation 58, 66
  see also class formation
 and risk 15, 59–60, 89
 as spatial structure 72
  see also spatial fix
 studies of 57–62, 174–6
 undesirable consequences 48, 73
migration theory 58–62
 and methodological nationalism 58,
  62, 66, 67, 70, 73, 228
 new economics of labour migration
  (NELM) model 60–1
 'push–pull' model (neoclassical
  approach) 58–60, 61, 65, 174
Mohammad, R. 134
Movement for Democracy and
 Liberties 209
Mubarak, Sheikh (Kuwait) 11
Al-Mudarissi, Hadi 203
Muharraq 119, 203
Muntazeri, Hussein Ali 203
Al-Murbati, Mohamed 202, 205, 206
Mushaima, Hassan 209
Muwatana citizenship 50

Naficy, H. 205
Na'im tribe 154
Nasserism 21, 47
nation-state 39, 40–1, 49, 58, 62, 66,
 72, 73
National Democratic Action (Bahrain)
 208
National Guard (Bahrain) 158, 159,
 160, 166
National Liberation Front-Bahrain
 (NLFB) 201, 202
National Safety Law (Bahrain) 214, 215
neoliberalism 63, 64–5
 creating conditions for migration 64